Experimental Film and Artists' Moving Image

Series Editors
Kim Knowles
Aberystwyth University
Aberystwyth, UK

Jonathan Walley
Department of Cinema
Denison University
Granville, OH, USA

Existing outside the boundaries of mainstream cinema, the field of experimental film and artists' moving image presents a radical challenge not only to the conventions of that cinema but also to the social and cultural norms it represents. In offering alternative ways of seeing and experiencing the world, it brings to the fore different visions and dissenting voices. In recent years, scholarship in this area has moved from a marginal to a more central position as it comes to bear upon critical topics such as medium specificity, ontology, the future of cinema, changes in cinematic exhibition and the complex interrelationships between moving image technology, aesthetics, discourses, and institutions. This book series stakes out exciting new directions for the study of alternative film practice – from the black box to the white cube, from film to digital, crossing continents and disciplines, and developing fresh theoretical insights and revised histories. Although employing the terms 'experimental film' and 'artists' moving image', we see these as interconnected practices and seek to interrogate the crossovers and spaces between different kinds of oppositional filmmaking.

We invite proposals on any aspect of non-mainstream moving image practice, which may take the form of monographs, edited collections, and artists' writings both historical and contemporary. We are interested in expanding the scope of scholarship in this area, and therefore welcome proposals with an interdisciplinary and intermedial focus, as well as studies of female and minority voices. We also particularly welcome proposals that move beyond the West, opening up space for the discussion of Latin American, African and Asian perspectives.

More information about this series at
http://www.palgrave.com/gp/series/15817

Kim Knowles

Experimental Film and Photochemical Practices

palgrave
macmillan

Kim Knowles
Aberystwyth University
Aberystwyth, UK

ISSN 2523-7527 ISSN 2523-7535 (electronic)
Experimental Film and Artists' Moving Image
ISBN 978-3-030-44311-5 ISBN 978-3-030-44309-2 (eBook)
https://doi.org/10.1007/978-3-030-44309-2

Cover image: A strip of phytogram imagery from *It Matters What*, Francisca Duran, 2019
Cover design by eSTudioCalamar

This Palgrave Macmillan imprint is published by the registered company Springer Nature Switzerland AG
The registered company address is: Gewerbestrasse 11, 6330 Cham, Switzerland

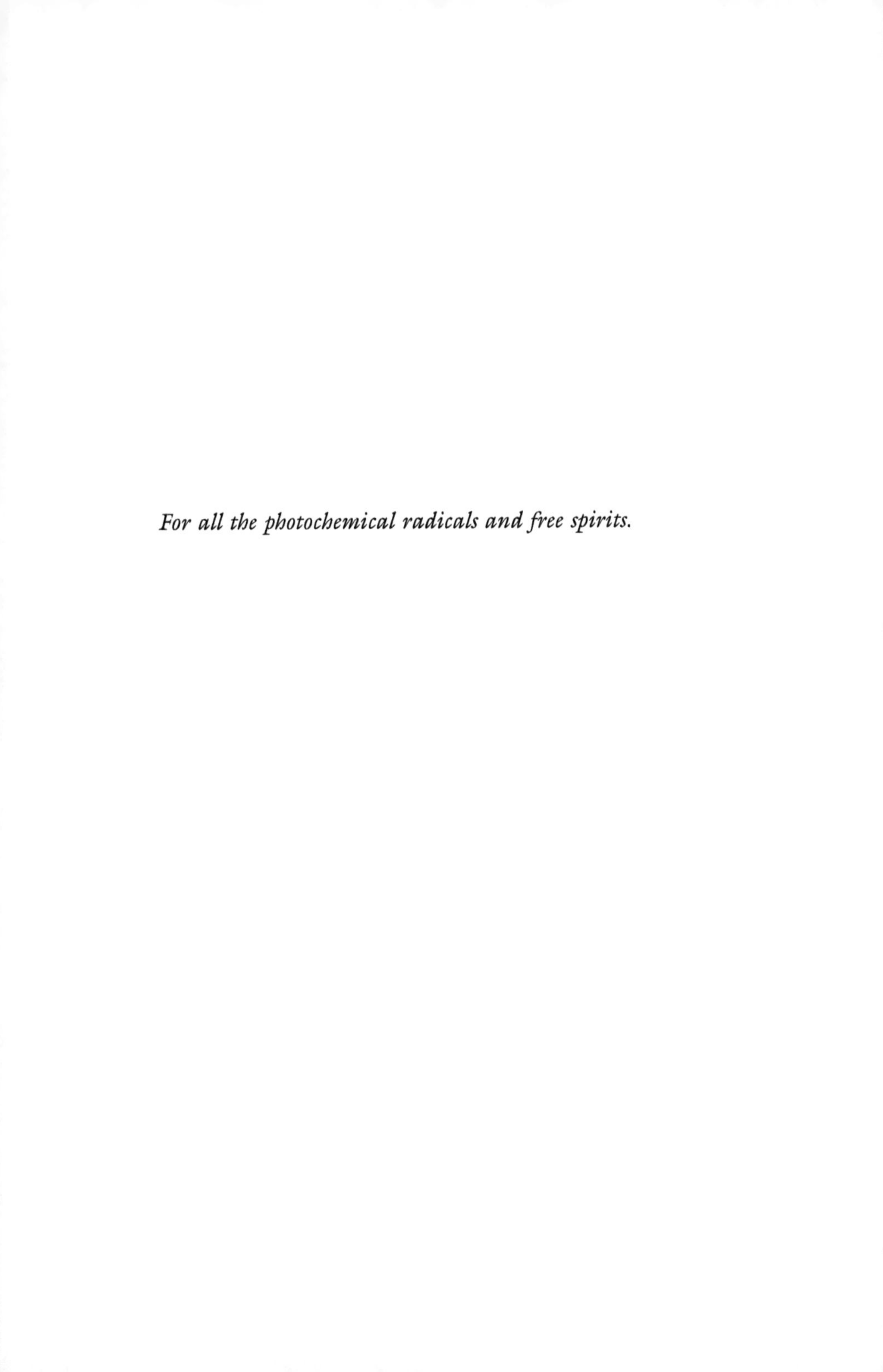

For all the photochemical radicals and free spirits.

Acknowledgements

My interest in photochemical film practice in the digital era was first ignited in 2008 when I saw Jeanne Liotta's *Loretta* (2003) projected on 16mm at the Filmhouse cinema in Edinburgh. I was running a small film festival called Diversions and Teale Failla, a postgraduate student from New York, had put together a screening of work by Liotta, Jennifer Reeves, M. M. Serra, Joel Schlemowitz among others. She probably has no idea how much that screening changed my life. Since then, most of my academic work and much of my curation has been devoted to contemporary engagements with a medium largely deemed obsolete. I have returned to *Loretta* constantly and I am deeply thankful to Jeanne for those images that led me on a long and exciting journey. Over the years, I have crossed paths with a great many people with a similar passion and I have been inspired by their creativity, warmth and openness. It's difficult for me to imagine this book being written without them, but it's equally difficult to name them all. Every encounter, every conversation and every film screening somehow resonate through these pages. Heartfelt thanks to Jenny Baines, Erika Balsom, Dianna Barrie, Christopher Becks, Lydia Beilby, Martine Beugnet, Stephen Broomer, Brad Butler, Guillaume Cailleau, Stefano Canapa, Pip Chodorov, David Curtis, Karel Doing, Helen de Witt, Anja Dornieden, Franci Duran, Kelly Egan, Phillip Fleischmann, David Gatten, Sandra Gibson, Sally Golding, Juan David González Monroy, Nicky Hamlyn, Bea Haut, Gabriele Jutz, Chris Kennedy, Eva Kolcze, Karl Lemieux, Luis Macías, Pablo Mazzolo, Penny

McCann, Lindsay McIntyre, Miles McKane, Peter Miller, Noor Afshan Mirza, Tomonari Nishikawa, Jem Noble, Elena Pardo, Aurélie Percevault, Sasha Pirker, Greg Pope, Charlotte Pryce, Sarah Pucill, Luis Recoder, Nicolas Rey, Daïchi Saïto, Vitkoria Schmid, Tanya Syed, Richard Tuohy, Sarah Turner, Esther Urlus, Sami van Ingen, Erwin van't Hart, Adriana Vila, Christo Wallers and Antoinette Zwirchmayr. Thank you particularly to all the artists who went out of their way to provide me with viewing materials and images, and who let me into their creative world, explaining in detail their working methods and philosophical approach by phone, Skype or in person.

Emmanuel Lefrant, Vicky Smith and James Holcombe have been loyal friends and mentors, endlessly generous with their technical knowledge and intellectual insight and patiently explaining and re-explaining the workings of this or that machine. They have guided me throughout this journey and have inspired me to keep going. My friends at Bristol Experimental and Expanded Film (BEEF) were instrumental in helping me to understand film communities from the inside: Stephen Cornford, Matt Davies, Louisa Fairclough and Marcy Saude in particular gave me fresh insight into film processes and the spirit of invention. Marion Schmid and Angela Piccini were the most attentive readers, offering thoughtful advice and encouragement each step of the way.

It's fair to say that this book took a slight change of direction after my trip to The Independent Imaging Retreat (Film Farm) in Canada. I cannot thank Phil Hoffman, Terra Long, Chris Harrison, Scott Miller Berry, Rob Butterworth, Deirdre Logue and Janine Marchessault enough for an experience that moved me physically, spiritually and intellectually. They inspired me to think, feel, see and write differently, as did my fellow travellers on that journey: Alix Blevins, Gerry Fialka, Tara Khalili, Annapurna Kumur, Markus Maicher, Elian Mikkola, Ramey Newell, Kelly O'Brien, Emily Pelstring, Mike Rollo, Ángel Rueda, Cindy Stillwell and Hagere Selam 'shimby' Zegeye-Gebrehiwot.

I have been assisted by several organisations over the years, who have always been eager to help with the research process: Light Cone in Paris (Eleni Gioti, Emmanuel Lefrant, Mariya Nikiforova), LUX in London (Matt Carter, Ben Cook), Sixpack Film in Austria (Brigitta Burger-Utzer, Isabelle Piechaczyk, Dietmar Schwärzler, Gerald Weber), Vtape (Wanda vanderStoop) and the Canadian Filmmakers Distribution Centre (Genne Speers, Lauren Howe, Jesse Brossoit, Shannon Gagnon, Madison More) in Toronto. My long involvement with the Edinburgh International Film

Festival and Filmhouse has fed my passion and has given me important access to films and filmmakers that I might never have encountered. I have several people to thank there—employees past and present—for always having faith in my ideas and for continuing to provide a vital infrastructure for 16mm and 35mm screenings, as well as countless complicated set-ups: Mark Adams, Ali Blaikie, Emma Boa, David Boyd, Ali Clarke, Chris Fujiwara, Niall Greig Fulton, Diane Henderson, James Rice, Evi Tsiligaridou and Rod White.

A special thank you to all my colleagues at Aberystwyth University for their patience and the best home-baking I've ever tasted, and to Emily Wood, Lina Aboujieb and the anonymous peer reviewers at Palgrave Macmillan for helping me through the crucial publication stages.

Most importantly, much love and endless gratitude to Tree, who, with the patience of a saint, has been my rock, my reality checker, my deadline setter and my proof-reader.

Contents

List of Figures

CHAPTER 1

The Matter of Media

Throughout the recent wave of books and articles on the current state of film in the digital era one finds more or less the same conclusion: film, or cinema, in its previous incarnation is no longer. The technological shifts that have been taking place since the 1990s have dislodged the ontological foundations of the medium as well as its spaces of reception.[1] As several writers have demonstrated, we now live in an era of digital 'convergence', where the moving image manifests in numerous forms and contexts, sliding across a multitude of platforms and implicating the spectator/consumer in new ways.[2] What was previously associated with the cinematic experience has exploded into a moving image environment that resists any unified definition and infiltrates almost every aspect of our lives, from small handheld devices to gigantic public screens. Accordingly, current scholarship sets out to navigate this heterogeneous terrain and to make sense of its multifaceted and dispersed nature, revisiting and revising established theories whilst developing new ones. For André Gaudreault and Philippe Marion, 'cinema is going through a major identity crisis',[3] whilst for Janine Marchessault and Susan Lord the scope is wider—'digital technologies are transforming the semiotic fabric of contemporary visual cultures', they state, appropriating Gene Youngblood's concept of 'expanded cinema' to account for the new landscape of 'immersive, interactive, and interconnected forms of culture'.[4] Clearly, it is not just cinema that is questioned in the digital era, but the entire realm of human experience: artistic expression, forms of communication and modes of being.

K. Knowles, *Experimental Film and Photochemical Practices*,
Experimental Film and Artists' Moving Image,
https://doi.org/10.1007/978-3-030-44309-2_1

Disentangling one from the other is a challenging task, and their interrelatedness demands theoretical approaches capable of teasing out the complexities.

Until quite recently, discussions of technological transition were dominated by the problematic concept of 'new media', a term that, like a stone skimming across the surface of water, gained momentum with each successive scholarly text dedicated to it. In Wendy Hui Kyong Chun's introduction to the revised 2016 edition of *New Media, Old Media: A History and Theory Reader*, aptly titled 'Somebody Said New Media', several key issues are put into play. 'To talk of new media in the early twenty-first century', observes Chun, 'seems odd: exhausted and exhausting.'[5] Not least because, tied to corporate interests, the increasing rate of technological replacement means that nothing is ever new for very long. 'To call something new', Chun continues, 'is to guarantee that it will one day be old; it is to place it within a cycle of obsolescence, in which it will inevitably disappoint and be replaced by something else that promises, once again, the new'.[6] This intricate relationship between the old and the new is central to understanding what is at stake when we talk about 'new media' or 'new technology', and it has certainly been one of the focal points in criticisms of 'newness'. From Charles Acland's perspective:

> An inappropriate amount of energy has gone into the study of new media, new genres, new communities, and new bodies, that is into the contemporary forms. Often, the methods of doing so have been at the expense of taking account of continuity, fixity and dialectical relations with existing practices, systems and artifacts.[7]

In the heady rush to embrace and theorise the 'new', we have neglected to consider the wider cultural, economic and ideological implications of the recent technological (r)evolution, including the ever-changing notion of the 'old' and its precarious position in art, culture and society.

The New and the Obsolete

New technologies, like all consumer commodities, are aggressively marketed on their ability to improve on an existing product in terms of cost, speed, efficiency or style, to such an extent that the old is invariably framed as 'undesirable, dysfunctional and embarrassing, compared with what is new'.[8] In order to lock the consumer into a perpetual cycle of consumption, a visible dichotomy must be established that elevates the status of the new whilst denigrating and devaluing the old. Obsolescence, a concept that gained currency in the post-Fordist era, is the linchpin of this dichotomy and the buzzword of contemporary accounts of technological 'progress'. It is useful here to draw on Evan Watkins's remarks on the fabrication and ideological implications of the concept of the outdated. In what is perhaps one of the most rigorous investigations into the subject, Watkins argues that 'obsolescence is far from being a natural phenomenon—the invention of a new technology does not automatically render the old ones obsolete; rather, the concept of the "outmoded" or the "outdated" arises from very specific and targeted maneuvers by a consumer-led industry that functions in the interests of capitalism, itself "an economy of change"'.[9] 'Obsolescence', he states, 'must be produced in specific ways'.[10] Or, as Michelle Henning outlines in her discussion of obsolescence in relation to photography, it 'is an ideologically produced designation. To study the production of obsolescence necessarily means to attend to social and cultural processes, to the production of a "field of equivalence"'.[11] Here, Henning picks up on Watkins's concept of equivalent use to demonstrate how technologies are developed and marketed in such a way that 'one thing [is viewed] as replacing the other'.[12] The process by which digital image production renders obsolete old analogue systems, for example, depends heavily on a particular narrative that bypasses their material specificities in order to place emphasis on the same basic functions. Thus, digital photography essentially does the same as analogue photography, only better, cheaper, faster and, importantly, in ways that allow more control over the final image.

Indeed, in the analogue-to-digital paradigm, the tendency to reduce the intricate dialectics of media change to a historical-theoretical standpoint that reinforces the cultural dominance of the new is often couched in such narratives of continuity, which see new media as not simply replacing old practices but perfecting the means through which their creative potential may be realised. Slavoj Žižek refers to this discourse as 'the historiography of a kind of *futur antérieur* [future perfect]' that involves 'the well-known phenomenon of the old artistic forms pushing against their own boundaries and using procedures which, at least from our retrospective view, seem to point towards a new technology'.[13] This view to a large extent characterises early accounts of new media, particularly Lev Manovich's now well-cited *The Language of New Media*, in which one finds the statement that 'the computer fulfils the promise of the cinema as a visual Esperanto'.[14] The narrative of equivalent use is problematic because it encourages the understanding of digital technology as simply a replacement for film, in much the same way that the desktop computer replaced the typewriter, CDs replaced vinyl and the e-book is gradually replacing printed material.[15] Mark Hansen, for example, criticises Manovich's 'circular history', which 'effectively reimposes the linear, teleological, and techno-determinist model of (traditional) cinema history'.[16] Hansen, along with other critics such as D. N. Rodowick, have pointed out that this approach, with its emphasis on 'overdetermined similarities', has largely prevented the digital from finding its own creative voice as a medium with distinct technical properties and possibilities.[17] Recent media archaeological approaches have challenged dominant trajectories of technological progress, pointing out the discontinuities and circumstantial decisions that punctuate the history of the moving image and unearthing alternative material histories.[18] Garnet Hertz and Jussi Parikka's exploration of 'zombie media' as a form of critical art practice, for example, demonstrates how discarded technologies condemned to the rubbish heap enter new ecologies of repurposing and reinvention.[19] In their refusal to disappear, these undead objects complicate and reimagine understandings of history, temporality, functionality and intended use, working against the grain of capitalist desire.

Florian Cramer's notion of 'post-digital' aesthetics follows a similar line, arguing that creative forms of technological reuse and misuse are the primary means through which individuals are able to navigate an alternative agenda to that of 'digital high-tech and high-fidelity cleanness'.[20] For Cramer, using old media is 'no longer a sign of being old-fashioned. It is instead a deliberate choice of renouncing electronic technology, thereby calling into question the common assumption that computers [...] represent obvious technological progress and therefore constitute a logical upgrade from any older media technology'.[21] This is, of course, intricately tied to questions of nostalgia and retro-fetishism, both bourgeoning fields of scholarly enquiry in the digital era and inseparable from any discussion of media transition. Since the turn of the millennium, and particularly in the ten or so years since the publication of Acland's *Residual Media*, a number of studies on cultures of retro, vintage and nostalgia have emerged, opening up differing perspectives on contemporary society's fascination with the past in an era of rapid technological and stylistic change.[22] Svetlana Boym's work has been particularly influential in developing more nuanced understandings of how nostalgia operates not simply as a 'yearning for yesterday', but also as a productive means of negotiating the past.[23] Nostalgia, she argues, 'is not always retrospective; it can be prospective as well'.[24] Whilst restorative nostalgia is associated with a reconstruction of the past, reflective nostalgia moves towards a process of deconstruction, 'calling into doubt' the certainties of the past and acknowledging the complexities of our relationship to the past in the present. As we shall see, interrogations of obsolete media still carry with them negative associations of retro-fetishism, but adapting Boym's concept of 'reflective' nostalgia as a form of resistance provides a starting point for more fruitful theoretical formulations of technological appropriation.

We must not forget, however, that the past is also often packaged as a commodity and now appears in many forms of mainstream media, fashion and design. From retro Instagram filters to the explosion of vintage clothing and furniture shops, looking back has proved to be a highly lucrative gesture. This complicates any straightforward reading of appropriation as an exclusively counter-cultural practice and asks us to navigate both mainstream and alternative positions. In an artistic context, how might looking back—at past forms, practices and techniques—create new possibilities in the present and forge alternative creative pathways into the future?

In *Obsolescence: Ouvrir l'impossible*, Mathias Rollot argues that obsolescence relates less to the object or technology itself than to the social context that determines its perceived relevance and functionality. In reality, nothing in the essential makeup of the obsolete object changes; rather, the needs and demands of society—often driven by capitalist notions of 'progress'—give rise to new tools that are considered to be more adapted to the milieu in question. In relation to this, Rollot emphasises the constructive impetus inherent in obsolescence, countering the dominant tendency to approach it as negatively inflected:

> Obsolescence is not a question of disappearance or destruction of a subject or object, but, on the contrary, of its profound conservation, *despite everything*, despite the changes to which the milieu is submitted, cultural displacement, paradigmatic metamorphosis, technological evolutions. Obsolescence is the hyperconservation of an entity that becomes unsuited to its times.[25]

It is this quality of anachronism that seems to drive much artistic interest in film. Let us take the comment by British artist Tacita Dean: 'Everything that excites me no longer functions in its own time'.[26] Clearly this isn't simply a case of refusing to move with the times, but of cultivating a deeper sensitivity to the way that different temporalities rub up against each other to produce alternative perceptions and artistic possibilities. No longer functioning in its own time is not ceasing to function altogether; it is, as Rollot points out, and as Dean suggests, continuing to function according to different rules, via a different pathway, '*despite everything*'. Anachronism plays a crucial role in the forms of material understanding that I outline in the next chapter, since the obsolete object is almost always defined by a material excess that is somehow out of kilter with the modern world. In the case of film, it is the bulky and cumbersome equipment with its stubborn mechanical presence that signifies times past, but which also stimulates a counter-cultural impulse to travel in opposite directions. Dutch artist Esther Urlus refers to the pleasures of working with 'useless media', where use value relates to the potential to generate profit through perpetual 'innovation'.[27] Having dropped out of this cycle, photochemical film finds itself in a position of relative freedom, no longer useful in one sense, but endlessly valuable in another. Innovation becomes multidirectional and (re)invention often involves looking backwards in order to move forwards.

Reinventing the Medium

As a result of its declared obsolescence or 'crisis' (both as photochemical film-making practice and as a film theatre experience) cinema has become a sought-after object for art institutions and amateurs of vintage media alike and is being subjected to all forms of recycling and re-appropriation—actual as well as virtual. One might suggest that with the increasing cognisance of film's disappearance comes to a stage of mourning, where the qualities of analogue are afforded special cultural significance. This can be seen on the one hand in the digitally simulated material characteristic of celluloid, such as camera flares, scratches and faded colour, and, on the other, the abundance of archive, found footage or 'ruin' films, such as those by Bill Morrison and Gustav Deutsch, as well as more contemporary compilation films by artists like Christian Marclay, whose 24 hour sampling exercise in *The Clock* (2010) is an overt exercise in cinematic remembrance. Indeed, the archive or the 'lost object' of film has been one of the main focal points in discussions of analogue aesthetics in the digital era, with attention firmly placed on the reworking of existing material through various material interventions.[28] It is perhaps here that the complexities of film as a residual media emerge—the tension between working with film in a manner that brings to light its historical status and reinventing a medium that is considered a thing of the past. In Acland's brief discussion of analogue film, only one of these avenues—film as history—is suggested, that is, through works that 'explicitly announce their historicity [...] through aged and aging [material] qualities.'[29]

This book argues for a wider understanding of photochemical film practice in relation to discourses of technological transition and material culture. It takes the view of film as persisting in the contemporary moment, framed by obsolescence but developing in new directions as a result of alternative networked cultures of collectivity and DIY skills sharing. Although many artists have embraced the creative potential of digital technology, photochemical film practice continues in a new, one might say reinvigorated, form, despite—or in some cases because of—the challenges posed by a scarcity of resources and rising costs associated with analogue technology. It is within this field that the model of equivalent use highlighted by Watkins and perpetuated in the dominant accounts of new media and technological change is most problematic, and indeed problematised. To this end, we might take as our starting point Tacita Dean's response, published in *The Guardian* on 22 February 2011, to the discontinuation of 16mm printing services at the London-based Soho Film Lab, then recently taken over by the American company Deluxe:

> Many of us are exhausted from grieving over the dismantling of analogue technologies. Digital is not better than analogue, but different. What we are asking for is co-existence: that analogue film might be allowed to remain an option for those who want it, and for the ascendency of one not to have to mean the extinguishing of another.[30]

In her powerful and militant stance against the reduction of artistic choices driven by commercial interests, Dean draws attention to the politics of obsolescence underlying the phasing out of film: 'Culturally and socially, we are moving too fast and losing too much in our haste. We are also being deceived, silently and conspiratorially.'[31]

The potential loss to which Dean refers is a range of practices particular to, and characteristic of, experimental cinema, where investigations into the material support—celluloid—are an integral part of the artistic process. Because experimental filmmaking is, by definition, a quest, no matter how precise and meticulous the process, it remains dependent on approaches to technology and practice—experimenting with or diverting machines and techniques away from their intended use—that represent salutary alternatives to what Sean Cubitt, in his introduction to Malcolm Le Grice's writings, describes as the 'human, and specifically capitalist tyranny over technology': our present-day culture of utmost technological functionality and performance.[32] Artisanal or materialist filmmaking is exemplary here because it relies not only on technologically mediated processes, but also on direct human intervention—an involvement that is inherently flawed and inconsistent: the result is never certain; in effect, randomness and 'defect' are fully integrated features of the aesthetics of the artisanal or handmade. The film is a physical testimony of the artist's intricate, painstaking work on the surface of the celluloid, the trace of which is felt in the uneven, raw quality of the finished product. The process is the film, which continually reasserts its own tactile character.

Since the publication of Dean's article and her campaign to save film, a growing number of artists have been (re)turning to this 'old' medium in all its gauges—8mm, Super 8mm, 16mm and 35mm—quietly picking up the pieces of a dismantled industry and reconstructing it in the image of alternative artistic enquiry.[33] Questions of materiality and medium-specificity emerge in a new context, re-igniting some of the old debates and stimulating a host of new ones. But why continue to talk about photochemical film in a digital era? What is the value of working with outmoded technologies and what can scholarship in this field contribute to the ongoing redefinition of film studies as an increasingly dispersed and hybrid discipline? Would our energies not be better directed towards film futures rather than harking back to old technologies and methods? With the exception of a few high-profile die-hards such as Christopher Nolan and Quentin Tarantino, for the commercial film industry celluloid film is largely a thing of the past. Its cultural relevance has dwindled and shifted to a position now so marginal that few people are even aware of its existence. However, this marginal position is crucial from both an aesthetic and a political perspective and, as I will argue throughout the course of this book, opens out to wider questions of matter and materiality that dominate contemporary intellectual discourse. The consideration of celluloid film within the context of technological progress and obsolescence—the dialectic of old and new—reveals a vista of theoretical positions that coalesce to create fresh perspectives on moving image practice in the digital era.

One of the most important recent discussions of 'old media' within a contemporary context is Erika Balsom's *Exhibiting Cinema in Contemporary Art*.[34] This insightful study of how cinema is reconfigured within a gallery context considers, amongst other issues, the ways in which 'analogue film has reasserted its uniqueness within a digital landscape through works that stage the material specificities of 16mm and 35mm film'.[35] Balsom's position is incredibly valuable in pushing back against the stigma of medium-specificity and 'the term's inevitable invocation of the spectres of modernism, formalism, essentialism, and of Clement Greenberg'.[36] To speak of medium-specificity in an era of media fluidity and convergence risks appearing to idealise a state of pre-digital purity. Yet, as Balsom argues, exploring the contours of analogue image-making as it is reframed and redefined in new contexts is not tantamount to media fetishism, nor does it reject the new in favour of the old. The new exists only in relation to the old (and vice versa), yet previous accounts of technological transition have tended to privilege the ways in which new media technologies refashion or reinvent older forms. Considering the myriad ways in which photochemical film practice responds to its now marginal status is thus central to pursuing an alternative approach to media transition and the ever-evolving definition of 'cinema'. Balsom's book is a vital step in that direction, but the scope of her study is limited to works made for and exhibited within a gallery context, and out of necessity presents a rather skewed impression of contemporary interactions with analogue film.

In *The Virtual Life of Film*, published several years earlier, D. N. Rodowick paints a similar picture, highlighting the 'renewed interest in celluloid' in a digitally dominated era. Although he mentions the 'persistence of experimental filmmaking devoted to both 16mm and super-8 formats', attention is focused on the new status of 35mm as art object:

> Fabricated from a precious metal and installed in galleries and museums, where they are meant to be viewed in unique situations as autonomous artworks, films are regaining a sense of aura, and, finally film is becoming Art.[37]

Indeed, it is via the gallery that theme of analogue obsolescence has been played out most visibly, through installations and exhibitions that celebrate precisely these precious qualities (I will return to this topic in Chapter 5). Tacita Dean's *FILM*, installed in the Turbine Hall of the Tate Modern between October 2011 and March 2012, is a perfect example.

For this 12th commission in the Unilever Series, Dean drew inspiration from René Daumal's *Mount Analogue*, an allegorical novel first published in 1952 that centres on a mysterious mountain reaching into eternity, hidden from normal perception by the laws of time and space, but visible to those who believe in its existence.[38] This became, for Dean, a metaphor for film itself as it enters 'the illusory domain of being there only for those willing to board The Impossible'.[39] Standing thirteen metres high at the far end of the vast darkened Turbine Hall, the majestic image of a floating 35mm strip easily conjured up feelings of awe and a sense of the sublime. It was, in many ways, a powerful reminder of the beauty of the film medium, but in its hyperbolic self-referentiality it edged into a problematic rarefication of celluloid as an institutionalised form of mourning that seemed to preclude critical reflection. Its status as 'Art', with its auratic glow, thus turned film into 'film', an object or relic to be gazed upon lovingly with a hint of nostalgia.

FILM was presented again a few years later at the Eye Museum in Amsterdam. Taking a similar approach, the exhibition 'Celluloid' (September 2016 to January 2017) celebrated the 'remarkable qualities of analogue film', through works by renowned gallery artists Rosa Barba, Sandra Gibson and Luis Recoder, João Maria Gusmão and Pedro Paiva and Tacita Dean. This time, 16mm was presented alongside 35mm in installations described as 'striking' and 'sensational' that displayed the 'magic of the material'.[40] It is easy to detect, here, a zeitgeist of collective celebration/mourning of film in a gallery space, its material specificity now the object of wonderment and veneration as it fades into the horizon. In Jennifer West's recent interactive exhibition 'Flashlight Filmstrip Projections', presented at New York's Microscope Gallery in 2016, the audience lights up plexiglass frames containing 35mm and 70mm film strips with torches, turning the entire gallery space (including the bodies of the participants) into a projection surface. The exhibition is described as being originally conceived as a 'swansong to celluloid', not dissimilar to Dean's monumental homage to film at the Tate Modern and other swansongs such as Peter Kubelka's *Monument Film*. A pivotal figure in avant-garde film history, Kubelka made a series of 'metrical' films during the 1950s and 1960s that interrogated the material properties of film and isolated the single frame as the basic unit of expression.[41] With *Monument Film*, he returns to the most minimalist of these works *Arnulf Rainer* (1958–1960)—an early example of flicker film that works on the basis of alternating black and white frames with a soundtrack that also oscillates between the presence and absence of white noise—to produce from it an opposite corresponding version. The old and new versions are presented in various constellations: individually, together, side-by-side, and, crucially, as exhibited filmstrips that allow the rhythmic patterns to be understood from a spatial as well as temporal perspective. Significant in each of these examples is the weight of the artist's gesture—the presentation of film as rare and precious, and something to be contemplated with awe and amazement.

By way of contrast, and to open up the discourse on materiality, I would like to draw attention to another recent exhibition—lesser-known but no less noteworthy—that took place at the Kunsthalle Exnergasse—WUK in Vienna from 8 November to 16 December 2018. 'Slow Down! Cinematic approaches on reduction' was conceived by a group of Austrian filmmakers (Philipp Fleischmann, Susanne Miggitsch, Sasha Pirker, Viktoria Schmid and Antoinette Zwirchmayr) in collaboration with the architect Michael Klein. What immediately distinguishes this example from those mentioned above is the element of scale and the relative subtlety of the gesture. Although the exhibition focuses exclusively on photochemical film (predominantly 16mm), there are very few references to the status of the medium as precious or endangered and the installations are certainly not presented as any kind of swansong. In its material and sculptural form, film is celebrated as a living rather than dying thing, with an infinite range of expressive possibilities. This is not to say that the exhibition ignores or denies the precarious status of film in the digital era; in Sasha Pirker's *Closed Circuit* (2013), a roll of 16mm film captures the gradual appearance of a Polaroid image, the temporal correspondence of the two media doubly mirrored in their commercial disappearance. 2013 was a crucial year for both Kodak and Polaroid—the former was declared bankrupt, re-emerging as a restructured and redirected company, whilst the latter officially went out of business.[42] A dual reflection on appearance and disappearance, Pirker's installation draws on chance parallels between two 'obsolete' analogue mediums. A Polaroid photograph takes three minutes to fully develop, the same duration of a 100ft roll of 16mm film.[43] In *Closed Circuit*, Pirker films the gradual appearance of a Polaroid image, which turns out to be the filmmaker herself pointing a Bolex camera towards the viewer. Filming the photochemical process allows the temporal regimes and material substrate of both mediums to merge into a hybrid form, with the original image, displayed alongside the 16mm projection, creating a tension between still and moving, the original and the record. The intimacy of the image folds the viewer into its self-reflexive circularity as his/her gaze meets that of the camera lens (Fig. 1.1).

One of the key features of the Slow Down! exhibition is the sense of playfulness and discovery that is also inscribed into the architectural design of the installation space, where basic wooden shelves and cardboard screens contrast knowingly with the sophisticated sleek surfaces of

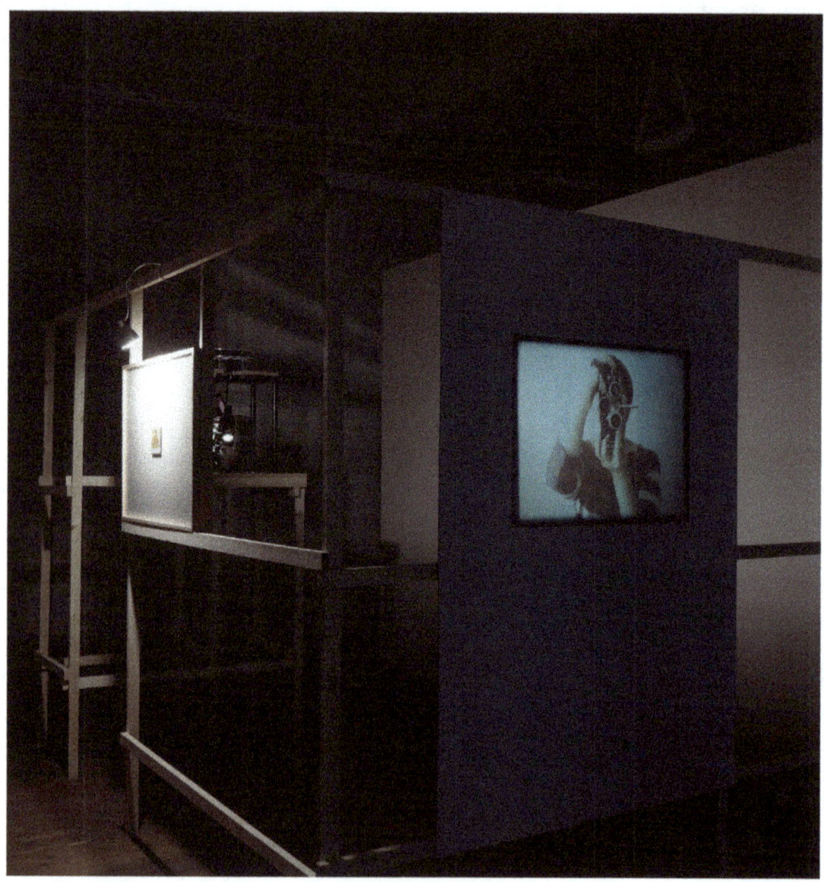

Fig. 1.1 *Closed Circuit*, Sasha Pirka, 2013. Installation view, 'Slow Down! Cinematic approaches on reduction', 8 November—16 December 2018, Kunsthalle Exnergasse, Vienna © Kunsthalle Exnergasse (Photo: Wolfgang Thaler, 2017)

many gallery interiors. This approach plays with visitor expectations—is the exhibition still under construction? Where does it begin and end? Can I sit on these wooden surfaces or are they part of the 'work'? The architecture creates fluid, open spaces that allow a dialogue to take place between the individual works as the eye follows a light here and a reflection there, or the line of a shadow tracing the wall, moving the attention constantly back and forth. The room is alive with the rhythmic chatter of 16mm projectors scattered throughout the space, which provides a mechanical soundtrack to this vibrant celebration of film technology. From Peter Miller's *Phenadiscoscope* (2010), a 16mm loop of a dancing figure projected onto a disco ball, to Björn Kämmerer's *Remote/8* (2008), in which a rotating 16mm projector atop a scaffold sends the image of an airplane flying around the gallery ceiling, there is an acute sense of artists reinventing the medium, finding new ways to engage with its physical properties and opening up new pathways to spatial and corporeal engagement. This desire to reinvent film does not preclude historicity, however, since an acute awareness of the historical rootedness of their practice runs through many of the artists' works. Miller playfully references the pre-cinematic Phenakistoscope, for example, whilst Viktoria Schmid's *The Clouds Are Not Like Either One—They Do Not Keep One Form Forever* (2015) returns to James Clerk Maxwell's method of additive colour mixing—a technique that produced the first colour photograph by Thomas Sutton in 1861—for her meditative multi-projector, multi-screen piece. Schmid uses three 16mm loops of clouds, filmed on black and white stock, through red, green and blue filters and projected through a filter of the same colour onto three staggered screens. The closest screen presents a triptych, with each colour presented separately; as it bleeds through on to a second translucent screen the image now overlaps, the clouds sliding past each other; finally, the third opaque screen presents all three colours in one single image—the culmination of the technique and a creative staging of process.[44] What if colour film ceased to exist? This is the premise of Schmid's installation, which triggers the desire or necessity to look back into the history of photographic technology. Yet this shouldn't be confused with a nostalgic return to the past—let us not forget the spirit of creative playfulness in this act, as well as the intention to create from it something entirely new. Indeed, as we shall see in Chapter 2, a number of contemporary film artists have been involved in such a historical reworking, returning to early cinema in order to trace an alternative path. Freed from its association with the commercial industry, film is thrown into a moment of soul-searching and a compulsion to reinvent itself; it re-emerges as 'art', but not exclusively in the sense described by Rodowick or Balsom (Fig. 1.2).

Through its counter-cultural embrace of outmoded technologies and slower working practices, photochemical film culture emerges as a gesture of resistance to modern society's emphasis on speed and efficiency, rejecting the imperative to update and upgrade in favour of an ecology of recuperation and restoration. As an antidote to our throwaway society, the value placed on film as an ongoing creative endeavour rather than cultural garbage must be viewed as more than mere nostalgic fetishism or another retro fad, as some writers have suggested. Catherine Elwes, for example, in her otherwise lively survey of moving image installation, takes a vehemently critical attitude to the interrogation of forms and technologies she deems irrelevant in a contemporary context, arguing that

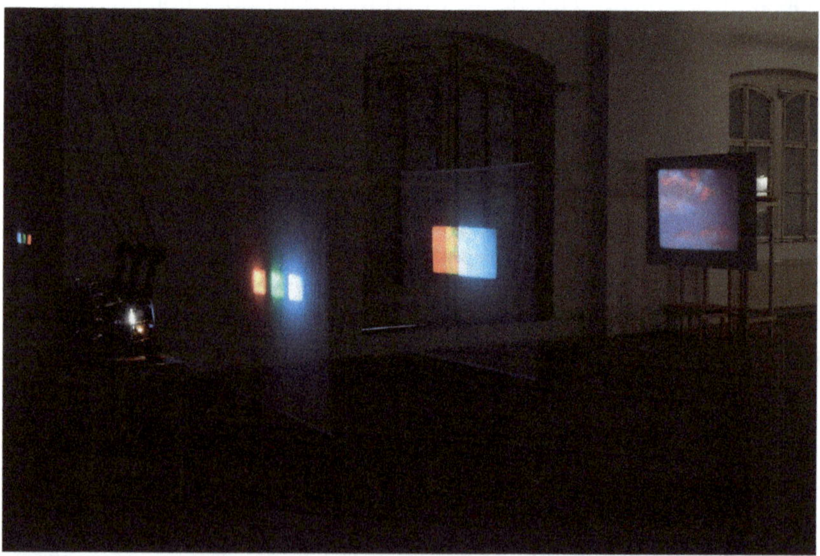

Fig. 1.2 *The Clouds Are Not Like Either One—They Do Not Keep One Form Forever*, Viktoria Schmid, 2015. Installation view, 'Slow Down! Cinematic approaches on reduction', 8 November—16 December 2018, Kunsthalle Exnergasse, Vienna © Kunsthalle Exnergasse (Photo: Wolfgang Thaler, 2017)

> the more time artists spend peering down the retrospectoscope of the cinema and television archive [...] or tinkering with the toys of yesteryear, the less time they spend forging a language to address the more urgent issues that attend the perilous, uncomfortable realities of the modern world.[45]

This unfortunate and unimaginative response to artistic practices that involve 'residual media' is problematic from a number of perspectives: firstly, by dismissing as infantile and regressive those artists who work with commercially outmoded materials and techniques, Elwes glosses over the very complex negotiations of historicity that are inscribed into these practices; secondly, she fails to acknowledge the critical potential of the outmoded, as outlined most succinctly in the writings of Walter Benjamin.[46] That Benjamin has experienced something of a revival in recent years attests to the ongoing relevance of his theories of materiality and commodity production to the contemporary technological landscape. In this context, we must also be mindful of the creative and critical potential of play, which, in the case of artists working against the grain of technological progress and exploring new uses of 'old' materials, is less inward-looking than Elwes's 'tinkering' might suggest.

Photochemical Practices

This book maps out some of the complex issues at stake when considering the field of photochemical film practice in the digital era, which, following the demise of celluloid in the commercial industry, now flourishes in the field of experimental and artists' film. It negotiates theories of technological obsolescence and material culture with a view to providing a more coherent critical understanding of how these marginal creative endeavours move beyond the restrictive confines of retro-fetishism. My interest lies in the emphasis on film's material properties and the very specific modes of representation that are opened up through diverse forms of physical intervention. I argue that this strong current of materialist film practice demands new theoretical formulations capable of drawing out its aesthetic and political relevance in a contemporary context. This requires a reformulation of materialist film theory that takes into consideration the shifting cultural coordinates and technological tensions of the twenty-first century.

Although the arguments I make in the book address the topic of technological transition, materiality and representation in a broad sense, the examples I refer to are largely drawn from a growing field of practice that receives relatively little attention in comparison with the topic of artists' film in the gallery space.[47] Many of the works discussed throughout this study are positioned within a tradition of experimental filmmaking that spans the work of early animators such as Len Lye, Robert Breer, Hy Hirsch and Marie Menken, through structural and structural-materialist filmmakers such as Kurt Kren, Paul Sharits, Lis Rhodes, Annabel Nicolson and Malcolm Le Grice, to the embodied explorations of Stan Brakhage and Carolee Schneemann. In drawing attention to this lineage, I do not wish to restrict discussions of contemporary experimental film to a fixed historical trajectory, nor do I suggest that these artists are working exclusively outside the gallery context. Indeed, some artists that feature in the following pages problematise the cinema/gallery division, or, in the case of Jennifer West, use the gallery as a performative space where material interventions are carried out in front of a live audience. Likewise, as I will go on to discuss, the field of expanded cinema finds its way into a plethora of screening contexts, including pop-up micro-cinemas and disused buildings, as well as high-profile gallery and museum spaces. A significant proportion of the films discussed, however, are exhibited in cinemas, or at least in spaces that approximate the immersive cinema experience, whether as single-screen, multi-screen or performative projections.

Experimental Film and Photochemical Practices has numerous threads and folds, tracing a path through diverse fields of thought to arrive at a new theory of materialist film in the digital era. It aims to unravel ways of thinking about photochemical film practices and forms of material engagement at a time when our physical connection with the material world is being reconsidered through cross-disciplinary perspectives and innovative methodologies. The framing question is: what new insights can be uncovered by connecting the wave of interest in film as a tactile medium with the desire to conceive of new material understandings of the world in the twenty-first century? In approaching this issue, the book looks back to previous formulations of materialist film as a form of political engagement in order to recast these gestures in a contemporary context and against a very different sociopolitical background. Drawing methodological inspiration from the work of Rosi Braidotti, Jane Bennett, Joanna Zylinksa, Timothy Morton, Bruno Latour and Graham Harman, my approach weaves together several strands of thinking that relate to post-human, post-anthropocentric ways of seeing and sensing. The intention here is not to create a singular theoretical approach, but rather to suggest different angles for a politics of resistance, where the critical power of the outmoded object meets the radical potential of the material surface.

Chapter 2 fleshes out a context for thinking about material engagements in contemporary photochemical film, reflecting on some key historical reference points from Man Ray to Paul Sharits. Emphasis is placed on the continuous quest for alternative forms of vision and the potential of physical contact with the celluloid surface to open up a broad experiential range. I argue that a heightened corporeal awareness can be evidenced in a number of recent works, drawing out parallels between the mortal human body and the culturally fragile medium of film through a focus on death, decay, memory and mourning. But the question of fragility also allows us to think about film in relation to broader political concerns. If, as Peter Gidal argued in his 'Theory and Definition of Structural/Materialist Film' in the mid-1970s, drawing attention to the material processes of film constitutes a deconstruction of representation and thus a critique of dominant ideology, what new critical positions are developed in contemporary practice?[48] In addressing this question, I approach the subject of materiality more generally and the relatively recent 'material turn' in both arts and science disciplines. Perspectives derived from the growing field of 'new materialism' can be mobilised to understand the significance of film in the digital era, particularly in relation to the performativity of matter and the challenge to perceptual norms. Timothy Morton's 'ecological thinking' and Jane Bennett's concept of 'vibrant matter' are important reference points for the development of a new theory of materialist or artisanal film in the digital era. Artistic gestures that explore the expressivity of the celluloid surface through direct physical encounters with the world are discussed in terms of what I call the 'aesthetics of contact'—a form of (re)visioning that counters the dominant tendency towards perceptual clarity and celebrates modes of making 'sense'.

In Chapter 3, I unravel this theoretical framing in relation to a number of contemporary practices that involve either direct manipulation of the film (scratching, drawing, painting, cross-processing, optical printing, contact printing, burying, chemically treating or a combination of these) or a heightened awareness of the material constraints of the Bolex camera. I explore materiality from a wide range of perspectives, beginning with the relationship between film and ecology in the work of Rose Lowder, Emmanuel Lefrant, Alia Syed, Greta Snider and Pablo Mazzolo, where the surface of the film is implicated in the representational process or where extensive artisanal manipulations elicit a sensuous form of understanding. Surface intervention as a form of cinematic close-up is at the centre of my analysis of the films of Vicky Smith and Charlotte Pryce, leading into a section that considers how innovative and playful experiments with colour and chemistry are pushing the art of photochemical filmmaking into new terrain. Questions of materiality are interrogated from a different perspective in the work of British artists Bea Haut and Jenny Baines, whose slapstick film performances draw attention to the physicality of the frame and highlight resistant approaches to space and place. Engaging with Gidal's theory of structural/materialism, I place particular emphasis throughout this Introduction on the politics of process, pointing to the significance of material interventions in the wider context of worldly re-imaginings. In order to draw out the complexities of the films I discuss, my analyses are based largely on in-depth discussions with the artists about their working practices. This has allowed me to develop an intimate relationship with the works, providing for the reader what I hope will be a valuable and insightful personal journey through a range of tactile engagements with the medium.

A personal approach also permeates Chapter 4's overview of the communities and networks, which, to a large extent, facilitate the ongoing reinvention of photochemical film. One of the most interesting developments in recent years is the expansion of the artist-run film lab scene, modelled on the London Filmmakers' Co-op and centred on the recuperation and repurposing of abandoned film equipment. From Studio Één in Arnhem to Atelier MTK in Grenoble, L'Abominable in Paris and no.where in London, the seeds of an alternative culture of creative autonomy, artistic experimentation and technological reinvention were sown throughout the 1990s and 2000s. The dwindling of film as a commercial medium and the subsequent closing of film printing labs, along with the removal of photochemical film from educational programmes, cinemas and art centres, has led, in recent years, to a technological surplus that has allowed an alternative DIY scene to flourish to the extent that there are now some fifty labs worldwide. Differing in size, structure and ethos, the labs are brought together through a shared counter-cultural spirit and a desire to explore the possibilities of a medium deemed obsolete by the mainstream film industry. Not a lab as such but crucial to the artisanal aesthetic that defines DIY film culture, the Independent Imaging Retreat—a 'film camp' established in 1994 by Philip Hoffman and his late wife Marian McMahon—offers a compelling example of grassroots community and alternative pedagogy. My own auto-ethnographic account of Hoffman's Film Farm demonstrates how artisanal film practice can open up entirely new experiences of the world that connect art and politics in very physical ways. The chapter concludes with a consideration of the Film Farm aesthetic across films by Hoffman, Eva Kolcze, Jennifer Reeves, Penny McCann and Deirdre Logue.

Alternative spaces and DIY communities play a key role not only in the practice of photochemical film, but also its presentation, and in Chapter 5. I consider the broader implications of obsolescence in terms of exhibition and projection. The shift to digital in most cinemas and art centres has made the experience of film on film a rarity, creating challenges for filmmakers and curators alike. Although contemporary discourses on the transformation of viewing environments from fixed screens to fluid experiences seem to consider the theatrical projection context a marker of times past, I argue that the immersive, collective space of the cinema is one of ongoing radical potential. This is evidenced in the bourgeoning of DIY venues, many of them dedicated to 16mm film projection and performance. But film projectors also find themselves in a variety of spaces, increasingly presented in galleries either as 'auratic' material objects or as looped installations, where the film strip takes on a sculptural presence alongside the warm glow of the whirring mechanical projector. At play here is the 'to-be-looked-at-ness' of analogue technology that reverses the fetishistic gaze of the traditional filmic diegesis; but gallery artists such as Louisa Fairclough and Sandra Gibson and Luis Recoder have shown how projectors can be repurposed in a gallery space to 'flesh out' their materiality in new affective ways. The body is also a crucial consideration in the growing field of expanded cinema, which, I argue, demonstrates an overwhelming interest in material excess and the staging of mechanical performativity. I consider a number of performances by Sally Golding, Greg Pope, the French collective Nominoë, as well as the Dutch lab Filmwerkplaats, in teasing out the importance of photochemical gestures, interactions and 'attractions' in a contemporary context.

This book is both a document of a moment and a celebration of resistance. Positioned precariously within a period of technological transition, it is written with the knowledge that things may look very different very soon, but also with the desire to capture the essence of a wave of contemporary experimental practice and to build new theoretical paradigms that can shed fresh light on the relationship between the present and the past. Art has always ridden the wave of technological change and cinema history in particular is a history of industrial shifts and developments, with technological innovation creating new aesthetic pathways. But the seismic shifts that have taken place in the past twenty years have altered the cinematic landscape in ways that have no real historical precedent. A time of radical change is a time for radical reimagining. What new insights might emerge from this cultural debris?

Notes

1. See D. N. Rodowick, *The Virtual Life of Film* (Cambridge, MA; London: Harvard University Press, 2007) for the most thorough discussion of film ontology in the digital era.
2. In his account of convergence culture, Henry Jenkins' points out that 'Convergence does not occur through media appliances, however sophisticated they may become. Convergence occurs within the brains of individual consumers and through their social interactions with others.' Henry Jenkins, *Convergence Culture: Where Old and New Media Collide* (New York and London: New York University Press, 2006), p. 3.
3. André Gaudreault and Philippe Marion, *The End of Cinema? A Medium in Crisis in the Digital Age* (New York: Columbia University Press, 2015), p. 10.
4. Janine Marchessault and Susan Lord (eds.), *Fluid Screens, Expanded Cinema* (Toronto: University of Toronto Press, 2007), pp. 6–7.
5. Wendy Hui Kyong Chun, 'Introduction: Somebody Said New Media', in Wendy Hui Kyong Chun and Anna Watkins Fisher (eds.), *New Media, Old Media: A History and Theory Reader*, Second Edition (New York: Routledge, 2016), p. 1.
6. Ibid.
7. Charles R. Acland, 'Introduction: Residual Media', in Charles R. Acland (ed.), *Residual Media* (London and Minneapolis: University of Minnesota Press, 2007), pp. xix–xx.
8. Giles Slade, *Made to Break: Technology and Obsolescence in America* (Cambridge, MA and London: Harvard University Press, 2006), p. 50.
9. Evan Watkins, *Throwaways: Work Culture and Consumer Education* (Stanford: Stanford University Press, 1993), p. 1.
10. Ibid., p. 27.
11. Michelle Henning, 'New Lamps for Old: Photography, Obsolescence, and Social Change', in Acland (ed.), *Residual Media*, p. 51.
12. Ibid.

13. Slavoj Žižek, *The Art of the Ridiculous Sublime: On David Lynch's Lost Highway* (Seattle, WA: University of Washington, Walter Chapin Simpson Center for the Humanities, 2000), p. 29.
14. Lev Manovich, *The Language of New Media* (Cambridge, MA: MIT Press, 2001), p. 79.
15. The main reference remains Friedrich Kittler and his vision of technological development as increasingly autonomous, and of man becoming a technological inscription. Friedrich Kittler, *Gramophone, Film, Typewriter* (Stanford: Stanford University Press, 1999).
16. Mark Hansen, *New Philosophy for New Media* (Cambridge, MA: MIT Press, 2006), p. 39.
17. Chun, 'Introduction: Somebody Said New Media', p. 3.
18. See, for example, Thomas Elsaesser, 'The New Film History as Media Archaeology', *CIN* QUOTE *MAS*, Vol. 14, Nos. 2–3, 2004, pp. 71–114; Erkki Huhtamo and Jussi Parikka (eds.), *Media Archaeology: Approaches, Applications, Implications* (Berkeley: University of California Press, 2011); Jussi Parikka, *What is Media Archaeology?* (Cambridge: Polity Press, 2012); Siegfried Zielinski, *Deep Time of the Media: Toward an Archaeology of Hearing and Seeing By Technical Means* (Cambridge, MA: MIT Press, 2006).
19. Garnet Hertz and Jussi Parikka, 'Zombie Media: Circuit Bending Media Archaeology into an Art Method', *Leonardo*, Vol. 45, No. 5, 2012, pp. 424–430.
20. Florian Cramer, 'What is Post-Digital?', in David M. Berry and Michael Dieter (eds.), *Postdigital Aesthetics: Art, Computation and Design* (Basingstoke: Palgrave Macmillan, 2015), p. 15.
21. Ibid., p. 17.
22. Svetlana Boym, *The Future of Nostalgia* (New York: Basic, 2001); Louise Crew and Nicky Gregson, *Second-Hand Cultures* (Oxford: Berg, 2003); Elizabeth Guffey, *Retro: The Culture of Revival* (London: Foci, 2006); Amy Holdsworth, *Television, Memory and Nostalgia* (Basingstoke: Palgrave Macmillan, 2011); Jake Kinzey, *The Sacred and the Profane: An Investigation of Hipsters* (Winchester: Zero, 2010); Katharina Niemeyer (ed.), *Media and Nostalgia: Yearning for the Past, Present and Future* (Basingstoke: Palgrave Macmillan, 2014); Kim Knowles, 'Locating Vintage', *NECSUS_European Journal of Media Studies*, Vol. 4, No. 2, Autumn 2015: https://necsus-ejms.org/locating-vintage/; Simon Reynolds, *Retromania: Pop Culture's Addition to Its Own Past* (London: Faber and Faber, 2011).
23. Fred Davis, *Yearning for Yesterday: A Sociology of Nostalgia* (New York and London: The Free Press, 1979).
24. Svetlana Boym, *The Future of Nostalgia*, p. xvi.

25. 'l'obsolescence ne témoigne pas d'une disparition ou d'une destruction d'un sujet ou d'un objet, mais au contraire de sa profonde conservation, malgré tout, malgé les changements que peuvent subir le milieu, les renversements culturels, les métamorphoses paradigmatiques, les évolutions technologiques. L'obsolescence est le hyperconservation d'une entité que devient inadaptée à son milieu.' Mathias Rollot, *L'obsolescence: Ouvrir l'impossible* (Geneva: Metis Presses, 2016), p. 33.
26. Tacita Dean, 'Artist Questionnaire: 21 Responses', *October*, Vol. 100, Obsolescence Special Issue, Spring 2002, p. 26.
27. Personal interview with the artist, 3 June 2019.
28. See, for instance, Christa Blümlinger, *Cinéma de seconde main—Esthétique du remploi dans l'art du film et des nouveaux médias* (Paris: Klincksieck, 2013); Nicholas Chare and Liz Watkins, 'The Matter of Film: Decasia and Lyrical Nitrate'; Dirk de Bryn, 'Recovering the Hidden Through Found-Footage Films', both in Estelle Barrett and Barbara Bolt (eds.), *Carnal Knowledge: Towards a 'New Materialism' Through the Arts* (London and New York: I. B. Tauris, 2013), pp. 75–87 and pp. 89–104 respectively.
29. Acland, 'Introduction: Residual Media', p. xvii.
30. Tacita Dean, 'Save Celluloid, for Art's Sake', *The Guardian*, 22 February 22 2011: https://www.theguardian.com/artanddesign/2011/feb/22/tacita-dean-16mm-film (accessed 14 May 2018).
31. Ibid.
32. Malcolm Le Grice, *Experimental Cinema in the Digital Age* (London: BFI, 2001), p. xi.
33. On February 2012, 800 industry professionals came together at the Tate Modern in London to celebrate and call for the protection of photochemical film. This culminated in a proposal—initiated by the Mexican cinematographer Guillermo Navarro and led by Stuart Comer (film curator, Tate) and Tacita Dean—to UNESCO to declare film a World Heritage. In their proposal they state: 'Many in the cinema industry and in the art, museum and archive communities are reaching the consensus that such cultural irresponsibility and short-sightedness cannot be allowed to take place in what is seen as a critical moment in film's survival. We are therefore coming together as a body to petition UNESCO to protect the medium of film as a World Heritage so that future generations will be able to experience film as we have done': http://www.imago.org/index.php?new=604 (accessed 20 April 2018).
34. Erika Balsom, *Exhibiting Cinema in Contemporary Art* (Amsterdam: Amsterdam University Press, 2013).
35. Ibid., p. 15.
36. Ibid., p. 71.
37. Rodowick, *The Virtual Life of Film*, p. 158.

38. René Daumal, *Mount Analogue: A Novel of Symbolically Authentic Non-Euclidean Adventures in Mountain Climbing* (London: Vincent Stuart, 1959).
39. Tacita Dean, 'FILM', in *Catalogue for the Exhibition* FILM, *11 October 2011–11 March 2012* (London: Tate Publishing, 2011), p. 27.
40. https://www.eyefilm.nl/en/exhibition/celluloid (accessed 13 February 2020).
41. See Peter Kubelka, 'The Theory of Metrical Film', in P. Adams Sitney, *The Avant-Garde Film: A Reader of Theory and Criticism* (New York: Anthology Film Archives, 1978), pp. 139–159.
42. Polaroid photography has continued on a smaller scale with The Impossible Project, a company that started life as a sales outlet for Polaroid film called Unsaleable. When Polaroid closed its last film factory in 2008 as a result of bankruptcy, the founder of Unsaleable, Florian Kaps, bought the plant and renamed the company after a quote by Polaroid's founder Edwin Land: 'Don't undertake a project unless it is manifestly important and nearly impossible.' David Sax, *The Revenge of Analog: Real Things and Why They Matter* (New York: Public Affairs, 2016), pp. 66–71.
43. British filmmaker Neil Henderson has similarly focused on the relationship between photographic and filmic temporality in a series of works based on Polaroid images. *Candle* (2009), for example, 'is a film that documents a Polaroid developing. It is shot on a 100-foot roll of black and white 16mm film. This standard film length is roughly equal to the time it takes for the Polaroid to fully develop, about three minutes. The film presents this photographic event in reverse. Over the duration of the film the image of a candle disappears back into the emulsion of the photograph. [...] The developing image is a time-based event and acts as an interval between the taking of the picture and the final settled image. Film preserves this moment, and makes possible its manipulation.' Neil Henderson, 'Emptying Frames', *Animation Practice, Process & Production*, Vol. 1, No. 1, 2011, p. 78.
44. This description was originally written for the Reset the Apparatus! online database: http://www.resettheapparatus.net/corpus-work/the-clouds-are-not-like-either-one.html.
45. Catherine Elwes, *Installation and the Moving Image* (New York: Wallflower Press, 2015), p. 256.
46. See, in particular, Walter Benjamin, 'Surrealism: The Last Snapshot of the European Intelligentsia', in Michael W. Jennings, Howard Eiland and Gary Smith (eds.), *Walter Benjamin, Selected Writings, Volume 2, 1927–1934* (Cambridge, MA and London: Belknap Press, 1999), pp. 207–221.
47. See, for example, Erika Balsom, *Exhibiting Cinema in Contemporary Art*; Erika Balsom, Lucy Reynolds and Sarah Perks, *Artists' Moving Image*

in Britain Since 1989 (New Haven: Yale University Press); Maeve Connolly, *The Place of Artists' Cinema: Space, Site and Screen* (Bristol: Intellect, 2009); Catherine Elwes, *Installation and the Moving Image*; Tamara Trodd (ed.), *Screen/Space: The Projected Image in Contemporary Art* (Manchester: Manchester University Press, 2012).

48. Peter Gidal, 'Theory and Definition of Structural/Materialist Film', in Mark Webber and Peter Gidal (eds.), *Flare Out: Aesthetics 1966–2016* (London: The Visible Press, 2016), pp. 37–68. Originally published in 1976 in *Studio International* Vol. 190, No. 978, pp. 189–196.

CHAPTER 2

Materials, Materiality, New Materialism

The arguments made in this book relate primarily to a mode of experimental film practice commonly referred to as 'materialist', that is, works that draw attention to the material of the filmstrip through tactile intervention and obscure vision by creating multiple layers, tangible surfaces, proximal views and haptic images. In this chapter, I sketch out a foundation for thinking about materials, materiality and materialism in a contemporary context, finding new points of connection between film aesthetics and current political concerns that demand new ways of seeing, sensing and experiencing our physical world. I navigate overlapping avenues of thought that relate to the value of photochemical film as an artistic tool capable of communicating across multiple materialities: bodily, earthly, human and non-human. I emphasise materiality, therefore, as both aesthetics and politics, necessarily framed by film's obsolete status, which, as I outlined in the introduction, bestows on it a critical and oppositional force and allows it to articulate alternative subject positions. That the demise of celluloid film as a commercial medium coincides with both a rising awareness of the finite physicality of the planet and a wave of scholarly discourse calling for a more attuned material sensibility suggests that the time is ripe for a reassessment of materialist film's radical potential and theoretical implications. Far from looking backwards into film's glorious past, artists working photochemical resources are, I argue, resolutely focused on present-day issues and future challenges. Accordingly,

K. Knowles, *Experimental Film and Photochemical Practices*,
Experimental Film and Artists' Moving Image,
https://doi.org/10.1007/978-3-030-44309-2_2

new theoretical paradigms are mobilised here to take into account this cutting-edge position.

However, no contemporary phenomenon exists in a vacuum, and only by returning at times to the historical context will the current situation be effectively unfolded and more concretely understood. To a large extent, materialist film has its roots in the 1960s and 1970s, with the establishment of the London Filmmakers Co-op and the emergence of a set of theorisations—notably through the filmmaker-critic Peter Gidal and his 'Theory and Definition of Structural/Materialist Film' of 1975—in which interrogating the physical substrate and laying bare the means of production were framed as anti-representational political gestures in opposition to the illusionism of narrative cinema.[1] As I will outline throughout the current and subsequent chapters, there are some key resonances between this period and the contemporary moment, particularly in terms of the re-appropriation of industrial equipment for fine art purposes, the emphasis on artistic autonomy and the exploration of material processes that bear the trace of the artist's hand. But although the 1960s and '70s might be considered the origin of the first systematic examinations of materialist filmmaking from a theoretical perspective, many earlier examples serve as precursors to the kinds of material reflection that have accompanied the recent 'renaissance' of photochemical film. Ever since Man Ray's first film *Le Retour à la raison* (1923), artists have sought out ways to activate and interrogate the material properties of film, directing attention towards film as a surface rather than a transparent window. Man Ray's sequences of 'rayograms', produced by placing objects directly onto or above the filmstrip and exposing it to light, subverted the norms of photographic representation by rejecting the camera and embracing the material support, creating direct imprints and traces rather than perspectival representations. These sections of the film pass by as a flurry of forms, a frenetic dance of objects barely perceptible at sixteen frames per second. Certain details are discernible—pins, sequins, a spring—whilst others appear only as abstract impressions, dusting the surface of the screen, as well as the eye of the viewer. Consistently discussed in terms of its association with the Dada movement, and thus its purely destructive features, the film might also be considered as opening up an alternative visual order.[2] How else, Man Ray seems to ask, are we to present on the screen matter such as salt and pepper, pins and drawing pins? Such material—the banal and the everyday—demands a new aesthetic that allows it to transcend its purely functional status, communicate its physical qualities and elicit affective responses in the viewer.

The challenge to perception was largely the driving force of 1920s avant-garde cinema, grounded in the modernist desire for anti-realist and non-linear modes of representation that swept through all the arts. Bill Nichols has referred to these modernist films (by Man Ray as well as his contemporaries Fernand Léger, René Clair, Hans Richter, Walter Ruttmann, Dziga Vertov and others) as a form of documentary, subverting the traditional understanding of documentary as essentially representational. He argues that the techniques of fragmentation, defamiliarisation and abstraction are 'less a retreat from the social world into aesthetic reverie' than a critique of the very notion of realism.[3] Politics, in this sense, begins with the question of vision, and the challenge to normative ways of seeing the world is the first step in a movement towards social transformation. Although there is no mention in Nichols' account of Man Ray's foray into camera-less filmmaking, this alternative approach to representation seems crucial to the consideration of avant-garde filmmaking techniques in terms of the relationship between an alternative documentary impulse and the embrace of a materialist aesthetic.

Material Bodies

Scattered throughout the history of experimental film are attempts to draw out the expressive potential of the celluloid material, from the camera-less animation of Len Lye, Norman McLaren, Harry Smith and Hy Hirsch between the 1930s and 1960s, through techniques of painting, scratching, burning, tearing and bleaching in the Lettrist films of Isidore Isou and Maurice Lemaître in the 1940s, to the myriad material interventions by artists such as Paul Sharits, Birgit and Wilhelm Hein, Pierre Rovère, Jose Antonio Sistiaga, Takahiko Iimura, Owen Land, Stan Brakhage, Carolee Schneemann, Peter Tscherkassky, Frédérique Devaux and Aldo Tambellini, to name just a few. Underlying these divergent approaches is not only an interest in the medium-specific properties of film, but also, more importantly, a desire to create embodied cinematic experiences and alternative forms of knowledge that rely on material entanglement and physical connection. Although many examples of materialist film involve the staging of physicality through destruction, the emphasis often lies in what is revealed through this process rather than on the act of destruction as an end in itself. Paul Sharits's *3rd Degree*

(1982), for example, pushes his intensely physical series of flicker films in the 1960s (*Piece Mandala/End War*, 1966; *Razor Blades*, 1966; *T,O,U,C,H,I,N,G*, 1968; *N:O:T:H:I:N:G*, 1968) further into the realms of bodily implication by breaking through the material surface. A three-screen installation that can also be shown as a single-screen piece, *3rd Degree* visualises the gradual breakdown of the filmstrip as it is burnt in the projector. By manually running the strip backwards and forwards and slowing it down to increase the time of exposure to the projector bulb, scars gradually appear and bubble out to the sides leaving a gaping absence but also a very tangible material presence. The film contains the image of a woman's face being threatened with a lit match that is thrust towards her. The soundtrack occasionally emits the sound of the striking match followed by the words 'Look. I won't talk'. The second screen is a film of the first, which is also subsequently burnt and represented in a third screen, by which point the layers of deterioration render both the image and sounds barely perceptible. Sharits's own account of the film draws attention to the interlacing of bodies—the body of film and the filmed body:

> This film is 'about' the fragility of the film medium and human vulnerability, both the filmic and the human images resist threat intimidation/mutilation, the victim is defiant and the film strip also struggles on, both 'under fire'. It is a somewhat violent drama but it is also an ironically comic work and there is a formal beauty in the destructiveness of the burning film.[4]

Fragility, defiance, material destruction and vulnerability: all of these terms capture in some way the current status of film—both materially and culturally—but they also resonate with the contemporary theoretical positions on environmental instability that I will go on to outline below. I thus use Sharits's film, and his comments about it, as a springboard for thinking about trajectories of materialist film and the centrality of both body and vision to these practices.

Sharits highlights the body of the film—its physical struggle and persistence 'under fire'. It is, in fact, through the use of bodily metaphors and mortality that photochemical film has often been discussed in the contemporary era, particularly in the field of film preservation. At the turn of the millennium—the point at which film's obsolete status was thrown into relief by the increasing embrace of digital technology—Paolo Cherchi Usai lamented that '[m]oving image preservation will be redefined as the science of gradual loss and the art of coping with the consequences, very much like a physician who has accepted the inevitability of death, even while he fights for the patient's life'.[5] In D. N. Rodowick's view, film's chemical substrate makes it:

> perhaps the most impermanent and variable substance for the registration of images yet found in the history of art-making: what doesn't explode in flames [...] will slowly dissolve [...] one may say that the material basis of film is a chemically encoded process of entropy. This is one of the many ways in which watching film is literally a spectatorship of death.[6]

It is revealing to juxtapose the two statements by Sharits and Rodowick, both of which emphasise film's inherent entropic character and its relationship to destruction. However, whilst Sharits celebrates the point of resistance or the edge of entropy as a creative force, Rodowick seems resigned to dissolution as an end point—death pure and simple. The 'death of cinema' discourse may have subsided in recent years, but the focus on the chemical instabilities of film is still very much present in preservation and conservation practices, as well as the artistic field of 'ruinophilia', where death and decay become the subject of aesthetic enquiry. A sub-category of experimental found footage film or cultural recycling, the ruin film revels in the physical beauty of chemical decomposition, the traces of time that register as marks and scars on the body of the celluloid and shift attention from the photographic images to the material surface. In the films of Bill Morrison and Peter Delpeut, along with recent examples such as Leandro Listorti's *La película infinita* (*The Endless Film*, 2018) and Sami van Ingen's *Polte* (*Flame*, 2018), decay becomes a lens through which to interrogate the intertwined poles of film history and film materiality (Fig. 2.1).[7]

In this sense, the ruin film occupies quite hazy territory in relation to materialist film aesthetics. What can seem in one instance (or instant) to be offering a critical perspective on the instability of the archive can easily shift into the display of deterioration as an object of mere pleasurable consumption and nostalgic lament. Nicholas Chare and Liz Watkins, in their discussion of *Decasia* (Morrison, 2002) and *Lyrical Nitrate* (Delpeut, 1990), argue that the 'underlying materiality of film is usually disavowed

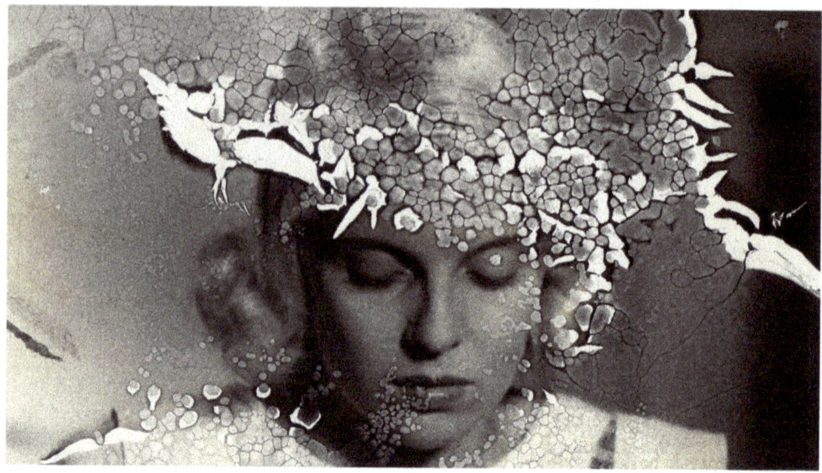

Fig. 2.1 *Polte* (*Flame*), Sami van Ingen, 2018 (Image courtesy of the artist and testifilmi)

in studies of cinema', where narrative content and questions of representation and signification are the main focus of enquiry.[8] Decomposed found footage film, however, makes manifest this materiality as the veneer of photographic realism breaks down and exposes the underlying organic substance. In their view, this process 'functions to undermine the grammar and syntax of the films', making possible alternative readings.[9] The physical matter—those 'bubbling, troubled and troubling images'—reveal latent meanings and repressed traumas that the authors, via the semiotic theory of Julia Kristeva, trace to the psychic scars of the Holocaust.[10] In his reworking of structural/materialist theory, Dirk de Bruyn similarly associates materialist film practice with what he refers to as the 'performance of trauma'.[11] Although de Bruyn's notion of materialist film is not limited to the physicality of the film strip, it is clear that the rupture produced through the passage of moving image culture from the photochemical to the digital has thrown into relief a bodily awareness and a heightened sense of physicality that manifests in both creative approaches and theoretical formulations. As Laura Marks states in her discussion of faded films and decaying video tapes: 'These images appeal to a look that does not recoil from death, but acknowledges death as part of our being'.[12]

Jeanne Liotta's *Loretta* (2003) is an example of how questions of materiality, the body, death and mourning come together in a forceful appeal to the senses. In many ways, *Loretta* stages the 'death of cinema' discourse by making visible and tangible the physical surfaces, edges, scratches and grain of the celluloid, folding them into the ghostly image of a human figure that seems to undergo its own traumatic experience. 35mm negative photographs were contact printed onto 16mm film by exposing the images with a flashlight section by section, even frame by frame. Strips of positive and negative are combined and yellow food colouring rubbed into the film by hand—a painstakingly labour-intensive process reminiscent of Georges Méliès. The film explodes onto the screen with a burst of yellow light, a corresponding explosion on the soundtrack immediately creating a complex fusion of the senses. A confusing array of abstract and figurative visual stimuli lashes out at the spectator with frenzied, hypnotic speed. From between the flickering images a disembodied human figure continually appears and disappears as if being washed onto the surface of the screen, only to be dragged back into a sea of film fragments, sprocket holes and material debris. The figure oscillates between black against yellow and yellow against black in a constant movement between figure and ground. A hand reaches out, as if appealing to the viewer, who helplessly watches the writhing, suffering body as it slowly dissolves into the abstract matter (Fig. 2.2).

Made in the wake of her mother's death after a lengthy period of illness, Liotta employs 'visceral excitation'[13] or what Walter Benjamin calls the 'physical shock effect',[14] to explore and translate the experience of grief. Mourning is expressed *through* the body (of the filmmaker) *on* the body (of the film), to be felt physically *in* the body (of the spectator)—a process of tactile translation that, as I will discuss further in this chapter, hinges on the communicative power of the celluloid surface. In its collage-like construction, *Loretta* presents what could be understood as a series of elusive sensory memory fragments that continually cancel each other out through film's insistence on presence in the moment of projection. Fragments of sound—a ringing telephone, the barely audible hum of human voices, snippets of music—seem to merge with the flicker of the images as if drifting in and out of focus and demonstrating the ungraspable yet evocative nature of sense-related memory. The trapped figure attempts to free itself from the gradually deteriorating forward movement of memory, represented in the fragility of the film itself, to stop itself from 'suffocating in the emulsion'.[15] Representation and

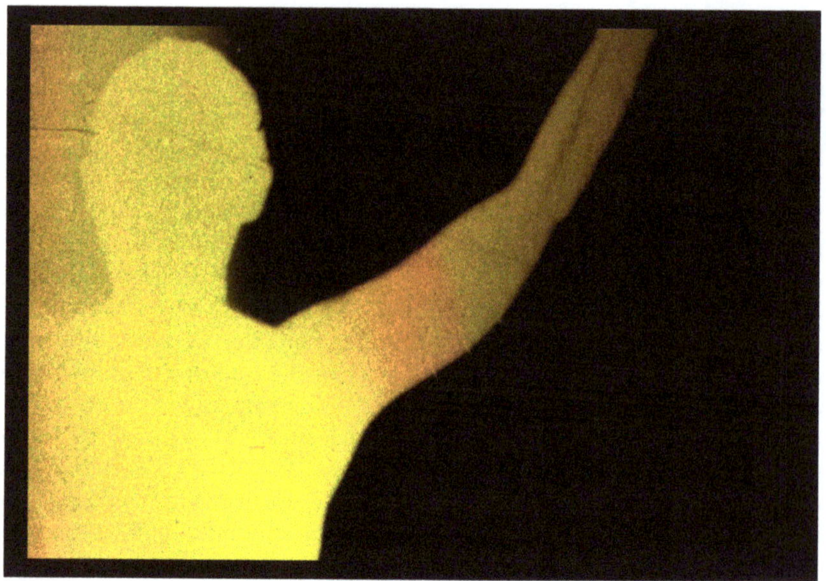

Fig. 2.2 *Loretta*, Jeanne Liotta, 2003 (Image courtesy of the artist)

the difficulty of vision are central to how the film functions on an affective level: our eyes do not—cannot—fix or contain the image. Form and content, figure and ground are in a constant state of flux, a process of becoming that prevents one from dominating the other. Matter washes over matter in a ritualistic cinematic burial that sees death as an inevitable part of the earthly continuum (Fig. 2.3).

Wake (2015) by Eric Stewart is another recent example of how the materiality of film can be employed to express loss and mourning on a very intimate scale. Echoing Man Ray's approach in *Le Retour à la raison*, Stewart scattered his deceased father's ashes onto 35mm film, leaving an indexical trace of the body and opening up another level of corporeal understanding. In an attempt to represent death—the absent body—the filmmaker turns to the expressive potential of matter and the representational possibilities of contact. Just as Man Ray found a way to allow everyday objects to reveal their soul through the rayogram technique, so too does Stewart draw on the physical nature of film in order to perceive the ashes as a new body and to experience death differently. He describes

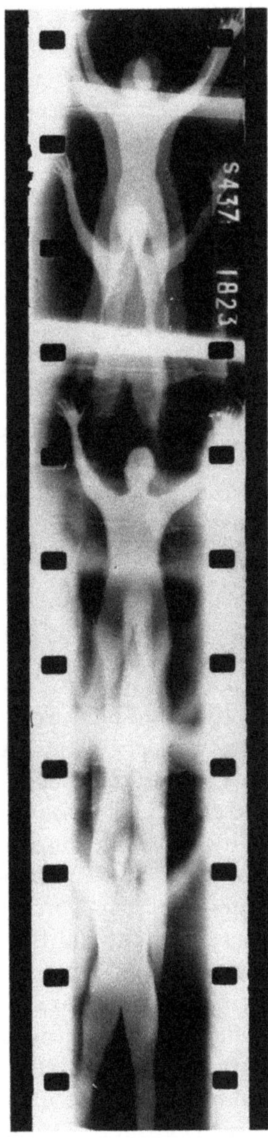

Fig. 2.3 *Loretta*, Jeanne Liotta, 2003. Black and white rayograms prior to the addition of colour (Image courtesy of the artist)

the film as creating presence through absence, opening up an in-between space: 'What we see in this process of photogramming is not the object in the photographic sense, but instead a representation of the space surrounding an object. The photogram is a shadow charting the distance between things'.[16]

The organic nature of the film strip, and its ability to communicate death, destruction and decay, provides a context for thinking through shared materialities and alternative forms of vision, particularly in relation to the body. But in order to consider materialist film more clearly within a contemporary context and to understand the relevance of its creative persistence as an apparently obsolete technology, it is necessary to broaden the scope of the argument slightly, taking into consideration the slippery nature of the word 'material'. This will assist us in moving towards a fuller appreciation of how the terms of materialist film shift from one historical period to the next. If we state that photochemical film practice, through its material specificity, is able to articulate alternative positions, what exactly are these positions and how do they operate in a world of material excess, fluid subjectivities and political unrest?

Materiality and the Ecological Thought

What does it mean to speak about materiality in the twenty-first century? In today's digital world, the concept is fraught with anxieties, contradictions and paradoxes. As more and more of human experience migrates to the virtual domain, the rate of commodity production and disposal increases, giving rise to an overabundance of things. Novelty trumps durability, and while humans live longer, most material goods have a lightning-fast life cycle that condemns them to the rubbish heap within just a few years. Whilst the virtual world promises to make our lives cleaner, clearer, more efficient and less cluttered, the reality is a growing pile of technological waste—what Jonathan Sterne calls 'the other side of innovation'.[17] Furthermore, as Jussi Parikka has argued, '[t]he immaterialization of digitality as a service on the cloud has forced us to consider that we need new political vocabularies that address the double bind of technical materiality and conceptual immateriality'.[18] Parikka's account emphasises the (literal) grounded-ness of the digital, dependent as it is on precious geological resources extracted from the earth and invariably bound up in 'unsustainable, politically dubious, and ethically suspicious practices'.[19] The relationship between technology and ecology is an increasingly prevalent concern in the field of media history and theory, with writers such as Jennifer Gabrys, Sean Cubitt and Parikka calling for a more heightened awareness of the complex material entanglements at play in the process of innovation and obsolescence.[20] Parikka's concept of 'medianatures'[21] points towards the '*weird materialities*' that constitute the hardware of modern technological devices and their potential after effects on the environment in the form of e-waste or electrical signals, whilst Gabrys, in her 'natural history of electronics', offers a mode of thinking about objects and commodities in terms of their spatial, temporal and political effects—a form of archaeological excavation that 'works through cast-off objects in order to take up the "scatter" of electronic materialities'.[22]

The discussion of film as an obsolete medium—the emerging micro-ecologies of artisanal production and the flourishing practices that interrogate the material specificities of the celluloid substrate—is therefore situated within a broader field of material reflection and negotiation. The discourses that framed materialist film practice in the 1960s and 1970s in terms of its radical gestures and political significance are now replaced (or at least supplemented) with perspectives that take into account both the shifting technological landscape and the related questions of environmental instability in an increasingly computerised and networked society. Medium-specificity is no longer an issue of materials alone (in the sense of representational relations), but of *materiality* as a more far-reaching concept, and it is my contention in this book that the continuation of photochemical film practice can be understood within the context of the 'material turn' taking place across the social sciences. Against the backdrop of rampant consumerism and increasingly invasive marketing campaigns for new products, lifestyles and experiences, emergent writings on material culture take up much-needed critical positions on the importance of 'stuff' and how we relate to it.[23] This is accompanied by a global populace waking up (albeit to varying degrees and, for some commentators, perhaps too late) to the effects of air pollution, plastic pollution, resource depletion and the many devastating by-products of the manufacturing and farming industries. In the following pages, photochemical film is considered in relation to technological obsolescence, material culture and ecological thinking in order to stimulate reflection on how creative practices of material engagement offer alternative ways of seeing and sensing the world. Thinking through the ecological issues of our time will allow us to assess some of the wider political implications of an artistic field so invested in the material possibilities of what is now largely considered as the waste product of a past industrial era.

Waste—the discarded, the cast-off, the abject—is, in fact, one of the key concerns of our time, even more so in the context of rising global population numbers and the parallel increase in the production (and rapid disposal) of consumer technologies.[24] As Evan Watkins already observed in 1993, the discarded relates not only to material consumables but also to human bodies—particular societal groups, whose 'throwaway' status derives from their inability to contribute productively to the capitalist economy.[25] Writing in the context of obsolescence, Watkins refers to 'isolated groups of the population, who haven't moved with the times, and who now litter the social landscape', into which category we might place the elderly, the poor and the deskilled. As we edge towards ever-more technologically automated systems, the human workforce itself becomes increasingly disposable, leading to fears about 'a future in which computer and robotics technology replaces human labour not just in traditional domains such as agriculture and manufacturing, but also in sectors ranging from medicine and law to transportation'.[26] The material consequences of technological obsolescence extend well beyond the objects themselves, affecting traditions, practices, human relations and ways of life. In terms of throwaway social groups, we might also add the spatially and geographically displaced—refugees, migrants and the homeless.[27] Political and ideological borders are also material, their embodied effects resonating through the more abstract 'body' of society. If we consider as related (how could we not?) the issues of obsolescence and climate change, then it follows, as Bruno Latour convincingly argues, that displacement, immigration panic and the subsequent closing of borders all stem from the same material concerns. In Latour's words, 'the climate question is at the heart of all geopolitical issues […] it is directly tied to questions of injustice and inequality'.[28] Understanding our relationship to waste, then, involves thinking a complex set of interrelations that involve the human and the non-human, the animate and the inanimate.

In *The Ethics of Waste*, Gay Hawkins offers an approach to rubbish that reveals dominant social structures and normalised divisions, pointing to the ways in which subjectivity is constituted through our relationship to matter, from the things we produce and the objects we value to the stuff we throw away and the waste that lingers. The capitalist imperative of consume-discard-repeat creates material divisions that come to dictate other ethical encounters with the world, including the human–non-human hierarchy. 'A lot can happen when waste is noticed', suggests Hawkins. 'The waste that suddenly claims our attention, maybe by its repulsive smell, maybe by its ephemeral presence on the side of the road, can disrupt habits and precipitate new sensations and perceptions'.[29] In this 'sense', noticing waste, engaging with the tensions that arise from matter out of place and tuning into the energetic impulses of discarded objects—like the surrealist concept of 'convulsive beauty' or Walter Benjamin's 'revolutionary spark'—provides an opening to alternative ways of negotiating the world. It offers an antidote to the prescribed 'order of things' in which our relationship to the hierarchies of matter is always intrinsically, yet often imperceptibly, political.[30] As Michel Foucault points out, human behaviour is controlled and disciplined through a web of normalised power relations that range from the macro-level of social institutions to the micro-level of interactions with everyday objects and commodities. Perceptual rupture or renewal, as Hawkins suggests, is the starting point for unpicking and undermining these relations—the beginning of a politics of resistance that will be a key theme throughout this book.

The imperative to take up alternative subject positions in relation to the discarded is also central to Jane Bennett's theory of vibrant matter, derived largely from the seventeenth-century philosopher Baruch Spinoza's concept of 'vital materialism'. Here, the notion that a life force runs through all material phenomena forges a path of rediscovery, along which the relationship between things can be rewritten and reimagined according to a different set of rules. Describing an encounter with a littering of disparate items on a street in Baltimore—a plastic work glove, a chunk of oak pollen, a dead rat, a plastic bottle cap, and a stick of wood—Bennett argues that the affective draw of such a scene demonstrates how 'thing power [can rise] from a pile of trash'.[31] In the movement of emphasis from the radical act of simply noticing, or consciously sensing that which perceptual normativity relegates to the edges of our attention, to the recognition that objects themselves have an expressive interiority that goes beyond their surface function and form, a theoretical position emerges that has much broader implications for understanding the complexities of the material world and our position within it.

What is it about the discarded object specifically that triggers such strong feelings and compels both Hawkins and Bennett to argue for the political significance of trash? It is partly the sense of rediscovery that comes with a juxtaposition of objects that do not belong together, whose silent co-existence disturbs the natural order. We only need to think, here, of the surrealist definition of beauty (derived from the poetry of the Comte de Lautréamont) as 'the chance meeting on a dissecting table of a sewing machine and an umbrella'. In their random constellations, these objects ask us to perceive them anew, to look beyond the functional properties and traditional uses assigned to them. It is also, perhaps, the powerful obstinacy of these things in their refusal to disappear once their use value has been exhausted that affects us. Freed from their original purpose—be it natural or man-made—they enter into new relationships, their material form and surface textures taking on new significance. It is here that we can locate the first resonance with film technology as a discarded medium, its association with waste, as well as its critical position outside the mainstream. As this book aims to demonstrate, the contemporary status of film is one of liminality; used up, thrown out, a thing of the past, it continues to exist on the cultural periphery, disturbing notions of technological progress and replacement via its bulky mechanical presence and connotations of pastness.[32] It is, in many ways, an abject object in the sense of the living undead.

For Bennett, matter has expressive potential that manifests as an interconnected vibration across all things, both animate and inanimate. Her view that so-called inert or passive matter has agency and that objects 'act' as well as being acted *upon*, upends traditional Eurocentric assumptions about the primacy and privileged place of the human in a world of multiple materialities. Bennett's work is part of a wider intellectual trend loosely referred to as 'new materialism' and involving a number of overlapping philosophical positions on the material world—how matter behaves, how we perceive it and how it responds to encounters with other things. Although divergent in their specific theoretical articulations and epistemological foundations, we find in this reworking of ideas related to materiality a common commitment to challenging what Rosi Braidotti refers to as the 'hegemonic cultural model' of Humanism, which has led to man's unfettered dominance of the planet via a normalised system of power relations.[33] In this model, all life is subordinate to, and at the mercy of, human will. Braidotti imagines, in contrast, a non-human approach, a post-anthropocentrism that 'displaces the notion of species hierarchy and of a single, common standard for 'Man' as the measure of all things'.[34] In a similar vein, Graham Harman has stated that object-oriented ontology 'cannot be sympathetic to any form of human-centred politics, which treats the political sphere as if it were the product of human nature and purely human history. Object-oriented politics also means that non-human objects are crucial political actors'.[35] Although Harman refers to Bennett as a 'fellow traveler', he rejects her 'flat ontology' approach, which considers all matter—both organic and inorganic—as ultimately connected through a Bergsonian '*élan vital*' or life force. For Harman, objects pre-exist their relations with other objects, a view that also contrasts with Karen Barad's relational ontology, in which the notion of stable representational entities assumes a knowing (human) subject. 'It is through specific agential intra-actions', states Barad, 'that the boundaries and properties of the "components" of phenomena become determinate and that particular embodied concepts become meaningful'.[36] Agency, here, does not mean transposing human qualities onto non-human entities, but instead relates to a mode of thinking the world horizontally, 'rather than vertically as a hierarchy of being'.[37] In Bennett's view, this paves the way for a more ecological sensibility and a 'greater appreciation of the entanglements of humans and non-humans'.[38]

Framing these discussions and reconsiderations of materialism is the overwhelming sense that new directions are urgently required for the future survival of the planet and the various species that inhabit it. In recent years, this awareness has come under the grand moniker 'Anthropocene': the new 'geo-historical period, in which humans are said to have become the biggest threat to life on earth'.[39] First coined by Paul Crutzen and Eugene Stoermer, the concept has resonated across virtually all disciplines, giving rise to an explosion of scholarly materials and artistic projects that attempt to engage with the ethics and aesthetics of climate change and environmental catastrophe.[40] Anthropocene provides a catch-all term for thinking about our current ecological crisis—from global warming and species extinction to over-development and pollution—and might be said to increase awareness of such issues. As T. J. Demos points out, contributions to the Anthropocene discourse 'point to a massive transformation that is occurring in how we might comprehend the present intersection of human culture and the environment that is remaking the world as we know it'.[41] Environmental awareness in art and intellectual thought is certainly not a new phenomenon, but the force and urgency with which it has swept through our collective consciousness is. The state of the planet is daily news, as is the political corruption associated with it.

However, whilst no-one would deny the role of human activity (globalisation, urban expansion, economic growth at all costs) in the production of environmental fragility, the concept of the Anthropocene has come under criticism in many circles for, amongst other things, its paradoxical anthropocentrism. The vision of 'Man' as the sole agent of environmental destruction glosses over key cultural distinctions, social inequalities and political agendas, assuming equal responsibility across a seemingly homogenous 'Planet Earth'. Reinstating a problematic Humanism that so much intellectual and artistic discourse has worked to dismantle, the Anthropocene is our contemporary conundrum. Claire Colebrook argues that, 'To return to the "anthropos", now, after all these years of difference seems to erase all the work in postcolonialism that had declared enlightenment "man", to be a fiction that allowed all the world to be "white like me"'.[42] Clearly the Anthropocene is not a concept to be rejected entirely, but should be modified to take into account the complex entanglements that make up our material world. Donna Haraway's concept of the 'chthulucene', for example, suggests that rather than apocalyptic viewpoints or misplaced faith in technofixes, the only adequate response to environmental uncertainty is 'staying with the trouble'—working through the mess by cultivating multispecies kinship.[43] A similar direction is forged in Timothy Morton's series of ecologically engaged studies *The Ecological Thought*, *Dark Ecology* and *Humankind,* all of which propose new critical pathways based on a deep material interconnection between humans and non-humans.[44] Morton's concept of ecological thought involves a subtle but radical shift from thinking *about* ecology and environmental issues such as climate change to thinking *through* and being *with* ecology: from separation to integration or implication. He states:

> *The ecological thought* is the thinking of interconnectedness. The ecological thought is a thought about ecology but it's also a thinking that is ecological. [...] The ecological thought doesn't just occur 'in the mind.' It's a practice and a process of becoming fully aware of how human beings are connected with other beings—animal, vegetable, or mineral.[45]

This has important consequences for questions of representation, since building a more ecological awareness of materiality and material entanglements ultimately necessitates not just a form of rethinking, but also a kind of 're-visioning'. Indeed, Joanna Zylinksa has recently argued that new artistic approaches are needed in order to bring about such an awareness.

Citing Nicholas Mirzoeff's view that the Anthropocene eludes both vision and comprehension due to its vastness of scale,[46] she suggests that processes of '*unseeing*' this phenomenon offer potentially productive avenues of understanding through feeling.[47] Morton's conceptualisation of environmental crisis in terms of the 'hyperobject' works through similar issues of visualisation:

> Hyperobjects are real objects that are massively distributed in time and space. Good examples would be global warming and nuclear radiation. Hyperobjects are so vast, so long lasting, that they defy human time and spatial scales. They wouldn't fit on a landscape painting.[48]

Like Zylinska, Morton draws on the senses as the principle site of encounter. 'We are stuck with hyperobjects', he argues. 'They stick to us literally: our bodies absorb nuclear radiation and we are totally surrounded by global warming'.[49] The failure of traditional modes of visual representation to communicate the physical, yet largely inaccessible, aspects of our environment relates to a particular kind of separation that involves the objectification of nature—a version, perhaps, of Laura Mulvey's gendered gaze and the coding of the female body in mainstream cinema in terms of its 'to-be-looked-at-ness'.[50] The presentation of the natural world as visual spectacle—what Anat Pick has referred to as 'ocular inflation'—prevents a deeper awareness of and connection with ecology, glossing over the uncomfortable realities in the name of pleasurable consumption.[51] Inherent in these representations is the assumption that seeing is understanding, and that by making the world *more* visible through greater clarity, precision and proximity (facilitated by advances in technological sophistication) we can conquer and contain the otherwise unknown. A key point of reference here would be the vastly popular television documentary series *The Blue Planet* (2001), *Planet Earth* (2006) and *Frozen Planet* (2011), which revel in the spectacular scenes of natural beauty and primal brutality that amaze and entertain yet do little to create real affective bonds. Pick cites Paul Virilio's 'zero degree of representation' to describe how the kind of optical overexposure that plagues conventional attempts to understand the world actually moves us further away from this goal by suppressing the unseen.[52] Similarly, Morton's reference to landscape painting (to which nature documentaries might be compared) in his discussion of hyperobjects underscores the limitations of established visual languages for presenting the world; we do not need to see *better* or more clearly, but *differently* and with a deeper physical awareness.

(Re)Visioning the World: The Aesthetic of Contact

How does this relate specifically to photochemical film practice in the digital era? How can we bring together these avenues of thought relating to waste, obsolescence, new materialism, the Anthropocene and visuality to create new perspectives on the political and aesthetic potential of celluloid film? These are surely, one might argue, grand claims for a dying medium, part of a last-ditch attempt to claim artistic legitimacy for a technology that is now already historical in the minds of many. I have suggested that, as is the case with any outmoded object or technology, the marginal or residual status of film bestows on it a critical force that allows it to speak a form of resistance to capitalist cycles of consumption and disposal that arise from an incessant pursuit of the new. This has been one of the key critical models for recent accounts of technological obsolescence, often drawing heavily on Walter Benjamin's theories of history and progress.[53] A spirit of resistance certainly runs through this book, but it is accompanied by an investment and a belief in the power of alternative forms of vision that have long defined the field of experimental filmmaking and which now resurface in fresh contexts. For it is precisely through the attention to surfaces, namely the photochemical substrate that registers the indexical trace of a physical encounter, that materialist film opens up a language of perceptual complexity. This *aesthetic of contact*, as I would like to call it, responds to the call for a wholesale re-visioning of the world with material gestures and experiential awakenings. It privileges the unseen through an emphasis on sensation—that which cannot be comprehended through vision alone, but which points to the politics of the encounter, the hand of the artist, the layers of time and the communicative spaces between physical phenomena. Reworking Raymond Bellour's concept of *l'entre-images* (between the images), I propose, here, the notion of *l'entre-objets* (between the objects) to describe an in-betweenness that manifests both as the self-reflexive staging of materiality through the presence of the film strip and the transformation of perception through proximal relations.[54] As Eric Stewart suggests in relation to his film *Wake*, discussed earlier, meaning arises not necessarily from the object itself, but from the space around it, or through the expressive tension produced in the encounter with another surface.

Rebecca Coleman and Liz Oakley-Brown point out that surfaces are a means 'by which particular ideas, relations, aspirations may be visualized and materialized', that is, they are the carrier of meaning, functioning as a receptacle or container. On the other hand, surfaces are also meaningful in themselves, offering an alternative source of knowledge about the world where traditional representational approaches fail to fully translate the essence of things. In this sense, surfaces, 'may themselves visualise, that is be a spatio-temporal site through which relations and materialities become visible, or not'.[55] The authors refer to Tim Ingold's account of the earth's surface, not as pre-existent but rather undergoing 'continuous generation'.[56] A surface is never fixed, in Ingold's view, but always in the process of becoming as it enters into a range of shifting material relations with other physical phenomena. Surfaces are therefore defined by perpetual movement and redefinition that bring to mind Barad's notion of 'intra-action'. Barad argues that phenomena are inseparable from—do not precede—their interlocking relations, suggesting an open-ended dialogue between matter that blurs the boundary between subject and object.[57] This understanding of matter as flux and flow can be anchored to a discussion of how new conceptions of materiality give rise to forms of relational vision, where images are not mastered as a unity that is always inevitably partial, but perceived through an ongoing process of *surfacing*.

In *Surface: Matters of Aesthetics, Materiality, and Media*, Giuliana Bruno follows a similar path, mapping out some key avenues for thinking about materiality and the significance of surfaces in a contemporary context. 'Rethinking materiality', she states, 'means fostering new forms of connection and relatedness'. She argues that 'materiality is not a question of materials but, fundamentally, of activating material relations'.[58] Bruno acknowledges the importance of the moving image in her discussion of surface aesthetics, particularly within a shifting technological landscape and its corresponding changes in spectatorship. But whilst much of her discussion centres on the spaces and sites of reception, such as the gallery environment and its mobile viewer, she also touches on the issues raised by the renewed cultural status of celluloid as it passes into a space of obsolescence. Film, she observes, is a 'dense fabric', 'as porous as skin', which also, like the human body, displays 'wrinkles of age' that inscribe time into its material layers.[59] Bruno is sensitive to the ways in which these qualities of film are emphasised in the digital era, arguing that an interrogation of materiality does not, as I pointed out in the introduction to this book, have to entail 'uncritical nostalgia' or the pitting of film against digital. She describes, rather, an impulse to reinvent and rediscover materiality that characterises contemporary work in both film and digital media. It is striking, then, given Bruno's nuanced account of these issues, that so few examples of materialist film practice are cited beyond the work of artists such as Bill Morrison and Tacita Dean. It seems vital to connect these ideas about the radical potential of materiality and the significance of surfaces to the relatively lesser-known and under-theorised field of contemporary celluloid practice—precisely the focus of the present study.

It is here that we find resonances between new materialism or critical posthumanism and the field of sensuous film theory, where a crucial turn to the body as the site of meaning-making has shifted scholarly attention away from an exclusive focus on cognitive processing and intellectual reasoning. Emerging as a new theoretical paradigm towards the end of the 1990s, this phenomenological approach has been heavily employed as a critical tool in cinema studies, paving the way for more nuanced accounts of how bodies come to matter in both the making and the reception of films. Vivian Sobchack's essay 'What My Fingers Knew: The Cinesthetic Subject, or Vision in the Flesh', for example, is a key text in the theoretical formulation of how films can elicit synaesthetic responses that are a natural part of how our bodies *actually* exist in, and respond to, the world.[60] The body, she argues, is an entity that '*in experience*, lives vision always in cooperation and significant exchange with other sensorial means of access to the world, a body that makes meaning before it makes conscious, reflective thought'.[61] Sensuous film theory allows us to understand how particular kinds of images appeal directly to the body, emerging from the screen as a tactile, rather than a purely visual, experience. Importantly, as a multi-sensory model it asks us to be mindful of affective responses and resonances, much as the new materialism of Jane Bennett and others evokes a sensitivity to the interconnected energies and vibrations that escape the human eye but are real nonetheless.

Activating the political potential of film surfaces and drawing attention to tactile modes of vision, Carolee Schneemann's *Fuses* (1964–1967) is a key reference point in the history of materialist filmmaking. Schneemann's friendship with Stan Brakhage was a key influencing factor, and *Fuses* was apparently made in response to his films depicting his domestic space and sexual intimacy such as *Cat's Cradle* (1959), *Wedlock House, An Intercourse* (1959) and *Window Water Baby Moving* (1963).[62] *Fuses*, she claimed, was 'in part an answer to Brakhage's *Loving*', a film made in

1956, in which she appears with her partner James Tenney.[63] As M. M. Serra and Kathryn Ramey have argued, in capturing her intensely sexual relationship with Tenney over several years, Schneemann shifts from being the object of the gaze in Brakhage's film and 'returns to the "eye/body", which includes the eyes of the artist-as-subject, the eyes of the artist as filmmaker, and the gaze of the viewer'.[64] To this, we should add the body of the film itself, which is scratched, punctured, painted, burnt and overlaid to create a dense and tactile fabric of erotic expression. As in Brakhage's *Dog Star Man* (1961–1964), Schneemann blends the photographic images with an awareness of the film surface, making it difficult to discern one image from another. The sense of bodily folding and dissolving that characterises the sexual intercourse depicted is inscribed into the form of the film and envelops the viewer in waves of material excess. As Schneemann explains:

> I wanted the bodies to be turning into tactile sensations of flickers. For the viewer to be lost in the frame – to move the body in and out of its own frame, to move the eye in and out of the body so even as viewers could see everything desired, the perceptions would be in a state of dissolution, optically resembling some aspect of the erotic streaming in the bodies, which cannot be a literal translation. It is a painterly, tactile translation edited as a music of frames.[65]

Again, mirroring Brakhage, the cat, like the 'medium cat' in *Cat's Cradle*, is witness to these intimate scenes, with the restless movement—the rapid shifting from one perspective to another—pointing to a form of non-human vision, where the recognisable points of reference and clear divisions between figure and ground are conspicuously absent.

A form of feminist filmmaking, *Fuses* liberates the female body from dominant visual regimes, using the surface interruptions and tactile gestures as a means to disrupt a penetrating voyeuristic gaze. As Peggy Phelan has argued, representation 'is almost always on the side of the one who looks and almost never on the side of the one who is seen'.[66] Resisting these dominant power structures means 'resisting the reproductive ideology of visible representations' altogether, and it is within these realms that a feminist approach to materialist film emerges.[67] Schneemann challenges dominant structures of looking, firstly by producing her own sexualised image, and being both the subject and object of the gaze, and secondly by employing a radically new visual language that approximates the sensuous contact between the two bodies on screen. Surface awareness draws the viewer away from voyeurism and towards a form of visual empathy. In Jennifer Barker's account, the surface inscriptions in *Fuses* enact a form of spectatorial disavowal and 'make vision difficult'.[68] Like the flurry of forms in Man Ray's *Le Retour à la raison* (1923), attention is directed away from the photographic image, 'thus invit[ing] the viewer to feel rather than see the film, to make contact with its skin'.[69] Here, the tactile proximity is understood as taking place *on* the surface, relocating attention from one form of bodily contact to another and physically implicating the spectator in the process. Laura Marks's definition of haptic visuality is grounded in this 'dialectical movement from far to near, from solely optical to multisensory', where images seem to reach out and touch the viewer through their surface presence.[70] The film functions, for Barker, as a springboard for developing a theory of tactile vision, where skin is a powerful communicating membrane.

This resonates strongly with a recent interest in the aesthetics of blur and indeterminacy in visual culture—a response, across both theory and practice, to the cultures of hyper-visibility described above.[71] Hito Steyerl's landmark essay 'In Defense of the Poor Image', for example, maps out some of the ways in which substandard legibility disturbs the neoliberal consumerist drive that frames the visual hierarchies of contemporary culture. Although her argument focuses primarily on digital data and its degradation through circulation, reproduction and compression, many of her broader claims about the 'political punch' of the poor image relate to other forms of illegibility. Particularly relevant to the present discussion is her observation that these low status images constitute 'the debris of audio-visual production, the trash that washes up on the digital economies' shores'.[72] Since our consideration of materialist film practice is framed by its marginal position as a form of cultural trash, it is possible to draw some comparisons; yet one must also keep in mind the very different value systems at play here. Whilst Steyerl emphasises those images that are produced cheaply and circulated freely, this is not necessarily the case with photochemical film, even if, as I will discuss in Chapters 3 and 4, the cultures formed around it are often based on minimal means and DIY processes. To a certain extent, film still carries with it the elitist associations of the industry, particularly when installed in galleries, where its 'aura' and its unique status as 'Art'—to return to D. N. Rodowick—become part of its overall signification. Nonetheless, Steyerl's claim for the oppositional potential of low-resolution images might be reconceptualised here as a model for thinking through materialist visuality and its celebration of touch as an alternative representational mode.[73]

In her introduction to a collection of essays entitled *Indefinite Visions: Cinema and the Attractions of Uncertainty*, Martine Beugnet takes a similar approach to the politics of visibility. With the tightly bound relationship between the circulation of images and the reinforcing of dominant ideology, she argues, comes the proliferation of 'simplistic messages [...], threatening to reduce our view of the world to a set of preconceived, immediately graspable affirmations and one-dimensional oppositions'.[74] This has been a key characteristic of mainstream media throughout its history, against which all forms of alternative cinema have been positioned in their rejection of linear narratives and readable images, since 'cinema as a medium', states Beugnet, 'also has the means to explore, alter and *intensify* our experience of the world's constant transformation'.[75] Having developed as a realist art capable of creating a reflection of the world apparently *as it is* through representational clarity, film has developed an oppositional language of perceptual difficulty: that is, the non-visible, the blurred, the obscure, the indefinite, the indeterminate. The opaque image is one that poses questions rather than answers them; it speaks to and through layers of experience, creating impressions and eliciting sensations that cannot be named or tamed. That this challenge to dominant visual regimes has so often risen to the material surface, as demonstrated in the numerous examples of painted, scratched, burnt, buried, marinated, decaying and deteriorating film that weave their way through cinema history, attests to the enduring concern with physicality, the embodied and the haptic as key sites of resistance to the normalised and normalis*ing* modes of representation that so dominate our cultural landscape. In contrast with much mainstream media production, which transforms nature into entertainment, alternative forms of representation acknowledge the limitations of such Humanistic ocularcentrism. The turn to other modes of sensuous understanding can be considered as a rejection of objectifying hierarchies, shifting the perceptual register to accommodate a broader experiential range. It follows, then, that a haptic approach can be mobilised to envisage how Morton's stickiness of hyperobjects, the vastness of scale and the various forms of human–non-human entanglements might be elicited through an emphasis on touch and the process of 'unseeing'.

To illustrate these ideas, I would like to reflect for a moment on an example of contemporary film practice that to my mind encompasses key facets of the materialist approach. With a running time of under two minutes, Tomonari Nishikawa's handmade film *sound of a million insects, light of a thousand stars* (2014) is understated to say the least; yet behind its brevity lies an attempt to reconceptualise ecological thinking as an aesthetics of the unseen. On a clear summer night between sunset and sunrise, Nishikawa buried a 100ft roll of 35mm negative stock under fallen leaves 25 kilometres from the Fukushima Daiichi Power Station in Japan, where, in 2011, an earthquake in the region triggered a 15-metre tsunami that led to one of the biggest nuclear disasters. What registers on the film and how do we 'read' it? A rapid flurry of scratches and marks against a blue-green background suggests traces of the ground, residues of contact or a battle of surfaces. The abstract image pulsates in a scene of constantly shifting material tensions and transformations, each frame telling a different story of its encounter with the earth to the long continuous hum of what sounds like electrical discharge. A title card at the end reveals to the viewer that the images are a result of this process of burying, although given that most experimental screenings are accompanied by written information, either printed or online, it seems likely that most spectators would read the film through this filter from the start (Fig. 2.4).

Without wishing to over-inscribe Nishikawa's film with meaning, the gesture is nonetheless significant in the context of the previous discussion. If we return to Morton's concept of 'hyperobjects', we can see immediately the resonance of this and other films that attempt to visualise environmental phenomena through a form of material contact. In a way, *what* we see is less important than *how* we see, since meaning resides precisely in a form of resistance to either the power or the possibility of legibility. Different modes of understanding require different approaches to representation, which in turn challenge ontological certainties: 'I believe what I see' becomes 'I experience what I don't see'. Morton's hyperobjects may not fit on a landscape painting, but they might, in this respect, fit on a roll of film! It is from this perspective, I argue, that *sound of a million insects, light of a thousand stars* contains within it a forceful political gesture that can be read as an attempt to negotiate nuclear radiation by rendering visible—or tangible—its effects on the physical environment. Whilst physical effects, particularly within the field of environmental filmmaking, are usually thought of in largely figurative and measurable terms, this materialist film aesthetic opens the door to other forms of knowledge.

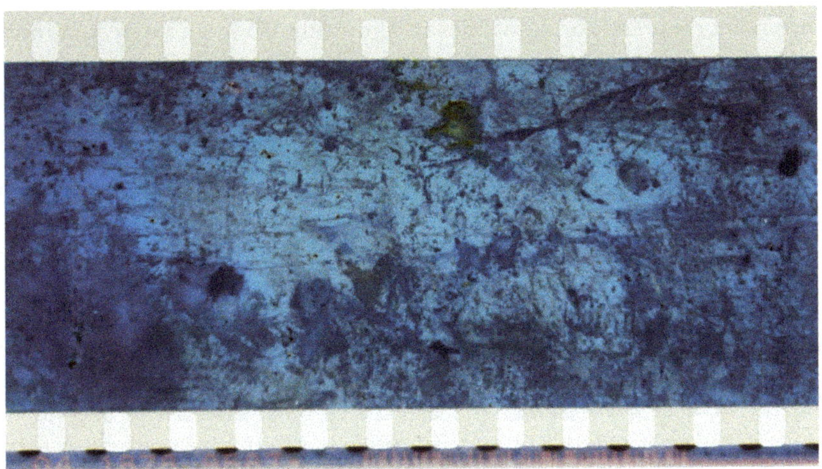

Fig. 2.4 *Sound of a million insects, light of a thousand stars*, Tomonari Nishikawa, 2014 (Image courtesy of Light Cone)

The title of Nishikawa's film is highly significant in this context, bringing together the microscopic and macroscopic and thus drawing attention to the interconnectedness of matter and the interrelated energies that elude human understanding. It attempts, as do many of the films discussed in this book, to connect with matter and to use the film as a metaphor for our own bodies. Although we do not see, in a literal sense, the effects of radiation in Nishikawa's film, we can understand the process as an attempt to make 'sense' of the physical world by other means, giving voice to the environment and allowing it to speak through the medium of film.

As Tess Takahashi suggests in an article on contemporary North American camera-less practice, the renewed attention to indexicality in materialist film contains within it a documentary impulse that goes beyond the limitations of purely photographic representations. The 'ability to physically record the influence of the material world on [the] celluloid body' of film is increasingly highlighted in experimental work as a means to shift the terms of documentary 'truth' and replace the traditional category of objective knowledge with material understandings that implicate multiple bodies of film, filmmaker and spectator.[76] Takahashi argues that the immateriality of digital—with its ability to 'seamlessly transcode, endlessly reproduce and recklessly disseminate images of all stripes'—throws into relief these indexical qualities of film, stimulating an interest in more embodied forms of image production. The aesthetic of contact hinges on this revised notion of documentary 'realism', reversing the terms by which the illegible and indeterminate image is understood and folding the haptic into a new formulation of materialist film. As we have seen, this resists the kind of inward-looking medium-specificity debates that have plagued interrogations of artistic materials by insisting on the radical revelatory possibilities of material engagement. Although Takahashi draws attention to the indexical image as a means to re-emphasise film's unique physical qualities in a digital world, this is arguably only a starting point for thinking about other forms of connectivity to those that dominate our always-online networked world. What *sound of a million insects, light of a thousand stars* articulates most effectively, beyond its own status as a material object, is a process of communication—a form of attentive 'listening', as suggested also by the title of David Gatten's series of submerged films *What the Water Said* (1997–2007). These collaborations with nature frame surface engagements as gentle political gestures, where anthropocentric visual perspectives are replaced with more grounded understandings of the planet we inhabit.

Material Entanglements

As Rosi Braidotti has argued, cultivating new perspectives involves building a greater sensitivity to the world as an interconnected network of human and non-human forces, through which flows what she calls *zoe*—'a posthuman yet affirmative life-force'.[77] She explains:

> Once the centrality of the anthropos is challenged, a number of boundaries between 'Man' and his others go tumbling down, in a cascade effect that opens up unexpected perspectives […] Animals, insects, plants and the environment, in fact the planet and the cosmos as a whole, are called into play.[78]

These posthuman perspectives ask us to think about the world differently, to train our eyes and minds to a more sharpened sensitivity to the energies, forces and multiple agencies that constitute our everyday environments, and to take up alternative subject positions to those pre-shaped by corporate capitalism and neoliberal agendas.[79] From the perspective of experimental film, we might look to a filmmaker such as Stan Brakhage, who, in the second half of his career, dedicated himself almost entirely to working directly on the surface of the filmstrip. In the opening lines of *Metaphors on Vision* Brakhage sets out a theory of vision that is not dissimilar to certain strains of the new materialist and posthuman theory cited above:

> Imagine an eye unruled by man-made laws of perspective, an eye unprejudiced by compositional logic, an eye which does not respond to the name of everything but which must know each object encountered in life through an adventure of perception. [...] Imagine a world alive with incomprehensible objects and shimmering with an endless variety of movement and numerous gradations of color.[80]

There are some clear resonances here between Brakhage's dream of 'a world alive with incomprehensible objects' and Braidotti's 'unexpected perspectives', both of which arise from the rearranging of perceptual hierarchies. Brakhage imagines a form of 'untutored' vision—a primal experience of the world before anthropocentric structures of language that privilege a human/non-human hierarchy. No wonder then that many of his films were an attempt to align human vision with that of non-human species—*Mothlight* (1963) for instance, or *Cat's Cradle*. Both works open up alternative modes of perception through attention to the film material, with representational clarity being replaced with haptic impressions. In *Mothlight*, moth wings, flower petals and grass placed directly onto clear film come to life on the screen as light and movement re-energise this earthly matter.

In a key section of *Metaphors on Vision*, Brakhage implores us to think differently about non-human vision not as limited and inferior, but as opening up new possibilities for human imaginings: 'To search for human visual realities, man must, as in all other homo motivation, transcend the original physical restrictions and inherit worlds of eyes'.[81] In other areas of his prolific artistic output, Brakhage explored the relationship between human and non-human forces. *Dog Star Man* (1961–1964), with its juxtaposition of the microscopic and the macroscopic, the intimate and the cosmic, might be understood from a posthuman perspective. Human and non-human rhythms are visually intertwined through the use of optical printing, where up to four rolls of film are layered one on top of the other to create a sense of interconnectedness through multiple and overlapping surfaces. As P. Adams Sitney observes, 'the birth of consciousness, the cycle of the seasons, man's struggle with nature and sexual balance' meet at the level of matter—the tangible textures of the celluloid strip.[82] In this sense, we might see Brakhage as a key precursor of contemporary materialist film, with its increasing interest in physical engagements and human–non-human entanglements.

The relationship between vision and ethics comes increasingly to the fore in contemporary accounts of how we relate to other living beings. Lori Gruen, for example, suggests that perception is the starting point for a more balanced coexistence with animals. Echoing the sentiments of both Brakhage and Braidotti, she states that:

> Once one's perception is altered, other relations move to the foreground. Entangled empathy can occur with those who are more distant. We are in relationships of all kinds with many, many animals and we may never have the opportunity to meet them or look into their eyes. But once we are attuned to some of them [...] we can begin to understand our relationships with and responsibilities to many others differently.[83]

Key to the current discussion is Gruen's reference to proximity and distance, reminding us of the importance of surface in materialist film. However, moving conceptually to the foreground does not necessarily mean seeing more clearly or with more detail, as we discovered in the previous section, and the aesthetic of contact entails precisely a form of reaching out to the physicality of things to capture the essence of experience. Although Gruen does not address the issue of visual representation in great detail, it is increasingly through images that the external world is communicated and understood, and thus shifting the terms of this mediated experience is a vital step in cultivating a new sensibility. Here, the re-visioning of Zylinska and the ecological thought of Morton meet the vibrant matter of Bennett and the entangled empathy of Gruen in a cross-disciplinary formulation of contemporary film aesthetics.

It is interesting to return to our consideration of death, loss and mourning in considering how entangled empathy is explored through the aesthetic of contact in materialist film. Brakhage, of course, used the wings of dead moths, into which the projector breathes back life. The resurrected moth parts dance on the screen alongside earthly debris, resisting any attempt to fix and hold them as a single identifiable image. Fragmented organic forms intermingle and fall into a maelstrom of matter. As we will see in Chapter 3, Vicky Smith's *Not (a) part* (2019) references

Brakhage's technique in an attempt to highlight loss on both a cultural and environmental level. Her camera-less film assembles various parts of dead bees collected on walks through Wales and the South West of England, printing them on the film through the rayogram process and, like Brakhage, mixing them with other physical matter such as the filmmaker's own hair and skin. Upon projection, the film creates a profound proximity that forces us into an uncanny relationship with these reanimated remains and invites us to see other bodies differently. Reflecting on obsolescence from the perspective of both species extinction and the potential loss of film as a unique way of representing the material world, *Not (a) part* is a powerful example of how contemporary materialist practice employs touch as a political gesture.

In a somewhat different vein, Matthew Ripplinger's *Sir Bailey* (2019) uses a range of physical interventions to portray the existential journey of a dog's last day. Through handmade film emulsion, contact printing and techniques of reticulation (the distortion of the emulsion layer that occurs when moved across baths of differing temperature in the developing process), Ripplinger turns the surface of the film into a site of material tension, through which the fragility of life plays out. Again, echoes of Brakhage's interest in the cycles of life and death, both human and non-human, can be detected. In *Sirius Remembered* from 1959, Brakhage records the gradual decomposition of the deceased family dog across the seasons as it lies in the woods, its corpse merging, like the wings of the moth, with the surrounding plant life—matter returning to matter. As with many of Brakhage's films, and particularly in the case of *Cat's Cradle*, the combination of whip pans, rapid editing, shifting focus, superimpositions and repetition draws the eye to the surface of the image, resisting a single stable viewpoint and emphasising tactility as the primary visual mode.

The Politics of Representation: Structural/Materialist Film Revisited

Approaching materiality from the perspective of human/non-human entanglements allows us to rethink the terms of medium-specificity and to consider photochemical film practice as engaged in a complex politics of vision. The new theoretical framings I am proposing here shift the emphasis away from film's auratic qualities, which have tended to dominate discussions of celluloid in the digital era, and towards a politics of representation that activates key contemporary discourses on the relationships between materiality and perception. Throughout its history, experimental cinema has consistently questioned the nature of cinematic representation, refusing the classical realist approach and drawing attention to surfaces, textures and sensations. But perhaps the most sustained discussion of how surface engagements are tied to the politics of vision and representation is Peter Gidal's 'Theory and Definition of Structural/Materialist Film', published in *Studio International* in 1975 and presented at the International Forum for Avant-Garde Film at the Edinburgh International Film Festival in 1976.[84] Along with Peter Wollen's 'The Two Avant-Gardes', this polemical piece was an attempt to formulate a theory of experimental practice against the backdrop of growing intellectual debate around film as an art form, and, despite the various criticisms it garnered in the wake of its publication, it remains a key reference point for thinking about material intervention as a political gesture. Particularly relevant in the context of the current discussion is the relationship between technology and artistic autonomy. Gidal's writings on materialist film responded primarily to the works emerging from the London Filmmakers' Co-operative (LFMC), an organisation that became central to histories of experimental cinema, particularly those that centre on artisanal interventions and DIY modes of working.

Established in 1966 primarily as an exhibition and distribution space, the LFMC incorporated film production into its activities with the arrival of Malcolm Le Grice and several of his students from Central Saint Martin's School of Art and Design. The LFMC's first workshop space was built in the New Arts Lab in 1969 with 16mm equipment (most notably a Debrie contact printer) that was built, bought and/or customised with the intention of creating access to production processes that were hitherto controlled by professional labs working to strict industry standards. With the newly acquired developing and printing machines, '[a] filmmaker could shoot footage and see it negative and then in positive within a few hours in black and white, within a couple of days in colour'.[85] The common 'desire to maintain control over every stage of the filmmaking process' led to a more artisanal practice than other forms of politically motivated filmmaking at the time, particularly the works of the Berwick Street Collective and Cinema Action.[86] As Simon Perry points out, the

1970s was a decade of intense activity in the folding of social struggles into a diverse counter-cinema, and although the aims and the means of the various groups that emerged during this period were far from homogeneous, a common fight against the dominant capitalist ideology could be discerned.[87]

Gidal's theory relates specifically to the politics of the image and the ideological workings of the film apparatus. Although, as this chapter has already illustrated, investigations into the material properties of film were by no means new at the time, the access to industry standard printing machinery opened the door to a different kind of material intervention that focused on the filmmaking process and conventional mechanisms of identification. 'Structural/Materialist film attempts to be non-illusionist', stated Gidal in the opening lines of the article. 'The process of the film's making deals with devices that result in demystification or attempted demystification of the film process'.[88] His anti-Hollywood, anti-narrative stance was articulated through a violent critique of representation, which he saw as reproducing dominant ideology and repressive structures of power. Only by negating representation and directing attention towards the act of viewing could the filmmaker mount a serious challenge to cinematic tradition. And only by refusing narrative content altogether and focusing on film's material conditions could a truly political cinema emerge. Gidal's notion of structural/materialist film built on P. Adam Sitney's description of the structural tendency in his survey of American avant-garde filmmaking from 1943 onwards. Emerging during the 1960s in the wake of Andy Warhol's durational films, the structural film, suggests Sitney, 'insists on its shape, and what content it has is minimal and subsidiary to the outline' He isolates four main characteristics that are present to varying degrees in the majority of films that fit this category: 'fixed camera position [...] the flicker effect, loop printing, and re-photography off the screen'.[89] Sitney describes a concern with formal structure, but lingering in the background of many of the films he mentions is an interest in what Malcolm Le Grice refers to as 'mechanical and physico-chemical processes', as seen, for example, in the work of Paul Sharits and Owen Land (particularly *Film in Which There Appear Edge Lettering, Sprocket Holes, Dirt Particles, Etc.*, 1966).[90] Indeed, many of the films mentioned by Sitney might fit into the category of materialist film.

However, as Stephen Heath has pointed out, the term 'materialist' in Gidal's usage follows the poststructuralist tradition of Althusser in deconstructing the identificatory mechanisms at play in the viewing situation. His theory, argues Heath,

> has to be understood away from any simple reference to the physical materiality of film. 'Materialist' stresses process, a film in its process of production of images, sounds, times, meanings, the transformations effected on the basis of the specific properties of film in the relation of a viewing and listening situation.[91]

Gidal warns against formalism, and his interest lies not in the material properties of film as such, but in the foregrounding of process as an anti-illusionist strategy. In films such as Malcolm Le Grice's *Little Dog for Roger* (1967), for example, the awareness of the film strip and its passage through the printer allows for a reflection on, and the deconstruction of, cinematic time. The film is a representation of a film, a staging of the tension between stasis and movement, visible in the passage from freeze frame to varying degrees of motion as the film, dragged manually, speeds up and slows down, blurs and becomes clear. An uncanny effect is produced through the combined presence of the film strip with its successive still images and the sudden animation *within* the frame—a technological effect that is usually hidden from view. Attention is thus drawn towards what Gidal calls the 1:1 relationship between the viewer and the viewed, or the coming into being of the film image. Other issues are at play in Le Grice's film, however, such as memory, nostalgia and the very obvious reference to technological obsolescence in the use of the 9.5mm format. Whilst the defamiliarisation of process and the deconstruction of spectatorship are clearly at play, I would argue that they do not preclude questions of form and the aesthetics of material engagement.

Although the works produced at the Co-op did not follow a single style or aesthetic, they were united through an interrogation of technology and an embrace of a craft-based approach to image-making. Several cameraless films such as *Dresden Dynamo* (Lis Rhodes, 1971) reflect the tradition of direct animation established in the 1930s and pursued by numerous filmmakers such as Harry Smith, Hy Hirsch, Len Lye, Takahiko Iimura and many others. The focus, here, lies in the ability of film to register images and sounds freed from figurative representation, and to create abstract patterns and rhythmic relations through basic means of drawing and printing images directly onto the film strip. To make *Dresden Dynamo*, Rhodes applied Letraset self-adhesive stickers to clear film, extending them into the soundtrack area to create parallels between what is seen and what is heard. Layering of the original image is produced during the contact printing process, with the final addition of colour filters. The resulting film is an exercise in synesthetic experience and the interplay of forms. If it draws attention to the viewing situation, it does so in the manner of early abstract films and the optical sound experiments of Norman McLaren. Furthermore, what emerges most forcefully in Rhodes's approach to the material is the sense of material proximity and a tactile awareness of the screen. This is similarly a feature of Annabel Nicolson's *Slides*, also dating from 1971, in which fragments of 35mm photographic slides and sections of 8mm and 16mm film are sewn together in a kind of filmic tapestry. The film disrupts any sense of continuous motion and resists a stable reference point. Presented with an onslaught of visual stimuli, the viewer must relinquish the game of identification and shift the attention to the surface, where the material drama plays out. This is undoubtedly a film about physicality, and Nicolson describes the process in distinctly tactile terms:

> 'Slides' came about through some fascination with the phenomena of matter, its frailty and transience, the oddness of tiny filmed images from my earlier work lying around. Working with these parts, 35mm slides cut into strips, thread, sewn film, light leaked footage, 8mm and 16mm fragments, I hand held this material in the contact printer. Images were created by movement and handling, literally keeping in touch with the elements.[92]

Manually pulling the film through the contact printer, in a manner similar to Le Grice's *Little Dog for Roger*, Nicolson was able to manipulate a process usually controlled by the professional film labs. Through this technological misuse, a new form of tactile materialism emerges that rubs up against Gidal's austere anti-representational stance.

For it is in these processes that we find a radical form of embodied vision that resonates through the work created by female filmmakers at the Co-op between the 1970s and the 1990s and which continues to the present day. A recent retrospective 'From Reel to Real: Feminism and the London Filmmakers' Co-operative' at the Tate Modern (23–25 September 2016), curated by Maud Jacquin, sought to wrest this work from the male-dominated historical discourse, highlighting the ways in which feminine subjectivity and bodily concerns were inscribed into materialist practices. As Jacquin states:

> Because they wanted to give voice to submerged aspects of women's personal and social experience, the women of the LFMC could not entirely subscribe to this modernist filmmaking approach. However, their practices undoubtedly emerged from the material experimentation that took place there. In fact, it is the combination of conscious feminist politics and this tactile engagement with film that made these works both highly singular at the time of their production and particularly relevant to our current context.[93]

Jacquin's assessment is valuable in its reconciling of material specificity with a form of political engagement anchored to the body. Such considerations are conspicuously absent from Gidal's theory, where physical encounters and tactile engagements are treated only as a means to disrupt the fabric of illusionism and draw attention to the actual production of images. That this shift in viewer attention towards process might involve a visceral awareness that carries with it its own political ramifications is a definite lacuna in Gidal's theoretical formulation.

Rhodes's *Light Reading* (1978) is a key example of work emerging from the LFMC that combines extensive material intervention with an interrogation of feminine interiority and embodied experience. Forms of subjectivity are negotiated through language, both written and spoken, articulating the impossibility of a unified subject position outside the patriarchal structures of looking. The first two minutes of the film denies the image altogether, presenting instead a black screen as an accompaniment to the spoken text. This is followed by a long period of silence as the film progresses through a series of visual dislocations and fragmentations that continually draw attention to the material as the site of representations. By disrupting narrative unity and by staging the act of filmic construction, Rhodes successfully questions the material as a neutral carrier. The images progressively deconstruct the illusion of cinema by showing cutout fragments, zooming into the image and shifting between surface and depth, abstraction and figuration. These self-reflexive material ruptures also gradually work their way into the voiceover narration in the second half of the film as a series of practical notes for the optical printing process:

lengthen the next frames
stretch hand in shadow
frame paper in mid-shot
move round from
top right of frame
in a complete circle
no sound
framed in reflection
her image fixed
mistake at the beginning of the camera movement
cut
start again—sound of running footsteps[94]

Light Reading appears in Gidal's later text *Materialist Film*, where it is described as 'an attempt at producing a different viewer and viewing through a different film'.[95] What Rhodes's film demonstrates most clearly is that material engagements entail an element of performativity that draws attention to the self as constituted in the image.

Mike Dunford's criticism of the materialist approach following the publication of Gidal's text in 1976 emphasised the incompatibility of self-reflexive formalism with real political engagement, arguing that

> Experimental film has evolved an insistent materialism and a form of perceptual dialectic, and this is supported by an existential and phenomenological philosophy which denies the intervention of this practice within social practice, ignores the existence of class struggle, and validates the existence of class ideology by omission.[96]

The demand that film intervene in class ideology clearly displays the concerns of the period, and the implicit distinction between form and politics in Dunford's article echoes Peter Wollen's 'The Two Avant-Gardes'. This frequently expressed view that a focus on materials precludes politics depends, of course, on the specific kind of politics in question. What the Co-op films demonstrated, however, was that politics resides to a large extent in hierarchies of vision, in the privileging of normative forms of representation that contribute to the subjugation of social groups, particularly women. In their search for a new language of the body, and through their interrogation of the material properties of film, artists such as Nicolson, Rhodes, Gill Eatherley and Marilyn Halford developed a politicised form of surface aesthetics, where 'handling' and 'keeping in touch' are as much a part of the process as the rejection of the traditional viewing situation. As Laura Marks argues, the haptic 'is a visual strategy that can be used to describe alternative visual traditions, including women's and feminist practices'.[97]

Although largely male-dominated in its theoretical discourse, the LFMC would later become an important site for the development of women's cinema and the expression of alternative subjectivities. The work of Anna Thew, Jean Matthee, Sandra Lahire, Jayne Parker, Nina Danino, Sarah Pucill, Ruth Novaczek, Sarah Turner, Alia Syed and Tanya Syed established a feminist counter-discourse that was rooted in the materiality of the medium but did not entirely refuse either photographic realism or narrative structure.[98] Various photochemical processes were employed to destabilise the image and challenge representational fixities in order to open up new languages of self-inscription and intersubjectivity. The optical printer, in particular, was exploited as a tool for deconstructing the gaze, with its ability to analyse, rework, freeze and stretch an image, freeing it from spatio-temporal norms. This is seen most effectively in Tanya Syed's *Chameleon* (1990), *Salamander* (1994) and *Delilah* (1995), where the female body is systematically defamiliarised and deconstructed.

In contemporary materialist film practice, these concerns re-emerge in a new context and with a renewed interest in the film surface. Naomi Uman's *Removed* (1999), for example, employs a chemical reworking of found footage to highlight and disrupt traditional representations. The artist used nail polish remover and household bleach to erase the female image from a 1970s soft-porn film, leaving a writhing white creature in its place. With the rest of the image left intact, this diegetic erasure reveals, through absence, the power structures inherent in the act of looking. Attacking the scopophilic impulse of mainstream cinema and the conventional representations of women as sexual objects, Uman's surface intervention combines Isidore Isou's Lettrist strategies of image chiselling with Laura Mulvey's critique of the heteronormative male gaze in her essay 'Visual Pleasure and Narrative Cinema'. Isou's approach in one of the key Lettrist films *Traité de bave et d'éternité* (1951) is centred on the shift from film's amplic (*amplique*) phase to the chiseled (*ciselante*) phase, that is, from a cinema where the technical elements cohere to produce narrative fluidity to one in which those elements are given expressive independence rather than interdependence. The formal dislocations produced through disjunctive editing are amplified by techniques of painting, scratching, tearing and bleaching of the filmstrip so that the very material of cinematic representation is implicated in its ideological critique. Although Isou's rejection of the gaze is a more generalised one, the destructive force that is unleashed on the material creates a space for oppositional image practices in the years that followed.

By framing these haptic engagements as a form of resistance, and by implicating the film surface in a kind of sensuous communication, we open up vital perspectives on the political potential of materialist film. This potential is rooted in the ability of film to create new perceptual hierarchies and visual experiences. To return to Bill Nichols, this is not simply as a retreat into abstraction, but as a *reframing* of abstraction as politically inflected. In this sense, it is perhaps necessary to also revise what is meant by politics and political intention as we move forwards in our assessment of contemporary photochemical film practice. The question is, therefore, not whether material engagement is capable of a new kind of politics post-Gidal, but rather what form this takes in a rapidly changing social, economic, environmental and technological landscape. The path forged in this book is one that folds Gidal's theory of materialist film into contemporary discussions of material thinking and haptic visuality as an ethical practice. For the current moment of technological transition and the resulting resurgence of photochemical filmmaking as an alternative practice seems to demand such a reassessment. Extending the issue of politics to an understanding of the world as constant transformation is key to formulating a new theory of materialist film that considers the contemporary context as a historical continuum. That a new materially aware wave of scholarship reaches its peak precisely at the moment of film's increasing uncertainty as a medium comes as no surprise.

Different forms of materiality weave their way through the next three chapters, unravelling and overlapping in their relation to process, performance, interconnected communities and technological specificities. The physicality of the body and the materiality of the support are of key concern, but so too are the affective bonds that constitute the enmeshed DIY working practices and alternative social structures that increasingly come to define photochemical film culture. Equally of interest are the specific materialities of different viewing situations and sites of encounter, whose importance is felt particularly in the context of expanded cinema and the performance of material excess. Contemporary approaches to materialism, including object-oriented ontology, allow us to reflect on filmic aesthetics as well as the creative practices from which they emerge. This forms a basis for thinking about how obsolete materials give rise to and necessitate particular modes of working, collaborating and engaging with the world.

Notes

1. Peter Gidal, 'Theory and Definition of Structural/Materialist Film', in Mark Webber and Peter Gidal (eds.), *Flare Out: Aesthetics 1966–2016* (London: The Visible Press, 2016), pp. 37–68.
2. Deke Dusinberre argues that historians of the avant-garde have 'stress[ed] the importance of the film solely in terms of its provocative intent and anarchic effect; it is never studied in terms of its content or construction.' Deke Dusinberre, '*Le Retour à la raison*: Hidden Meanings', in Bruce Posner (ed.), *Unseen Cinema: Early American Avant-Garde Film 1893–1941* (New York: Anthology Film Archives, 2001), p. 65. Whilst several studies seem to have redressed this balance in previous years, the wider relevance of the film, particularly in relation to materialist filmmaking and representation, has yet to be fully teased out.
3. Bill Nichols, 'Documentary Film and the Modernist Avant-Garde', *Critical Inquiry*, Vol. 27, No. 4, Summer 2001, p. 593.
4. http://film-makerscoop.com/catalogue/paul-sharits-3rd-degree.
5. Paolo Cherchi Usai, *The Death of the Cinema: History, Cultural Memory and the Digital Dark Age* (London: Reaktion Books, 2001), p. 105.
6. D. N. Rodowick, *The Virtual Life of Film* (Cambridge, MA and London: Harvard University Press, 2007), pp. 19–20.
7. Although the found footage film overlaps with discourses around obsolescence, nostalgia and material histories, it will not feature heavily in this book as it has already received a significant amount of scholarly attention in recent years. See, for example, Jaimie Baron, *The Archive Effect: Found Footage and the Audiovisual Experience of History* (New York: Routledge, 2014); Adrian Danks, 'The Global Art of Found Footage Cinema', in Linda Badley, R. Barton Palmer and Steven Jay Schneider (eds.), *Traditions in World Cinema* (Edinburgh: Edinburgh University Press, 2006), pp. 241–253; Sami van Ingen, *Moving Shadows: Experimental Film Practice in a Landscape of Change* (Helsinki: Finnish Academy of Fine Arts, 2012); Catherine Russell, *Experimental Ethnography: The Work of Film in the Age of Video* (Durham: Duke University Press, 1999), as well as more focused studies of particular found footage filmmakers: Wilbirg Brainin-Donnenberg and Michael Loebenstein (eds), *Gustav Deutsch* (Vienna:

Austrian Film Museum, 2009); Alexander Howarth and Michael Loebenstein, *Peter Tscherkassky* (Vienna: Austrian Film Museum, 2007).

8. Nicholas Chare and Liz Watkins, 'The Matter of Film: Decasia and Lyrical Nitrate', in Estelle Barrett and Barbara Bolt (eds.), *Carnal Knowledge: Towards a 'New Materialism' Through the Arts* (London and New York: I. B. Tauris, 2013), p. 75.
9. Ibid.
10. Ibid., p. 77.
11. Dirk de Bruyn, *The Performance of Trauma in Moving Image Art* (Cambridge: Cambridge Scholars Publishing, 2014).
12. Laura U. Marks, *Touch: Sensuous Theory and Multisensory Media* (Minneapolis: University of Minnesota Press, 2002), p. 91.
13. Steven Shaviro, *The Cinematic Body* (Minneapolis and London: University of Minnesota Press, 2000), p. 110.
14. Walter Benjamin, 'The Work of Art in the Age of Mechanical Reproduction,' in Hannah Arendt (ed.) and Harry Zohn (trans.), *Illuminations* (New York: Fontana/Collins, 1973), p. 238.
15. Laura U. Marks, *Touch: Sensuous Theory and Multisensory Media*, p. 95.
16. http://www.ecstatic-erratic.com/moving-image/ (Accessed 18 April 2019).
17. Jonathan Sterne, 'Out with the Trash: On the Future of New Media', in Charles R. Acland (ed.), *Residual Media* (London and Minneapolis: University of Minnesota Press, 2007), p. 27.
18. Jussi Parikka, *The Anthrobscene* (Minneapolis: University of Minnesota Press, 2014), p. 7.
19. Ibid., p. 6.
20. Sean Cubitt, *Finite Media: Environmental Implications of Digital Technologies* (Durham: Duke University Press, 2016); Jennifer Gabrys, *Digital Rubbish: A Natural History of Electronics* (Ann Arbor: The University of Michigan Press, 2013).
21. Jussi Parikka, 'New Materialism and Media Theory: Medianatures and Dirty Matter', *Communication and Critical/Cultural Studies*, Vol. 9, No. 1, 2012, pp. 95–100.
22. Gabrys, *Digital Rubbish*, p. 8.
23. On the subject of 'stuff', see Maurizia Boscagli, *Stuff Theory: Everyday Objects and Radical Materialism* (New York and London: Bloomsbury, 2014).
24. Scott MacDonald argues that these two factors are intertwined: 'The advances of digital technology have generally been instigated by the need, in a world increasingly crowded by humanity, for increased speed and efficiency in handling information and in getting services and products to citizens and consumers in the shortest possible time.' Scott MacDonald, 'The Ecocinema Experience', in Stephen Rust, Salma Monani and Sean

Cubitt (eds.), *Ecocinema Theory and Practice* (New York and London: Routledge, 2013), pp. 38–39.

25. Another notable point of reference here is William Rathje and Cullen Murphy's, *Rubbish!: The Archaeology of Garbage* (New York: HarperCollins Publishers, 1992).
26. Peter Frase, *Four Futures: Life After Capitalism* (London and New York: Verso, 2016), p. 2. See also Martin Ford, *The Rise of Robots: Technology and the Threat of a Jobless Future* (New York: Basic Books, 2015).
27. Evan Watkins, *Throwaways: Work Culture and Consumer Education* (Stanford: Stanford University Press, 1993), p. 3.
28. Bruno Latour, *Down to Earth: Politics in the New Climactic Regime* (Cambridge: Polity Press, 2018), p. 3.
29. Gay Hawkins, *The Ethics of Waste: How We Relate to Rubbish* (Lanham: Rowman and Littlefield Publishers, 2006), p. 15.
30. Michel Foucault, *The Order of Things: An Archaeology of the Human Sciences* (London and New York: Routledge, 1989).
31. Jane Bennett, *Vibrant Matter: A Political Ecology of Things* (Durham: Duke University Press, 2010), p. 6.
32. As I will go on to discuss in Chapter 4, this is also extends to the perception of people—human bodies attached to particular ways of working, resisting the loss of a skill set and knowledge base. Their refusal to let automation erase a whole area of mechanical expertise is central to keeping alive this very distinct art form.
33. Rosi Braidotti, *The Posthuman* (Cambridge: Polity Press, 2013), p. 14.
34. Ibid., p. 67.
35. Graham Harman, *Object-Oriented Ontology: A New Theory of Everything* (London: Pelican, 2017), p. 146.
36. Karen Barad, 'Posthumanist Perfomativity: Toward an Understanding of How Matter Comes to Matter', *Signs: Journal of Women in Culture and Society*, Vol. 28, No. 3, p. 815.
37. Bennett, *Vibrant Matter*, p. 10.
38. Ibid., p. 112.
39. Joanna Zylinska, *Minimal Ethics for the Anthropocene* (Ann Arbor: Open Humanities Press, 2014), p. 100.
40. Paul J. Crutzen and Eugene F. Stoermer, 'The "Anthropocene"', *Global Change Newsletter*, Vol. 41, No. 1, 2000, pp. 17–18. For accounts of artistic approaches to the concept of Anthropocene see, for example, Heather Davis and Etienne Turpin, *Art in the Anthropocene: Encounters Among Aesthetics, Politics, Environments and Epistemologies* (London: Open Humanities Press, 2015); Elizabeth M. DeLoughrey, *Allegories of the Anthropocene* (Durham: Duke University Press, 2019); Julie Reiss (ed.), *Art, Theory and Practice in the Anthropocene* (Wilmington: Vernon Press, 2019).

41. T. J. Demos, *Against the Anthropocene: Visual Culture and Environment Today* (Berlin: Sternberg Press, 2017), p. 11.
42. Claire Colebrook, 'What is the Anthro-Political?', in Tom Cohen, Claire Colebrook and J. Hillis Miller, Peter, *Twilight of the Anthropocene Idols* (London: Open Humanities Press, 2016), p. 91.
43. Donna J. Haraway, *Staying with the Trouble: Making Kin in the Chthulucene* (Durham and London: Duke University Press, 2016).
44. Timothy Morton, *The Ecological Thought* (Cambridge, MA: Harvard University Press, 2010), *Dark Ecology: For a Logic of Future Coexistence* (New York: Columbia University Press, 2016), *Humankind: Solidarity with Nonhuman People* (London and New York: Verso, 2017).
45. Timothy Morton, *The Ecological Thought*, p. 7.
46. Nicholas Mirzoeff, 'Visualising the Anthropocene', *Public Culture*, Vol. 26, No. 2, 2014, pp. 213–232.
47. Joanna Zylinksa, *The End of Man: A Feminist Counterapocalypse* (Minneapolis: University of Minnesota Press, 2018), p. 64.
48. Timothy Morton, 'Zero Landscapes in the Time of Hyperobjects', *Graz Architectural Magazine*, Vol. 7, 2011, p. 80.
49. Ibid., p. 83.
50. Laura Mulvey, 'Visual Pleasure and Narrative Cinema', in Gerald Mast, Marshall Cohen and Leo Braudy (eds.), *Film Theory and Criticism: Introductory Readings* (Oxford and New York: Oxford University Press, 1992), pp. 746–757.
51. Anat Pick, 'Three Worlds: Dwelling and Worldhood on Screen', in Anat Pick and Guinevere Narraway (eds.), *Screening Nature: Cinema Beyond the Human* (New York: Berghan Books, 2013), p. 25.
52. Pick, 'Three Worlds', p. 25. See also Paul Virilio, *The Vision Machine* (London: BFI, 1994).
53. See Walter Benjamin, 'Theses on the Philosophy of History', in *Illuminations*, pp. 255–266, *The Arcades Project*, trans. Howard Eiland and Kevin McLaughlin (Cambridge, MA and London: Harvard University Press, 1999). This path is well-trodden in the field of technological transition and media archaeology. See, for instance, Erika Balsom, *Exhibiting Cinema in Contemporary Art* (Amsterdam: Amsterdam University Press, 2013); Gabriele Jutz, *Cinéma Brut: Eine alternative Genealogie der Filmavantgarde* (Vienna and New York: Springer, 2010); Rosalind Krauss, 'Reinventing the Medium', *Critical Inquiry*, Vol. 25, No. 2, 1999, pp. 289–305; Catherine Russell, *Walter Benjamin and Archival Film Practices* (Durham, NC: Duke University Press, 2018).
54. Raymond Bellour, *L'entre-images: photo, cinéma, vidéo* (Paris: La Différence, 1990). Bellour's term relates, of course, to the relationship between the still and moving image. I have employed the French term

because, unlike its English translation, it expresses a connectedness that relates to this idea of contact.

55. Rebecca Coleman and Liz Oakley-Brown, 'Visualizing Surfaces, Surfacing Vision: Introduction', in *Theory, Culture & Society*, Special Section: Visualizing Surfaces, Surfacing Vision, Vol. 34, Nos. 7–8, 2017, p. 6.
56. Ibid., p. 8.
57. Karen Barad, *Posthumanist Performativity: Toward an Understanding of How Matter Comes to Matter*, p. 814.
58. Giuliana Bruno, *Surface: Matters of Aesthetics, Materiality and Media* (Chicago and London: University of Chicago Press, 2014), p. 8.
59. Ibid., p. 119.
60. Sobchack draws on Maurice Merleau-Ponty's view that synaesthesia—the involuntary experience of one sense through another, such as seeing sounds or tasting colours—is actually the normal functioning of the body that is inhibited through societal conditioning: 'Synaesthetic perception is the rule, and we are unaware of it only because scientific knowledge shifts the centre of gravity of experience, so that we have unlearned how to see, hear, and generally speaking, feel, in order to deduce, from our bodily organization and the world as the physicist conceives it, what are to see, hear and feel.' Maurice Merleau-Ponty, *Phenomenology of Perception*, trans. Colin Smith (London: Routledge & Kegan Paul, 1962), p. 229.
61. Vivian Sobchack, 'What My Fingers Knew: The Cinesthetic Subject, or Vision in the Flesh', in *Carnal Thoughts: Embodiment and Moving Image Culture* (Berkeley: University of California Press, 2004), pp. 53–84.
62. M. M. Serra and Kathryn Ramey, 'Eye/Body: The Cinematic Paintings of Carolee Schneemann', in Robin Blaetz (ed.), *Women's Experimental Cinema* (Durham and London: Duke University Press, 2007), pp. 108–109.
63. Scott MacDonald, 'An Interview with Carolee Schneemann', in *A Critical Cinema: Interviews with Independent Filmmakers*, Volume 1 (Berkeley: University of California Press, 1988), p. 142.
64. Serra and Ramey, 'Eye/Body: The Cinematic Paintings of Carolee Schneemann', p. 109.
65. Kate Haug, 'Interview with Kate Haug', in Carolee Schneemann (ed.), *Imaging Her Erotics: Essays, Interviews, Projects* (Cambridge, MA: MIT Press, 2002), p. 43.
66. Peggy Phelan, *Unmarked: The Politics of Performance* (London and New York: Routledge, 1996), p. 26.
67. Ibid.
68. Jennifer Barker, *The Tactile Eye: Touch and the Cinematic Experience* (Berkeley: University of California Press, 2009), p. 23.
69. Ibid.
70. Laura U. Marks, *Touch: Sensuous Theory and Multisensory Media*, p. 3.

71. See, for instance, Martine Beugnet, Allan Cameron and Arild Fetveit (eds.), *Indefinite Visions: Cinema and the Attractions of Uncertainty* (Edinburgh: Edinburgh University Press, 2017); Martine Beugnet, *L'Attrait du flou* (Liège: *Yellow Now*, 2017); Bernd Huppauf and Christoph Wulf (eds.), *Dynamics and Performativity of Imagination: The Image Between the Visible and the Invisible* (London: Routledge, 2009); Johanne Lamoureux, Christine Ross and Olivier Asselin (eds.), *Precarious Visualities: New Perspectives on Identification in Contemporary Art and Visual Culture* (Montreal: McGill-Queen's University Press, 2008).
72. Hito Steyerl, 'In Defense of the Poor Image', *e-flux journal* (10 November 2009), https://www.e-flux.com/journal/10/61362/in-defense-of-the-poor-image/ (accessed 21 January 2019).
73. Steyerl's reference to the cultural relegation of experimental and independent filmmaking, its relative invisibility in relation to commercial cinema, is not without significance, and provides another avenue for thinking about hierarchies of visuality in contemporary culture.
74. Martine Beugnet, 'Introduction', in Beugnet, Cameron and Fetveit (eds.), *Indefinite Visions: Cinema and the Attractions of Uncertainty*, p. 10.
75. Martine Beugnet, 'Introduction', p. 3.
76. Tess Takahashi, 'After the Death of Film: Writing the Natural World in the Digital Age', *Visible Language*, Vol. 42, No. 1, 2008, p. 49. See also Takahaski, 'Meticulously, Recklessly Worked Up: Direct Animation, The Auratic and the Index', in Chris Gehman and Steve Reinke (eds.), *The Sharpest Point; Animation at End of Cinema* (Toronto: YYZ Books, 2005), pp. 166–178.
77. Rosi Braidotti, *The Posthuman*, p. 115.
78. Ibid., p. 66.
79. An important reference point here is Félix Guattari's, *The Three Ecologies* (London: Bloomsbury, 2014). Originally published in 1989, this insightful essay argues that our ideas and behaviours are shaped by the homogenising force of mass media, a vital part of what Guattari call Integrated World Capitalism (IWC). 'A capitalistic subjectivity is engendered through operators of all types and sizes, and is manufactured to protect existence from any intrusion of events that might disturb or disrupt public opinion. It demands that all singularity must be either evaded or crushed in specialist apparatuses and frames of reference.' p. 33.
80. Stan Brakhage, 'From *Metaphors on Vision*', in P. Adams Sitney (ed.), *The Avant-Garde Film: A Reader of Theory and Criticism* (New York: Anthology Film Archives, 1978), p. 120.
81. Ibid., p. 125.
82. P. Adams Sitney, *Visionary Film: The American Avant-garde, 1943–2000* (Oxford: Oxford University Press, 2002), p. 190.

83. Lori Gruen, *Entangled Empathy, An Alternative Ethic for Our Relationships with Animals* (New York: Lantern Books, 2015), p. 79.
84. Despite the historical importance of this event, there is little scholarly information beyond fleeting references and brief overviews. The 1976 edition of EIFF also featured a five-day event on 'Psychoanalysis and the Cinema'. Both are discussed by Jonathan Rosenbaum in 'Regrouping: Reflections on the Edinburgh Festival 1976': https://www.jonathanrosenbaum.net/2018/10/regrouping-reflections-on-the-edinburgh-festival-1976/ (accessed 8 October 2019).
85. Peter Gidal, 'Technology and ideology in/through/and avant-garde film: an instance', in Mark Webber and Peter Gidal (eds.), *Flare Out: Aesthetics 1966–2016* (London: The Visible Press, 2016), p. 116.
86. David Curtis, 'A Tale of Two Co-ops', in David E. James (ed.), *To Free the Cinema: Jonas Mekas and the American Underground* (Princeton, NJ: Princeton University Press, 1992), p. 258. For more information on the context of film collectives in the UK during this period, see Petra Bauer and Dan Kidner (eds.), *Working Together: Notes on British Film Collectives in the 1970s* (Southend-on-Sea: Focal Point Gallery, 2012); Sue Clayton and Laura Mulvey (eds.), *Other Cinemas: Politics, Culture and Experimental Film in the 1970s* (London and New York: 2017).
87. Simon Perry, *Radical Mainstream: Independent Film, Video and Television in Britain 1974–90* (London: Intellect, 2020). See also Patti Gaal Holmes, *A History of 1970s Experimental Film: Britain's Decade of Diversity* (Basingstoke: Palgrave Macmillan, 2015).
88. Peter Gidal, 'Theory and Definition of Structural/Materialist Film', p. 37.
89. P. Adams Sitney, *Visionary Film: The American Avant-Garde, 1943–2000* (New York: Oxford University Press, 2002), p. 348.
90. Malcolm Le Grice, 'Material, Materiality, Materialism', in Malcolm Le Grice, *Experimental Cinema in the Digital Age* (London: BFI, 2001), p. 165.
91. Stephen Heath, 'Repetition Time: Notes Around 'Structural/materialist Film', in *Questions of Cinema* (London: Palgrave Macmillan, 1981), p. 165.
92. Annabel Nicolson, *A Perspective on English Avant-Garde Film Catalogue* (London: The Arts Council, 1978), p. 73.
93. Maud Jacquin, 'From Reel to Real—An Epilogue: Feminist Politics and Materiality at the London Film-makers' Co-operative', *Moving Image Review and Art Journal*, Vol. 6, Issue 1–2, 2017, p. 82.
94. Lis Rhodes, *Telling Invents Told* (London: Visible Press, 2019), pp. 61–62.
95. Peter Gidal, *Materialist Film*, p. 65.
96. Mike Dunford, 'Experimental/Avant-garde/Revolutionary Film Practice', *Afterimage*, Vol. 6, 1976, pp. 107–108.

97. Laura U. Marks, *The Skin of the Film: Intercultural Cinema, Embodiment and the Senses* (Durham, NC: Duke University Press, 1999), p. 170.
98. For further discussion of women in the LFMC, see Nina Danino, Jean Matthee, Ruth Novaczek, Sarah Pucill and Alia Syed, 'Roundtable Discussion: The Women of the London Filmmaker's Co-op', *Moving Image Review and Art Journal*, Vol. 4, Nos. 1–2, 2015, pp. 164–179.

CHAPTER 3

Process and Perception

In his overview of the artisanal film movement, Chris Gehman argues that experimental cinema has always been defined by its emphasis on alternative models of production, favouring individual, hands-on approaches to the large-scale industrial processes of commercial cinema. We have already seen how films like Man Ray's *Le Retour à la raison* (1923), as well as the many other early examples of creative rebellion, embraced the radical perceptual possibilities of the material substrate. As Gehman notes, however, the period between the late 1980s and 1990s marks a shift in these practices, with a move towards hand-processing and printing—stages which, up to that point, were still largely undertaken by professional labs. Experiments into different chemical treatments and biochemical decay also emerged, with filmmakers such as Jürgen Reble in Germany, Phil Solomon in the USA and Carl Brown in Canada producing works that emphasised, as the title of Reble's 1995 film *Instabile Materie* suggests, the instability and organic fluidity of the celluloid material.

This historical emphasis allows Gehman to counter recent arguments that locate the artisanal impetus within a wider reaction to the ubiquity of digital technology and its increasing threat to photochemical modes of working. Thus, 'by the mid-1990s, long before digital cinema systems created significant practical issues for filmmakers, a definite movement towards a highly material-oriented artisanal approach to filmmaking

K. Knowles, *Experimental Film and Photochemical Practices*,
Experimental Film and Artists' Moving Image,
https://doi.org/10.1007/978-3-030-44309-2_3

was underway'.[1] Gehman states that the more recent embrace of hand-made photochemical practices should be seen as emerging from this earlier period, which 'could be characterised as anticipatory, and motivated by aesthetic and philosophical concerns rather than reactionary, and motivated primarily by practical and technical concerns or naïve cultural allegiances'.[2] The naivety of which he speaks relates to the overemphasising of the 'natural' and of 'hand work' by both filmmakers and theorists, a tendency that seems, from Gehman's perspective, to put artisanal film in a backward-looking, ahistorical position. Two key issues arise from this account that relate specifically to the arguments developed in this book. The first is that an emphasis on the contemporary cultural framing does not preclude an acknowledgement of historical lineage; that is, it is entirely possible to discuss artisanal film practice in the context of the recent turn to the digital whilst acknowledging *at the same time* that these practices have their roots in the aesthetic and philosophical interrogations of the pre-digital era. The rich history of material engagements in experimental cinema is not in doubt when one concentrates on contemporary developments. Secondly, although several academic accounts of photochemical film culture have emphasised digital anxiety as a motivating factor in the emergence of artisanal techniques, celebrating the indexical and 'auratic' qualities of film, this has, as I have argued in the previous chapter, largely functioned as springboard for exploring a broader range of aesthetic, political and philosophical issues that are not limited to contemporary films.[3]

In this chapter, I discuss a range of photochemical film practices from the past twenty years—works that have emerged against the backdrop of a massive migration of our lives to the digital realm. This cultural framing invariably informs the discussion, but it does not dictate it; rather, my emphasis lies in teasing out the potential of artisanal techniques to uncover alternative forms of visual expression that privilege affect and experience. It relates specific film processes to languages of material understanding that both critique traditional representations and offer radical, more ethical approaches to seeing. Whilst the politics of representation is present to differing degrees in the works I discuss, the films are brought together by an overriding interest in visual defamiliarisation, attention to surfaces and the power of sensuous communication. My descriptions and theorisations are informed by in-depth conversations with the filmmakers about their specific working practices and wider philosophical approach, and whilst an explicit rejection of the digital rarely emerged in these discussions, it became clear that creative decisions often emerged through an embracing of physical modes of working that are only achievable with film.

The technical and chemical interventions outlined in this chapter include scratching, drawing, painting, cross-processing, optical printing, contact printing, burying, chemically treating, or a combination of these, as a way to explore the representational possibilities of film. These techniques always foreground the exploratory nature of process rather than following a pre-defined path, developing through multiple stages of experimentation where accidents, discoveries and unexpected chemical reactions direct the filmmaker into new creative avenues. The American experimental filmmaker Janis Crystal Lipzin explains:

> My conscious decision to begin with film is based on that medium's unduplicable and capricious response to light. I use darkroom processes to produce outcomes that allude to, but don't truly describe, color in the natural world – the outcomes become the visible evidence of a direct, yet surreptitious, conspiracy between artist, materials, and photochemical occurrences.[4]

In other words, rather than present themselves as a reflection of the world, these images emphasise the fact that they are *of the world*—their visual form resulting from the physical transformation of matter. Pip Chodorov, filmmaker and co-founder of the Parisian artist-run film lab L'Abominable, goes as far as to suggest that 'we don't work with "images", but with organic, physical material that comes from the earth: salts, silvers, minerals'.[5] The material substrate of film is therefore always already a complex combination of elements—an amalgam of vibrant matter whose chance constellations lead to a continually changing granular makeup. Chodorov's connection of film with earthly matter touches on issues largely absent from Peter Gidal's account of process; that is, the very grounded—in a literal sense—nature of film as a substance that holds within it the possibility for opening up new ways of seeing. From this perspective, material engagements with film bring us back to the kind of interconnectedness of which contemporary ecocritics and proponents of new materialism repeatedly speak, answering, in particular, Joanna Zylinska's call for a new form of visioning in the age of the Anthropocene.

Earthly Engagements and Radical Landscapes

That contemporary discussions of photochemical processes have tended to emphasise connections with the environment perhaps comes as no surprise when we consider that the decline of celluloid within the commercial realm coincides with the expansion of the scholarly field of ecocriticism, which 'takes an earth-centred, environmentally conscious approach to the study of texts'.[6] Technological obsolescence thus resonates with earthly fragility, as the urgent calls for more ethical and responsible forms of living extend to the kinds of images we create and *how* we create them. Ecological responsibility, as Lawrence Buell argues, is a matter for all disciplines, but it comes to bear particularly heavily on the production and study of film, given its highly influential cultural status, as well as its traditional association with objective realism.[7] Points of focus within eco-cinema studies differ quite radically, ranging from accounts of the film industry's historically toxic production practices[8] to arguments about how Hollywood cinema communicates environmental ethics by 'tapping into a latent hunger for connectivity within a broadly conceived ethical system of values'.[9] But the key question relates to the ideological function of representation and whether or not cinema is able to shake up the deeply ingrained human/non-human divide. Paula Willoquet-Maricondi asks: 'How can film bring about concern for and identification with the nonhuman without anthropomorphizing it, essentially inviting us to cross species lines in order to connect and empathize?'[10]

For Scott MacDonald, this evolves through an experimental 'tradition of filmmaking that [...] provides an evocation of the experience of being in the natural world' and which offers 'forms of visual/auditory training in appreciating the transitory'.[11] What MacDonald describes as the 'retraining of perception' elicits ecological consciousness through focused contemplation—the small acts of looking, listening and noticing espoused by many nature writers such as the late American poet Mary Oliver—offering an antidote to our media-saturated environment. But it also requires that we resist and challenge anthropocentric perspectives and turn the act of representation into a radical gesture, allowing new experiences and new embodied understandings to emerge. As Willoquet-Maricondi argues, 'it is not that representations directly shape nature but that they shape our perceptions of nature, perceptions that in turn inform and pattern our actions in relation to nature'.[12] The spectacularisation of nature, touched on in the previous chapter, arguably promotes an othering gaze, technologically mediated to give the impression of transparency and immediacy. It is also highly dramatised, privileging visually arresting wildlife and highly structured scenes to suggest exciting confrontations between animals.[13] Emphasising distant and exotic locations, epic views, hidden depths, staggering sights and jaw-dropping experiences, the rhetoric and visual language of the contemporary high-definition nature documentary is a uneasy mixture of colonialism and the amusement park. If nature is repeatedly presented as a visually appeasing distraction, something to care about only if it entertains, what kinds of quotidian relations does this encourage? It is easy to see from this perspective how representation—the ethics of the image—is intricately bound up with ecological responsibility, extending into everyday perception and affecting in different ways the choices we make. What we perceive and how we perceive it is thus central to the development of a political consciousness that does not stop at environmental and ecological issues.

From Jean Painlevé's fusion of documentary and surrealism in his intimate studies of underwater life to the landscape films of Margaret Tait, Marie Menken, James Benning and countless others, experimental cinema has developed multiple and diverse visual languages of the non-human. It has often been through nature that filmmakers have interrogated film's ontological specificities, both in theory and in practice and with or without a camera. Whilst Brakhage's *Mothlight* (1963) draws attention to the flat surface of the filmstrip and the sensation of proximity, works such as Larry Gottheim's *Fog Line* (1970) or Chris Welsby's *Entrance Island* (2015) emphasise cinematic temporality through a fixed, almost transcendental gaze onto a distant landscape, inviting a sensitivity to minute and subtle changes in the environment. And if these single-take films—pushed to the extreme in Benning's *Ruhr* (2009) and *Nightfall* (2011)—seem to represent a Bazinian celebration of objective realism by suppressing montage, then the ecological films of Rose Lowder challenge the supposed authority of the gaze through a sustained use of interruption.

Like Kurt Kren's *3/60 Trees in Autumn* (1960), Lowder brings a structural awareness to the single frame, meticulously composing her films in-camera with frame-by-frame modifications to focus and exposure. In works such as *Les tournesols* (1982), *Impromptu* (1989) and the *Bouquets* series (1994–2005), images are woven together by shooting clusters of alternating frames through a predetermined structure, winding the camera back and re-exposing as necessary. In this way, Lowder refers to the one-minute films in *Bouquets* as unique bunches of film frames, and the on-screen effect is indeed one in which different colours and forms burst forth in simultaneity. The frenzy of images coheres in what MacDonald describes as a 'retinal collage', where disparate spaces and places collapse into a single vibrating impression. This technique of rapid oscillation holds the spectator always at the edge of perception, unable to fully enter—and thus possess—the image, poised between reality and its representation. This self-reflexive space between invites an awareness of the film technology itself, whilst opening up what Guinevere Narraway describes as an 'expanded field of perception'.[14] Drawing attention to both the mechanical and material properties of photochemical film, Lowder elicits a very physical response to the images that is based not on continuity, fluidity and absorption but interruption, intrusion and fragmentation. The relentless flickering, however, can be understood as the destruction of only one form of (human) vision, which ultimately suggests the possibility of other ways of seeing and experiencing. How does the world see? How does nature experience time and space? What is experience? Without claiming to put us 'in the shoes' of nature, Lowder uses the film material and its sequential structure to problematise anthropocentric notions of temporality. From this perspective, the individual film frames in Lowder's work can be seen to 'perform' the act of perception, with the energetic impulses emanating from the interstices communicating a form of material agency. The artist, in this sense, does not entirely control the material, but harnesses its expressive possibilities through a form of structural collaboration (Fig. 3.1).

Although the austere formalism of British structural/materialism seemed to turn its back on the outside world, a number of artists from this period reintroduced representation into material interrogation via an engagement with the environment. As Deke Dusinberre observed in 1983, these 'new young film-makers', such as Chris Welsby and William Raban, 'embraced the radical vision of formalism but [...] felt uneasy with the strictures of "structural" film-making'.[15] In Welsby's double screen film *Wind Vane* (1972), two cameras were set-up with wind vane attachments so that the force and direction of the wind would control how the landscape was recorded. *Seven Days* (1974) works with a similar approach: employing an equatorial stand used by astronomers, the camera was mounted to align with the earth's axis, recording one frame every ten seconds over a period of seven days. Structure thus plays a defining role, but innovative modifications to the recording technology allow

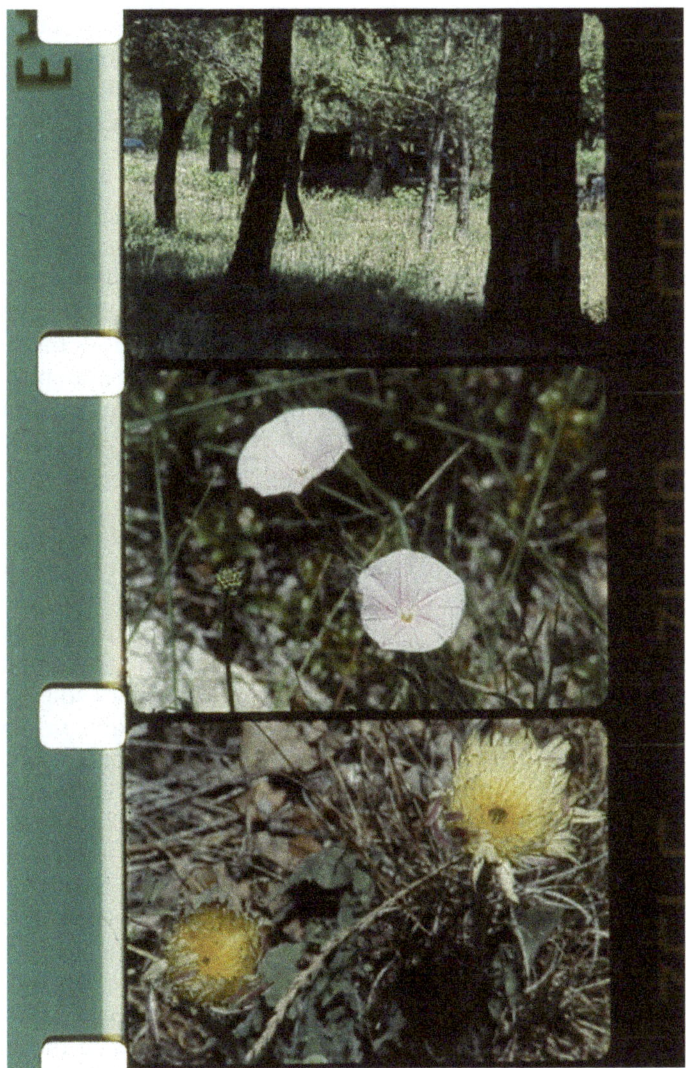

Fig. 3.1 Three frames from *Bouquets 9*, Rose Lowder, 1995, filmed near the town of Signes, Var, in the south-east of France (Image courtesy of Light Cone)

nature to determine the shape of its own representation. As Peter Wollen observes, 'the automatic procedures of science and technology, instead of being inflicted on nature in order to dominate it, were directed by nature itself'.[16] In this sense, nature is a collaborator in the artistic process, shifting power relations and uprooting the spectacularising tendency of more conventional film and television documentaries.

The renewed interest in celluloid film's material properties in the digital era has arguably given rise to a heightened awareness of film's power to engage with nature in a uniquely physical and embodied way. Tess Takahashi considers the indexical properties of film—the ability to register direct traces of contact—in terms of opening up possibilities for 'writing' the natural world, citing a number of North American examples where celluloid is brought into contact with the elements. 'Is film a medium closer to the natural world than the digital?' she asks. 'And, if so, does celluloid film allow nature to "speak" more directly?'[17] Gregory Zinman seems to answer in the affirmative when he asserts that the buried and drowned films of Tomonari Nishikawa, David Gatten and Jennifer Reeves 'draw our attention to the role of non-human actants in the creation of moving images and, in doing so, enable a political re-examination of the process and function of art'.[18] His analysis places particular emphasis on the 'relationship of filmmaking to ecological issues' and the importance of 'experiential knowledge' in eliciting environmental consciousness.[19]

One of the earliest examples of 'weathered film' is *Stadt in Flammen* (1984) by the German collective Schmelzdahin (composed of Jochen Lempert, Jochen Müller and Jürgen Reble). Meaning 'melt away', the group's name signalled a clear interest in the chemical substrate not as a fixed entity but as a malleable site of alternative visual representations, capable of communicating with other physical matter. No longer subservient to the mechanical optics of the camera, the composite chemicals of the film strip could find independent expression when brought into contact with the natural elements, taking on painterly and sculptural qualities. Super 8 images of B-movie action sequences were buried in Reble's garden during a hot and humid summer, causing the layers of colour emulsion to split apart and mix together. 'The colours remained very pure and intense, but departed from their previous form', says Reble. 'Indeed, they were laying themselves down upon the old action film to form veritable mosaics of color, remarkably like the stained glass of church windows'.[20] In a subsequent film *Aus den Algen* (1986) another found footage sequence is submerged in a pond, where, during the course of a year, algae and other lively bacteria contribute to the film's gradual biochemical decay. Although the alchemical transformations of Schmelzdahin do not explicitly state the visualisation of nature as their primary focus, they directly implicate earthly substances in the reconceptualisation of cinematic representation, incorporating ecological temporalities invisible to the human eye into the expansion of celluloid's expressive range.

The potential for material contact with the earth to open up modes of representation has been explored from a number of different perspectives.[21] Greta Snider's *Quarry Movie* (1999), for example, is 'an attempt to document a place ... not only its image as lensed, but its weather, its soil, and its toxins', which register on the surface of the film strip.[22] Like Nishikawa in the making of *sound of a million insects, light of a thousand stars* (2014), Snider relies on toxic material residues to inscribe themselves on the film, providing an experience of environmental destruction through the direct physical trace rather than the photographic image. Reversing traditional approaches to representing the environment, Snider emphasises that the motivation behind the film was 'not to use techniques to achieve a "look", but rather to achieve a presence, and then see what it looks like'.[23] What registers on the film couldn't be further from the images of conventional wildlife films and nature documentaries, where knowledge about, and insight into, a place are assumed to lie in the spectacular representational clarity of advanced recording technologies. In Snider's buried film, the image shifts from representational content to surface texture, with scratches and marks on the surface functioning as auto-inscriptions of a place.

A largely under-recognised example of buried film is Alia Syed's *Priya* (2011), a film that I have discussed elsewhere and thus limit my reflections here to several key details.[24] Syed filmed images of a classical North Indian dancer, suspending the camera from a rope above the dancer's head in order to create, as it unwinds, a corresponding circular movement to the filmed body. Finding the processed images 'too beautiful', and in an attempt to pierce the visual spectacle, the filmmaker buried sections of the film in her garden for varying lengths of time, from a few weeks to several months. The gradual breakdown of the material is evidenced in the uneven flashes of colour on the surface of the film that compete with the fluid gestures and saturated forms of the dancer, eventually obscuring them entirely as the deterioration becomes so advanced that the figurative image disappears. At work here is the refusal of the objectifying gaze that controls, fixes and penetrates the image, meaning that

> by literally penetrating and debasing the glossy surface of the film, Syed kills the dimension of the cliché in the image, eschewing the fetishization of the exotic 'other'. Drawing attention away from the superficial beauty of the image she pulls us back to the physicality of the celluloid material, its ability to produce an indexical trace of time's passing.[25]

But the exotic and fetishised 'other' also relates to nature itself, bestowing on the gesture a dual representational significance. Syed has referred to this physical engagement with the material as a way of 'working through the differences between film and [digital] video' by embracing film as something that can be touched and worked with manually.[26] Although this provides a starting point for thinking about photochemical specificities, addressing particularly Zinman's ontological questioning cited earlier, there is clearly much more at stake in Syed's film than simply marking out distinct material qualities. By destroying the visual cliché, Syed appeals to what Laura Marks refers to in her discussion of inter-cultural cinema as 'non-visual knowledge, embodied knowledge, and experience of the senses', problematising the separation of seeing and feeling, of objective and subjective.[27]

These ideas are teased out in the work of Emmanuel Lefrant, whose intricate photochemical processes offer a unique insight into the relationship between the film material and modes of perception. *Underground* (2001), a film made by burying strips of unexposed but processed Super 8 colour film stock in the ground during different weather conditions and in various geographical locations (France, USA and the UK) paves the way for his later, more complex environmental allegories. Like David Gatten's *What the Water Said* (1997–2007)—an early and now extensively analysed example of direct environmental contact, where spools of unprocessed film were submerged in water for extended periods of time—Lefrant dispenses entirely with the figurative image, beginning instead with the blank canvas of the celluloid itself.[28] The traces of underground life inaccessible to the human eye are registered through the material's prolonged exposure to micro-organisms in the earth that directly communicate their temporal existence through a process of biochemical transformation. This translates as a pulsating mass that spreads across the screen like volcanic lava, moving the eye in all directions as the colour palette shifts from fiery red to blue to a deep earthy green. It is a lively display of surface animation that at points resembles the painted films of Stan Brakhage (*The Dante Quartet*, 1987, comes to mind); the difference, of course, is that rather than applying paint to animate the surface, it is the surface that animates itself through a process of decomposition or erasure. And whilst the impression of abstraction is similar in both films, *Underground* is a radical reconceptualisation of the representational image as a material dialogue. 'The point', observes Lefrant, 'is to reach the extreme of realistic representation by way of an abstract image'.[29] This is precisely the paradox of the aesthetic of contact—in its refusal to conform to the conventions of visual recognition it opens up the spectrum of cinematic realism to incorporate the traces of matter.

Directly inspired by Maurice Merleau-Ponty's 1964 text *Le Visible et l'invisible (The Visible and the Invisible)*, Lefrant's later film *Parties Visible et Invisible d'Un Ensemble Sous Tension* (2009) takes these explorations further by interlacing figurative and abstract imagery.[30] Lefrant uses the process of making the film as a way of illustrating Merleau-Ponty's theory of perception, in which the body and the world—subjective experience and objective existence—are interwoven. This new conception of the body which emerges in the philosopher's later work is an attempt to articulate the relationship between 'what *seeing* is, and what *thing* or *world* is'.[31] Vision, for Merleau-Ponty, is inseparable from touch: 'The look, we said, envelops, palpitates, espouses the visible things. As though it were in a relation of pre-established harmony with them, as though it knew them before knowing them'.[32] In *Parties Visible et Invisible* material processes are employed to translate—through touch—an earthly experience that demonstrates the reversibility of perception. Whilst living in Togo in Africa, Lefrant shot the image he could see from his window using Super 8 film and time-lapse photography, condensing the twelve-hour period from dawn to dusk into just seven minutes. Several strips of Super 8 and 16mm colour film—again processed but unexposed—were also buried in the ground in various locations seen within the frame of the filmed image and then unearthed at different time intervals. The use of stocks with different kinds of emulsion composition introduced a greater variability into the way the earth would react with the layers of chemicals, giving rise to a wide spectrum of colour, texture and density. The two positive and negative versions of the time-lapse footage are brought together with the buried sequences through a process of bi-packing—an optical printing procedure where the layers of film are sandwiched together and rephotographed, superimposing the details of one image onto another. The end result is a startling animation of the figurative image by the colourful degradation and decomposition of the buried strip. Lefrant refers to the film as 'a bipolar world, where the invisible takes shape within the visible, where the first dissolves into the second and vice-versa'.[33] The transposing of these qualities—the invisible (underground) onto the visible (overground)—is emphasised by the visual impression of flipping that caresses the eye as a tactile flicker (Fig. 3.2).

Running under the surface of *Parties Visible et Invisible* is the theme of environmental catastrophe and earthly destruction. The fragility of the filmstrip and its susceptibility to physical intervention extends to the images of barren landscapes ablaze with energy and urgency. As beautiful as they might seem on one level, it is difficult not to read the explosions of colour as a deterioration not just of the celluloid material, but of the earth itself, and the destabilisation of the natural world by human activity. This becomes a much more explicit theme in Lefrant's subsequent work, where chemical and mechanical interventions are employed to create unsettling visions of ecological imbalance.

Le Pays Dévasté (2015) takes as its inspiration T. S. Eliot's poem *The Waste Land* (1922), an epic work of literary modernism that employs a disjointed, fragmentary structure. According to Lefrant, it is not so much the content of Eliot's masterpiece that feeds into the film but the evocative nature of the title and its significance in a twenty-first-century context (instead of the established French translation 'La Terre vaine' Lefrant proposes 'Le Pays dévasté' as a more accurate rendering). However, the allusions to earthly decay, emptiness and drought, particularly in the final section of the poem 'What the Thunder Said'—also an inspiration for Gatten's *What the Water Said*—arguably find their visual form in dried out and unpopulated dystopic spaces of Lefrant's film. Shot in geographically dispersed locations over a period of several years, the sequences of *Le Pays Dévasté* are brought together through the pursuit of a visual language for the Anthropocene. What might, in a different context, have been presented as a captivating travelogue—colour Super 8 footage of mangroves in Martinique, a riverboat journey through the Amazon rainforest, a water bird's graceful take-off into the air, a sacred baobab tree perched on the water's edge—are here reworked to expose the environmental tragedy that is the other side of nature as spectacle. Using cross-processing techniques—that is, experimenting with and harnessing the effects of developing film in the 'wrong' chemicals for that particular film stock—Lefrant is able to bring out latent alternative meanings embedded within the images themselves. 'The idea behind the film', he states, 'was to create a personal vision of what the world might soon become. I

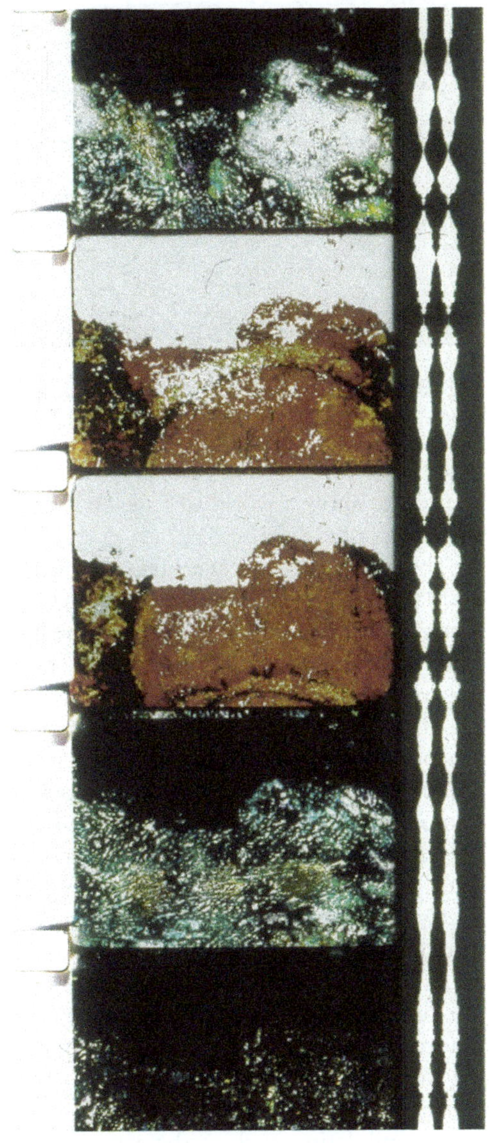

Fig. 3.2 *Parties Visible et Invisible d'Un Ensemble Sous Tension*, Emmanuel Lefrant, 2009 (Image courtesy of Light Cone)

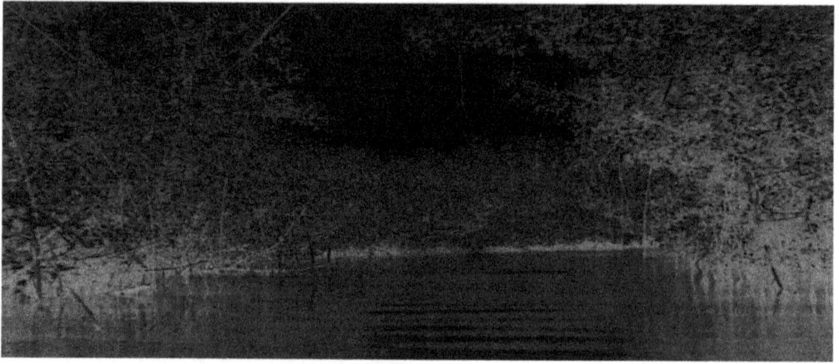

Fig. 3.3 *Le Pays Dévasté*, Emmanuel Lefrant, 2015 (Image courtesy of Light Cone)

wanted to show a world of rules in a state of absolute disruption. Images of catastrophe' (Fig. 3.3).[34]

The opening sequence takes us on a sepia-stained journey where sky and land are barely differentiated, the eye unable to fix a stable point of recognition. Double exposures of positive and negative images present both a living world we recognise and its scorched-out aftermath, an impression that continues with a subsequent negative image of trees moving through the frame to the sound of fire and wind. If we weren't, by this point, tuned into the film's post-apocalyptic vision, the next sequence shakes us out of our complacency, piling image upon image of the Sao Paolo skyline onto our retinas to the continuous sound of a car horn and the eerie use of a piece of audio taken from *The Misfits* (John Huston, 1961): 'Dropping a bomb is like telling a lie. It makes everything so quiet. Pretty soon you don't hear anything, you don't see anything'. Lefrant's intricate and dexterous use of optical printing techniques—already evident in *Parties Visible et Invisible*—creates a perceptual onslaught by alternating positive and negative versions of the same image. The alternations gradually increase and the flicker intensifies until the screen is a pulsating image of nothing. The reference derives from Lefrant's interest in the German philosopher Günter Anders and his writings on technologies of mass annihilation such as the atomic bomb, which for the first time, saw humanity create the means of its own destruction.[35] Lefrant thus draws a parallel between the gradual process of environmental catastrophe and the immediate effects of a nuclear war, both man-made forms of human obsolescence. The resonance can be found in Anders's statement that the bomb produces 'the effect of the daily growing gap between our two faculties; between our *actions* and our *imagination*; of the fact that we are unable to conceive what we can construct; to mentally reproduce what we can produce; to realise the reality which we can bring into being'.[36] In Lefrant's form of imaginative (re)visioning, the reality of this contemporary form of destruction is realised to chilling effect.

In *I Don't Think I Can See an Island* (2016), a film made in collaboration with Christopher Becks, Lefrant again shows how an otherwise visually appealing image of landscape—this time an island off the coast of Sicily—can, when subjected to a series of manipulations in the processing and printing stages, take on an intensely foreboding quality. Historically associated with home movies and poetic personal diaries, the Super 8 camera is here recharged with a different kind of energy that is no longer the carrier of happy memories, but rather the bearer of earthly premonitions. The act of seeing, suggested in the title of the film, is problematised through techniques of double exposure that bring together negative and positive imagery and flip perspective so that we appear to be drifting above the clouds. The transfer of Super 8 to 16mm, along with the traces of hand-processing, bring attention to the surface of the film as the site of this perceptual transformation. Does the film awaken an environmental consciousness? It certainly presents a dystopic world that elicits anxiety about our continued existence on this planet. The low electronic drone that draws out the copper tones of the image immediately sets us in an uneasy relationship with these drifting mounds of matter. But this film, like *Le Pays Devasté* and *Parties Visible et Invisible*, is not a political statement in the traditional sense. It asks us to think images differently, to see beyond the spectacle and to question the very status and authority of the image.

Images of landscape radically reworked through mechanical and chemical interventions permeate the field of contemporary experimental cinema, giving new significance to an artistic genre that, as Scott MacDonald observes, has its origins in the 'nineteenth-century fascination with "wilderness" and "nature".'[37] Whilst some film artists, such as Lefrant, address the theme of environmental destruction explicitly, imbuing the images with a dystopian and chilling atmosphere—see also Rosa Barba's *Bending to Earth* (2015), Christina Battle's *Oil Wells: Sturgeon Road & 97th Street* (2002), Dan Baker's *Transaension* (2006) and Karl Lemieux and David Bryant's *Quiet Zone* (2014)—there are many other examples of politics and ecology emanating from the surface of the film in less direct ways. Argentinian filmmaker Pablo Mazzolo works at the edges of documentary, creating experiential portraits of both urban and natural environments through material transformations. *Photooxidation* (2013) is a frenetic study of movement and light that begins with abstract bursts of illumination superimposed onto city scenes—clusters of concrete constructions, anonymous faces picked out from the crowd—and builds to a white-knuckle audio-visual crescendo. Echoing the nature-civilisation studies of Paul Clipson—for example, *Another Void* (2012), *Disporting with a Shadow* (2015), *Made of Air* (2014), *Feeler* (2016)—Mazzolo uses overlapping multiple superimpositions and shifting light play to create a haptic representation of matter and vital energies flowing through all things. Federico Windhausen, in his overview of the film, notes how Mazzolo's attention to the film surface weaves together the external world and its photochemical depiction, 'as if, in the sites of contact between the city and Mazzolo's filmic materials, the contents of the filmstrip had been transformed by a volatile admixture of urban energies and photochemical agents'.[38] Similarly, in *Oaxaca Tohoku* (2011–2012), shot on the coast of Mexico during a maximum tsunami warning brought about by an earthquake in Japan, the energy of tectonic plates is recreated through the instability of the image, which shifts restlessly across the densely populated landscapes.

Ecologies of (Small) Things

We have seen how a number of contemporary artists have explored the material properties of film in order to bring about alternative representations of landscape, shifting the ocular emphasis of traditional environmental film to a more tactile and embodied experience that privileges contact as a powerful communicating force. In these works, vision is not made 'better' by enhanced clarity but is rendered problematic through the emphasis on surface encounters and bodily engagements. As a result, the viewer is invited to activate other senses—to feel, rather than simply see, the physical world unfolding on the screen. In some works, particularly the 'weathered' films, the image might be described in terms of a filmic close-up, where details and textures become more pronounced and traditional perspectival reference points fall away. Given its emphasis on representational proximity, the aesthetic of contact in materialist film displays important overlaps with the cinematic close-up, particularly in its decentering and defamiliarising capabilities. However, despite the radical potential of the close-up, particularly in terms of haptic visuality, film theory has tended to neglect the development of this technique in experimental film, or even non-narrative cinema more generally. In her discussion of the close-up in dance film, Erin Brannigan observes in this respect:

> As a type of cinematic shot, the close-up has traditionally had a strong connection with narrative storytelling and the construction of the star personae. More specifically, it is the 'facial' close-up that has been with us since the earliest years of cinema and is most commonly cited in all manner of film discourse including critical theories of the cinematic image.[39]

From Béla Balázs to Gilles Deleuze, and from Jean Epstein to Laura Mulvey, the close-up has consistently been discussed in relation to the human body. For Deleuze, the close-up has a certain affinity with affect, which is most effectively expressed through facial expressions. '*The affection image is the close-up*,' he states, '*and the close-up is the face*'.[40] In Balázs's writings on early cinema, the close-up is associated with narrative intrigue, the 'inner drama' of characters being conveyed through the emphasis on facial expression and bodily gestures.[41] Jean Epstein's theory of *photogénie* is also based to a large extent on the transformative power of the close-up, with its ability to evoke emotional tension through magnified scale: 'A head suddenly appears on screen and drama, now face to face, seems to address me personally and swells with an extraordinary intensity'.[42]

In contrast to this emphasis on the exterior body, Vicky Smith's camera-less film *sobbingspittingscratching* (2012) makes innovative use of the close-up to turn the body inside-out, using the surface of the filmstrip as a repository for the titular excretions so that it functions as a kind of portal to a different engagement with the body. During a period of emotional turmoil, the artist collected tears in a pipette and transferred them directly onto strips of clear leader, combining these with sections on which she deposited globs of her own saliva.[43] Magnified on the screen, these fluids resemble microscopic images of bacteria and bring us into an uncanny physical proximity with the artist's body. Intricately connected to human emotion and drama, they nonetheless seem quite far from the kinds of bodily close-ups traditionally presented in the cinema. The materialist emphasis on the imprint or trace questions conventional modes of bodily representation but also explores an alternative language of the close-up that aligns it with the world of small things. And in this sense, we might understand the materialist gesture along the same lines as Man Ray's rayograms in its search for a mode of visualising matter that not only resists conventional cinematic representation but is also largely absent from the repertoire of things *worthy* of representation.

What happens when we narrow our field of vision and begin to notice the small things that surround us? Walter Benjamin, in particular, was sensitive to the capability of the cinema to open up a new awareness of the world through magnification. 'With the close-up, space expands', he states. It 'does not simply render more precise what in any case was visible, though unclear; it reveals entirely new structural formulations of the subject'.[44] The close-up was central to Benjamin's notion of the 'optical unconscious'—the technological means by which vision opens out into unexplored terrain—and it was certainly part of his interest in the rediscovery of material things and discarded objects. By comparing the work of Vicky Smith and Charlotte Pryce, I will try to draw out some of the ways in which materialist practice resonates with Benjamin's radical envisioning of the close-up, examining how tactile intervention facilitates quite different manifestations of proximity. A form of both perceptual and material reduction defines the working practices of both artists, meaning that their interest in the close-up goes beyond simply representing things in miniature. Whilst Pryce has described how her work is produced mainly within the confines of her home in Los Angeles, filming in her garden and hand-processing in her studio, Smith has a similarly intimate creative process, working with minimal means and simple gestures and responding to her immediate environment.[45]

Having been involved in the London Filmmakers' Co-op during the 1990s, Smith's early animated films demonstrate many of the concerns around subjectivity and identity politics that to a large extent defines the work emerging out of the Co-op, particularly by women, during this period.[46] With *sobbingspittingscractching*, Smith moved from a partly figurative to an almost entirely abstract camera-less practice that allowed her to consolidate a number of interests already present in her work related to touch, proximity and the expression of internal states. *Primal* (2016) continues this physical engagement with the surface of the film strip, this time with the marks acting as a metaphor for the inner body rather than emerging directly from it. Inspired by Max Ernst's technique of 'frottage', where a piece of paper is layered onto a hard surface and a pencil is used to trace the textures underneath, Smith rubbed old fogged negative film onto the walls and floors of her studio.[47]

As with *Chinese Series* (2003), the last film that Brakhage made before his death, spit was used to moisten the emulsion in order to make it more receptive to the marks, creating a connective tissue between different manifestations of matter, both solid and liquid.[48] The scratches—or rubbings—create an image that appears as a golden shard of light that quivers tentatively on the screen, barely perceptible at first but then rising in size and intensity. It flutters around like a moth or a butterfly trapped in the dark rectangular space until it gains strength and gradually fills the space with an all-encompassing glow. The 'primal' of the title refers to the stripped-back means of production, but it also points to a wider concern with how handmade marks on celluloid might allude to a vibrant life force. Like Jeanne Liotta's *Loretta* (2003), *Primal* was made following the death of a parent (the filmmaker's father) and represents an emotional and intellectual working through of both life and loss. In Smith's own words:

> I was meditating on life and the animating principle, and using the fogged negative film gave me these soft impressions that felt like the fundamentals of light and dark. Unlike the hard, graphic lines of Len Lye, these were more wavering, uncertain, wobbly and fragile kinds of marks.[49]

The specificities of the expired film stock allow Smith to create what is best described as a form of cinematic 'breath', which transcends the human through its universal abstract form. What makes this a powerful instance of materialist film is its sensitive connection to the physicality of things; rather than simply inscribing onto the surface of the celluloid, Smith allows, through her own repetitive gestures, multiple surfaces to communicate and describe an experience. This practice once again opens up an alternative perceptual regime through an aesthetic of contact, whilst developing a language of non-human agency and expressivity. Composed by Shirley Pegna, the soundtrack enhances this tactile energy through an audio assemblage of objects and surfaces interspersed with the abrasive rubbing of cello strings. Crisp packets, biscuit wrappers and other throwaway items are explored for their sonic properties, extending their otherwise limited lifecycle and suggesting alternative trajectories for the seemingly endless stream of 'stuff' that circulates in the world (Fig. 3.4).

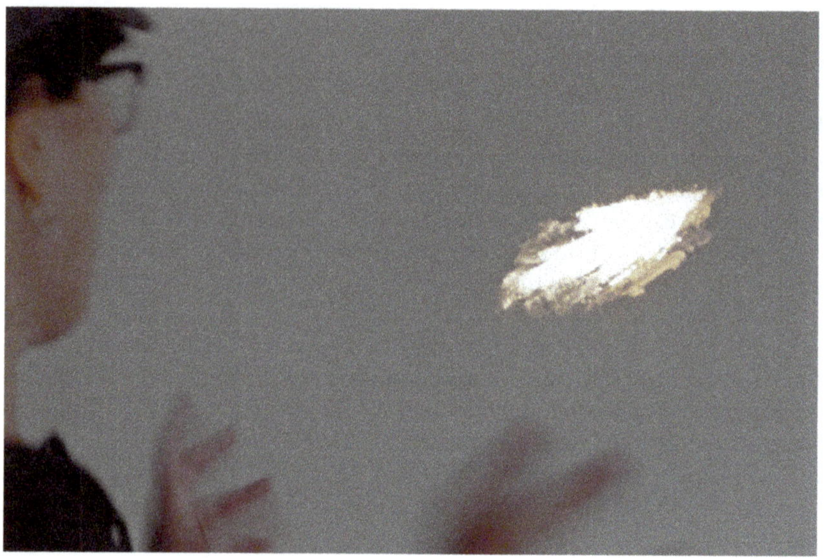

Fig. 3.4 *Primal*, Vicky Smith, 2016. Installation photo by Deborah Weinreb (Image courtesy of the artist)

In *Small Things Moving in Unison* (2018), Smith develops this interest in the performativity of matter and further explores the ability of small gestures to allude to broader philosophical concerns. In this intricate handmade animation, tiny perforations made frame-by-frame suggest clusters of animate matter that bustle around the screen, gathering together and falling apart with rhythmic precision. Visual associations shift from the macro to the micro—a starry sky, a flock of birds, communities of small insects, flecks of dust, clusters of bacteria—with the abstract simplicity of the marks giving free reign to these imaginative flights of scale. Every now and again, a perforation creates a tear in the celluloid skin, causing light to spill out in a less uniform way and drawing a parallel between the vulnerability of the material support and the fragility of those ecologies it represents. As attention constantly wavers between surface and depth, these interruptions are momentary reminders that what we are watching is not an image as such, but a series of absences made tangible by both the light and the repetitive mechanical movement of the projector (Fig. 3.5).

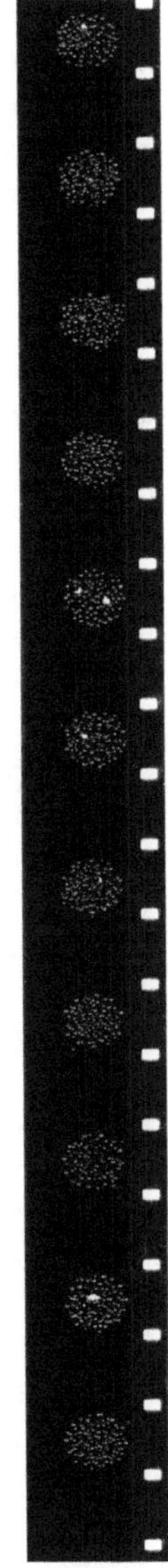

Fig. 3.5 Punched holes in successive frames in *Small Things Moving in Unison*, Vicky Smith, 2018 (Image courtesy of the artist)

With the increasing sophistication of contemporary animation techniques and the seemingly limitless possibilities of CGI for recreating worlds both familiar and strange, Smith's embrace of a pared-back, no-frills approach to filmmaking is a radical celebration of artisanal practice. Behind the apparent simplicity of the technique lies a process of painstaking physical labour that involves manually punching holes frame-by-frame and choreographing the fluid movements from one frame to another. This requires a significant level of bodily investment—a performance of process—that feeds into the on-screen movement and imbues the microscopic material world with a physical charge. Smith's working practice self-consciously looks back to the early pioneers of camera-less animation—Len Lye, Norman McLaren and Hy Hirsch—who scratched, painted and drew directly onto the film strip. In his biography, Lye describes how his wife, seeing him crouched over a piece of film, commented on his bodily contortions: 'I wriggled my whole body to get a compressed feeling into my shoulders—trying to get a pent-up feeling of precision into the fingers, and with a sudden jump I pulled the needle through the celluloid and completed my design'.[50] Referring to his bodily movements as having a 'spastic look'—a comment that feels somewhat dated now given its questionable body politics—Lye articulates a particular form of physicality that is channelled through material.

Marina Estela Graça identifies bodily implication as central to these alternative camera-less practices. 'There is an obvious direct physical relationship between the artist and the film itself', she writes. 'With their intimate connection to the body, handcraft processes reintegrate not only the physical senses into filmmaking, for both the maker and the viewer, but cinematic technology altogether'.[51] Handmade working processes, such as those pioneered by Lye, McLaren and generations of filmmakers after them, freed the artist from the constraints of complex technological procedures and restrictive industry standards. What emerges, as a result, is an approach to technology that not only widens the field of creative possibility, but also embraces—or indeed reimagines—imperfection. As Graça argues, this '[r]ecourse to the irregular (on the edge: verging on accident and mistake) rehumanizes the procedure, (re)aligning film with artisanal crafts that privilege the embodied relationship between the artist and their materials'.[52]

Primal and *Small Things Moving in Unison* draw together multiple bodies to refer to the interconnectedness and expressive power of matter, using the human body as a conduit in a process that relies to some extent on contingency—the ability of the material to 'act' in often unpredictable ways. By activating the vibrant surface of the film strip through touch, the artist reimagines scale and proximity, inviting us to reconsider what it means to look closely at the world. How might we expand our understanding of the close-up beyond lens-based, figurative formulations that privilege the eye? To this question, Smith proposes a haptic proximity that confuses perspective, refuses hierarchies and offers a playful collapsing of size and scale, opening up, in the process, an alternative ontology of things.

For Sean Cubitt, it is the material basis and physical groundedness of camera-less animation that bestows on it a particular status in relation to ecological and philosophical concerns:

> Direct animation flattens space to the dimensions of the medium: to the plane of the film-strip, the shape of the screen [...] Movement, as the root of animation, implies movement in and through, and in this case *of* space. It is in this sense that direct animation is the most ancient form, the prototype of all manipulations of the environment. This spatial identity of the animation and the animated belongs to a deep belief in the magical properties of animation, of breathing soul (*anima*) into the inert, of occupying the skin of an animal and so the forest or mountain where you live, and finally of animating the dead.[53]

This comment seems to relate directly to Smith's work, particularly given the centrality of breath as both image and rhythmic structure. The sequences of black frames that function as pauses between the inscriptions create a sense of inhalation and exhalation, not dissimilar to Hans Richter's description of his abstract animation *Rhythmus 21* (1921) in terms of 'going with the rhythm according to the successive rise and fall of the breath and the heartbeat'.[54] Shirley Pegna's soundtrack in both *Primal* and *Small Things Moving in Unison* uses breath to draw out the association of material with life, interspersing the sounds of objects with fragments of voice. In the later film, the appearance of the animated holes is accompanied by urgent whispers and sighs—sounds of communication that suggest–, but never fully describe, a recognisable language.[55] It is, however, in relation to the more recent film *Not (a) part* (2019) that one finds the life-giving power of direct animation most explicitly articulated. After several years of working in an abstract mode, using simple marks to problematise the division between animate and inanimate matter, this film sees Smith returning to the figurative image in the form of magnified insect parts, looping back in many ways to the earlier explorations of body fluids in *sobbingspittingscratching* and *Noisy Licking Dribbling and Spitting* (2014) (Fig. 3.6).[56]

As I briefly discussed in Chapter 2, the artist collected 53 dead bees on walks in Wales and the South West of England then created direct imprints of their bodies on 16mm negative film stock, exposing them to light using the rayogram method and hand-processing the results in caffenol.[57] Translating spatial relations into temporal rhythms, body parts are meticulously arranged frame-by-frame so that each bee takes up one second of film time, until, as an intertitle tells us 'parts become mixed'. Legs, heads, torsos and wings flicker across the screen, inviting us into an intimate study of the natural world whilst simultaneously emphasising a process of defamiliarisation. Unlike traditional representations of nature, Smith's camera-less technique resists visual complete-ness and highlights the material paradox of cinematic realism: although each body part leaves a physical trace on the surface of the celluloid, the intermittent nature of film projection produces only a fragmentary impression—a visual collapsing of the individual frames, 24 per second.

Here, the close-up finds a new expressive dimension, tied not, as is traditionally the case, to the magnifying properties of the camera, but to the mechanical relationship between the film surface and the film projector. The bee glimpsed at the very beginning of the film—the only camera-based section of the film—serves to draw attention to these visual differences. Our identificatory instincts are activated as we recognise the contours of head, body and wings *as* images, whilst the sections that follow reduce the representational field to tactile impressions. Ocular mastery is thus replaced with sensorial experiencing. This is, perhaps, the key defining feature of camera-less practice in relation to the ethical implications of looking closely. In its flattening of space, the aesthetic of contact disperses the gaze across the surface of the film, allowing the spectator to, in Cubitt's words, 'occupy the skin' of the onscreen bodies, just as Brakhage referred to *Mothlight* (1963) in terms of inhabiting the body of the deceased creature.[58]

Similar concerns are worked through in the films of Charlotte Pryce, particularly in relation to the ethical quandaries of the cinematic close-up and the expressive power of surface engagement. Since the 1980s, Pryce has developed an artisanal film practice in dialogue with the natural world, allowing the contingencies of material processes to open up new creative

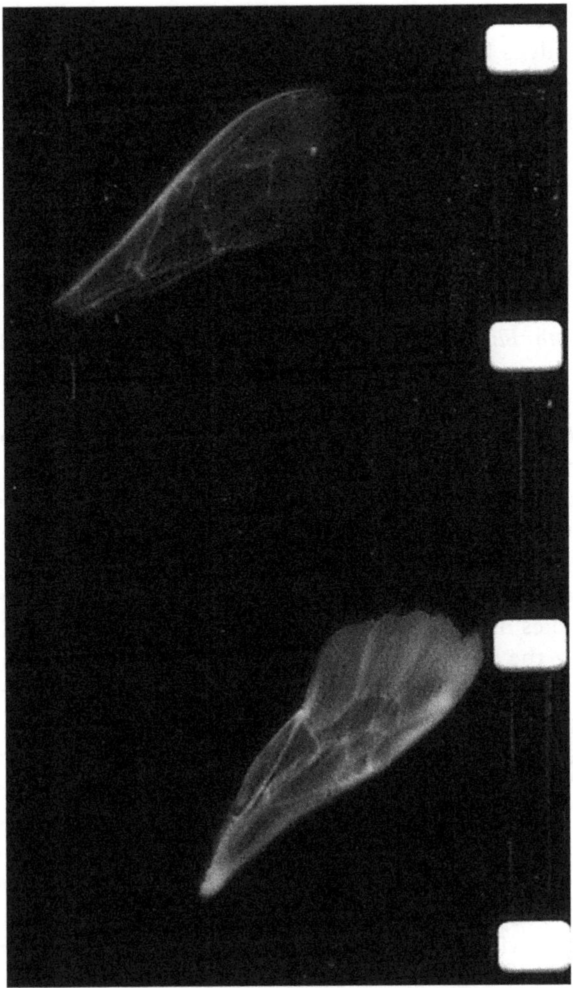

Fig. 3.6 Bee wings on individual frames in *Not (a) Part*, Vicky Smith, 2019 (Image courtesy of the artist)

pathways. She describes her films as 'observational reveries', where the object of study is filtered through imaginative wanderings and where scientific realism gives way to a more poetic interrogation of things. Pryce's material approach is determined to a large extent by what she describes as film's 'rich potential for metaphor', that is, its ability not simply to reflect reality but to describe it through material analogies.[59] Framing this interest in tangible realities and the sensuous experience of things is a desire to communicate with and via the natural world, and the development of her cinematic style over the past two decades can be understood largely from this perspective.

Concerning Flight—Five Illuminations in Miniature (2004) is the work that relates most closely to Smith's examination of non-human bodies in its search for an alternative language of insects. However, whilst Smith makes a political statement about the declining bee population by focusing on their dead bodies, Pryce treads a different path in celebrating the living form of various flying species, asking us to be attentive to their delicate movements and majestic presence. Consisting of five short films (*Thin Breath—Quivering; Landscape with the Fall of Icarus; Departure from the Garden; Conjuring forth the Firefly; Keepers of the Labyrinth*), this series of studies makes extensive use of close-up and macro cinematography to bring the viewer into another world and another temporal register. These brief 'illuminations' do more than simply bring us closer to the natural world; they invite us to experience the world differently through reference to non-human perception and movement, constructing stories around the insects that wrap us into their miniature existence. Inspired by Virginia Woolf's short story 'Death of a Moth', the first section *Thin Breath—Quivering* intersperses the rhythmic flapping of a moth's wings with rapid shifts in perspective, moving restlessly from one decentered image to another. The surfaces and edges of a windowpane, a vase of flowers and the view of buildings outside fly around the screen in a visual approximation of a moth's vision. The alternation of single frames produces an intense flicker effect that parallels the intermittent movement of the wings and forms a dialogue between the film material and the insect body. The 'thin breath' is material, mechanical and organic, and it is through this breath that we move beyond simply *looking* at the natural world to approach a form of *feeling with*.

Pryce's cinematic approach approximates Woolf's evocative and multilayered literary description of how the frenetic dance of a moth against the contours of her window seemed to encapsulate the interconnected energies of a fleeting moment one mid-September morning. Woolf's sensitive observation of the day moth—an in-between 'hybrid creature'—simultaneously narrows and expands the focus, collapsing multiple subjectivities and bringing together human and non-human perspectives. One key passage reads:

> The same energy which inspired the rooks, the ploughmen, the horses, and even, it seemed, the lean bare-backed downs, sent the moth fluttering from side to side of his square of the window-pane. One could not help watching him. One was, indeed, conscious of a queer feeling of pity for him. The possibilities of pleasure seemed that morning so enormous and so various that to have only a moth's part in life, and a day moth's at that, appeared a hard fate, and his zest in enjoying his meagre opportunities to the full, pathetic. [...] Yet, because he was so small, and so simple a form of energy that was rolling in at the open window and driving its way through so many narrow and intricate corridors of my own brain and in those of other human beings, there was something marvellous as well as pathetic about him.[60]

The relevance of Woolf's phenomenological accounts of experience to developments in ecological thought has been noted by a number of contemporary writers.[61] Kelly Elizabeth Sultzbach, for example, argues that Woolf's 'innovate formal strategies create an awareness of multiple animate beings within thick, sensory layers of earthly flesh'.[62] Little wonder, then, that Pryce's interest in the ability of film to translate the interconnected material layers of the natural world should gravitate towards Woolf's writings as a source of visual inspiration.

Central to Pryce's aesthetic in *Concerning Flight* is the experience of in-between-ness. In *Landscape with the Fall of Icarus* the persistent movement of the camera oscillates between a jerky and hesitant searching and urgent whip-pans across land, sky and sea that spread the image across the surface of the screen and create a sense of perceptual confusion. A dung beetle rolls a ball along the ground to the abrasive sounds of a whip, whilst a flying insect—the winged Icarus—falls through the air in slow motion in an epic and tragic descent. Throughout the five segments, the mixture of film stocks, variation of colour and texture, extensive optical printing and somatic camera constantly draw the eye to the material surface of the film strip, implicating it in the expression of landscapes and bodies, shifting temporalities and fluctuations of scale (Figs. 3.7 and 3.8).

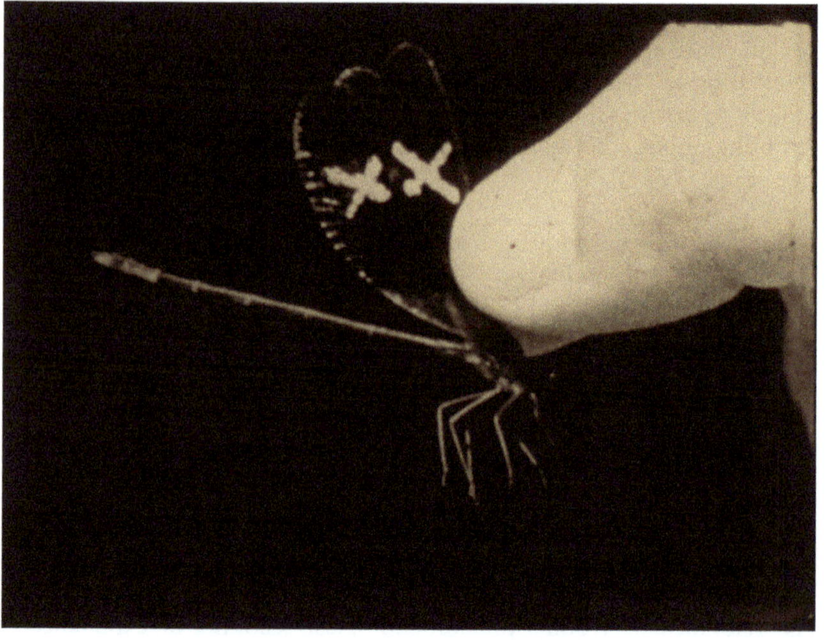

Fig. 3.7 An insect stilled in *Departure from the Garden*, part 3 of *Concerning Flight—Five Illuminations in Miniature*, Charlotte Pryce, 2004 (Image courtesy of the artist)

If *Concerning Flight* uses the material specificities of film to suggest the experience and behaviour of insects, *Discoveries on the Forest Floor* (2006) extends this to the plant world. This time, Pryce drew inspiration from Opal Whiteley's *Magical Nature Diary*, an American publication from 1920 that gathers together Whiteley's childhood observations about nature. Her imaginative reflections on and interactions with the 'little people' that lived in the woods beside her family home were scribbled with coloured crayons on various scraps of paper from the age of six. 'Most of the times, I looked looks out of the window', reads one passage in the diary. It continues:

> I had seeing of little plant folks just peeping out of the earth to see what they could see. I did have thinks it would be nice to be one of them, and

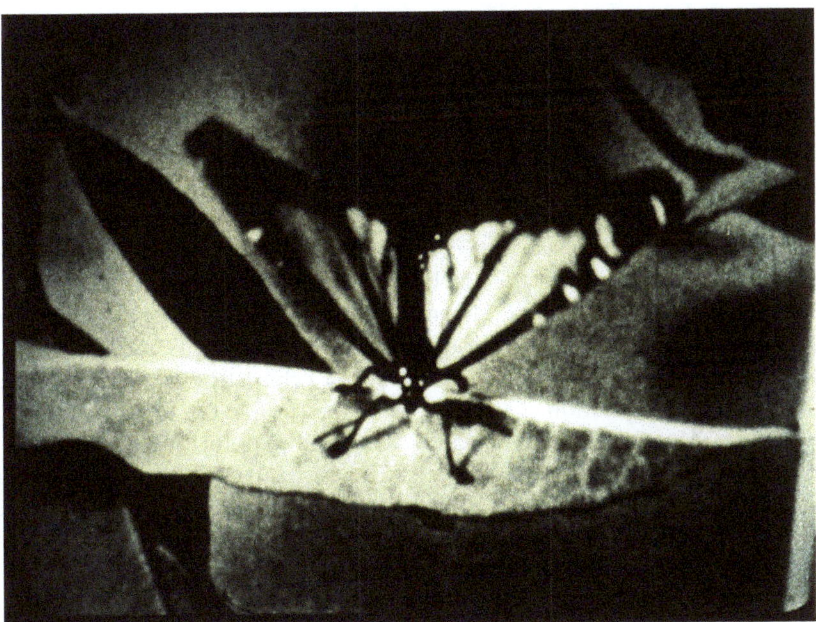

Fig. 3.8 The moth in *Thin Breath Quivering*, part 1 of *Concerning Flight—Five Illuminations in Miniature*, Charlotte Pryce, 2004 (Image courtesy of the artist)

> then grow up and have a flower, and bees a-coming, and seed-children at falltime. I have thinks this is a very interest world to live in.[63]

Approximating Whiteley's magical rendering of the natural world, Pryce explores a visual language of what she calls 'sympathetic resonance', where the celluloid material is manipulated to take on the distinct physical and behavioural characteristics of the plants themselves.

Divided into three interrelated sections, the film is a poetic study of the resurrection plant, lichen and the carnivorous plant, all with quite clear parallels with the medium of film in terms of capture, unfolding (the release of a latent image during processing) and attachment to surfaces. In the second section, 'The Talk of Lichen on a Lonely Day', Pryce treated the film with sulphuric acid—'a pretty drastic technique!'—to create an effect of lifting that imitates the crinkled texture of lichen: 'just as lichen sits on the surface of things, the image ended up being on the surface of the film itself'.[64] In trying to find a visual language, or 'textural response', for the carnivorous plant, Pryce draws on its almost complete absence of a root, represented in the evocative title 'Those Whose Attachment to the Earth is but Tentative'. Rapid alternations between the pages of an illustrated book and macro images of the plant's delicate tentacles and teeth create an ethereal mood somewhat removed from the objective representations usually associated with scientific study. The plant seems to emerge majestically from the air, held in a state of suspension that translates to the viewing process. Throughout the three sections, the emphasis on close-up details and attention to surface through the traces of hand-processing collapses figure and ground in a celebration of sensation and material communication.

Prima Materia (2015) takes as its starting point the investigation of substance and forms, inspired by the Roman poet and philosopher Lucretius in his six-book poem 'De rerum natura'. Pryce explores 'the nature of things' by alluding to the experience of earthly phenomena and material essences through processes specific to photochemical film. Threads, spirals and particles hover and weave through a thick background of a visually uncertain nature, where figure and ground become intertwined. Bursts of light reveal the grain and texture of the film whilst bringing into relief these primal, abstract forms suggestive of the first stirrings of matter. It is a perfect example of how the film surface—through chemical and mechanical interventions—comes to play a key role in creating a sense of perceptual ambiguity. As Pryce explains:

> I was trying to get a darkness and the sense of particles resting, coming to earth. The [Kodak] 7285 was no longer a possibility so I needed to find colour that was on the threshold of black and white. I thought, well, I can tone. By toning you get a solarization. Or I could do a slightly incomplete black and white reversal, which also leads to a kind of solarization. What I ended up doing was combining colour negative with black and white solarized images through a process of bi-packing in the optical printer: the colour negative positive and the black and white solarized copy of that same image.[65]

With an insight into Pryce's working methods one can begin to construct a narrative of materialist film research, which, as the filmmaker explains, is the result of several stages of process-based experimentation—'thinking

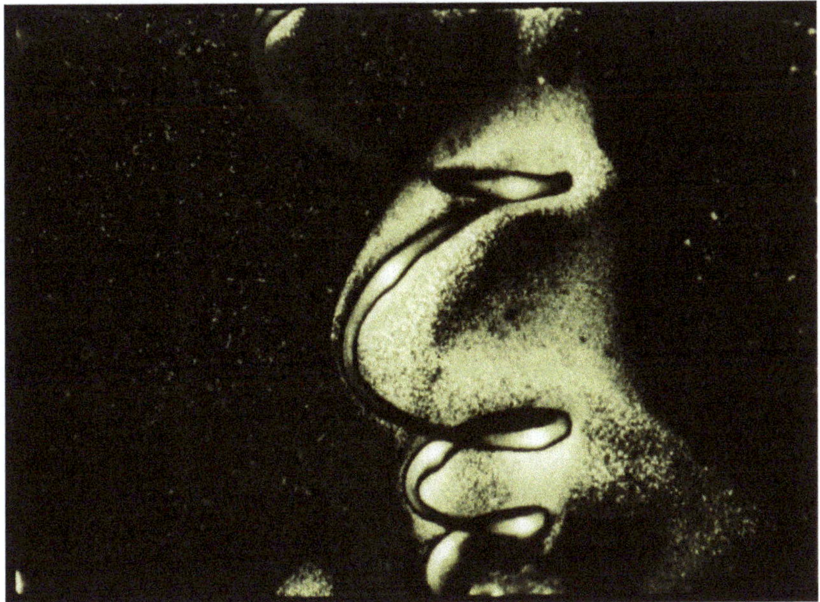

Fig. 3.9 *Prima Materia*, Charlotte Pryce, 2015 (Image courtesy of the artist)

through the material and the nature of that material'.[66] The otherworldly effects emerge to a large extent from the combination of unconventional approaches to the film material that emphasise a state of in-betweenness or alchemical transformation from one substance to another. Neither colour nor black and white, and suspended between surface and depth, the images speak a certain anxiety about the world, a sense of not knowing. In a period of earthly uncertainty, Pryce's filmic embrace of ancient questioning of the nature of things invites us momentarily into a space of reflection and reimagining, uprooting fixities and challenging traditional ways of seeing (Fig. 3.9).

Colour and Chemistry

What should be evident by this point is that, for most experimental film artists, the celluloid substrate is not simply the carrier of photographic images, but a site of creative expression and innovation in its own right.

Interventions into this complex gelatin layer through hand-processing, optical and contact printing, tinting and toning, reticulation, solarisation and other chemical transformations open up a world of metaphoric and experiential significance that takes us beyond the realms of photographic realism. Esther Urlus, for example, states: 'For me, film is a lot more than the representation of what a camera has recorded. [...] It's important for me that the emulsion has its own texture and can respond to chemicals differently than expected'.[67] This is akin to being taken on a walk, a form of filmic *flânerie* or a mindful meandering with the material, where the final destination is not known in advance. Japanese filmmaker and founder of the Double Negative lab in Montreal, Daïchi Saïto expresses this beautifully in his book *Moving the Sleeping images of Things Towards the Light*:

> Hand-processing has the aspect of negotiation between what's controllable and what's not, between predictability and unpredictability. [...] It's a rational and logical affair, to a certain extent. But no matter how precise you may be, some margin of error is inevitable, often yielding unexpected results. [...] Sometimes such accidents trigger new thoughts and make you see your work in a different light. You strive to control the medium and the medium betrays your intention. When the medium invites you for a walk, you walk with it – vulnerable though you may be. A medium is never simply a 'tool' for artists to express themselves.[68]

Allowing the work to emerge through the mysteries and contingencies of chemistry is central to a process-oriented approach to filmmaking that sees the world 'in constant change and movement— in a process of becoming'.[69]

Although, as Gehman points out, interest in the expressive possibilities of chemical manipulation and organic decay began to emerge in the 1980s and '90s, the decline of film as a commercial medium in the digital era has arguably intensified these activities, expanding them into exciting new areas of artistic reinvention such as homemade emulsion production and eco-processing. This has involved delving into the photochemical past in order to imagine possible futures, a process that Urlus describes as 'opportunistic backtracking'.[70] Urlus, along with several other filmmakers from around the world—Alex MacKenzie, Kevin Rice, Lindsay McIntyre, Robert Schaller, Etienne Caire, Guillaume Ferry, Juan David

González Monroy and Anja Dornieden, among others—has been instrumental in researching small-scale 'home-brewed' emulsion as an alternative to the industry-standard products manufactured by Kodak. Through a series of international meetings entitled Maddox Seminars (named after the nineteenth-century British photographer and physician Richard Leach Maddox), the group has attempted to refine various recipes and application procedures to arrive at a substrate capable of registering an image. It should be noted, however, that this passage from the industrial to the artisanal is both a search for creative autonomy and an embrace of alternative pathways. 'We're not going to repeat Kodak's years of hard work in our basement', admits Robert Schaller of the Handmade Film Institute, 'so why try? Let's do something else, something that they didn't do because it didn't match their objectives',[71] Looking into the past in order to map out new directions for the future is a defining feature of photochemical film culture, galvanised particularly through projects such as Re-Engineering Moving Image (RE:MI), a two-year artistic research collaboration between three artist-run film labs Labor Berlin (Berlin), Filmwerkplaats (Rotterdam) and MIRE (Nantes), which facilitated the exchange of industry skills and knowledge with the intention of fostering creative innovation in film.[72] The use of the term 're-engineering' is an important gesture in this sense, signalling not a return to the past but a reconfiguring of techniques that were developed to the industry standards of commercial film, and which now, in the hands of artists, offer a limitless field of reinvention.

This alternative aesthetic impulse can be seen particularly in Urlus's *Konrad & Kurfurst* (2013), a film that resulted from several stages of research into technical manuals by the early pioneers of both photography and film. Using a simple recipe of gelatin, potassium bromide and silver nitrate, and then hand-tinting in the spirit of Georges Méliès, Urlus immerses the spectator in a world of chemical transformation and vibrant matter. The film is a fictional re-enactment of a five-minute incident in the 1936 Berlin Olympic Games, in which Konrad Freiherr von Wangenheim was thrown violently from his horse Kurfurst, but nonetheless went on to win a gold medal. The fragmented image of a horse—documentary footage shot by Leni Riefenstahl—shifts in and out of view, struggling against a bubbling viscous background, revealing itself fleetingly, only to be dragged back into the sticky stuff of the film material. Movement animates the dried bubbles of emulsion and in the moment of projection appears to turn them back into liquid, reversing time in the process of moving the film forwards. The instability of the emulsion is described as a 'fragile metaphor for the heroism of Konrad and his horse Kurfurst', but the reference clearly extends to the fragile cultural status of celluloid and the pressing need for artists to explore alternatives to the dwindling commercial manufacture of film stock. Konrad's fall, and ultimate unforeseen triumph, could be read as a reflection on the narrative of film itself and its potential surmounting of the challenges of obsolescence. The struggle is an allegory—the fight to stay alive against all odds—and from this perspective the foregrounding of the material is multi-layered in all senses of the word (Fig. 3.10).

Konrad & Kurfurst emerged out of a curiosity about whether colour film stock could be made by hand from scratch. Having consulted with various industry professionals who advised her that this was near impossible on a small scale, Urlus pursued her own artisanal path, turning photochemical research into a fine art practice in its own right. This is, in fact, part of a larger enquiry into handmade colour mixing that manifests across a body of work spanning over ten years. Using a repurposed flatbed

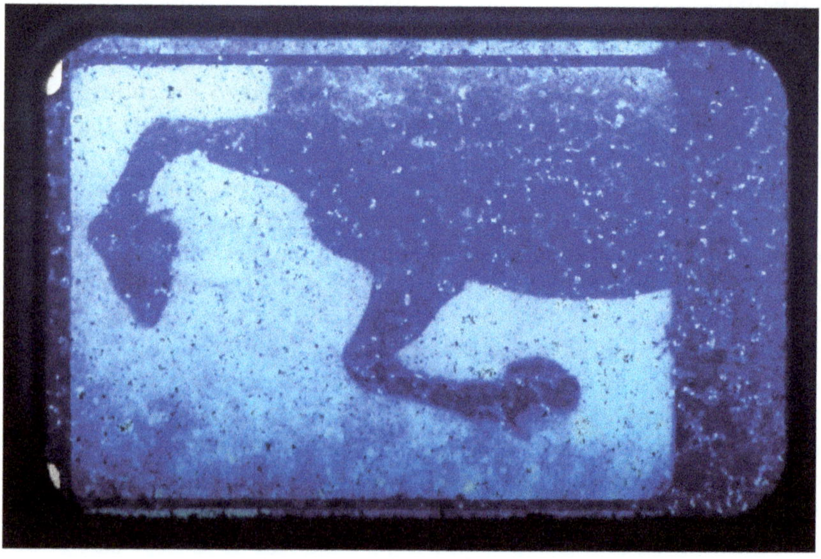

Fig. 3.10 Home-brewed emulsion with colour added in *Konrad & Kurfurst*, Esther Urlus, 2013 (Image courtesy of the artist)

editing table as a contact printer, Urlus employs a method of stacking, where multiple layers of film are reprinted as both positive and negative with colour filters. Objects and landscapes filmed in black and white are transformed into evocative flights of imagination through the successive accumulation of vibrant hues. In *Deep Red* (2012), a high contrast image of trees racing past the window of a car are pushed further and further into abstraction through the gradual build-up of different colours. As the layers accumulate, the screen turns into a tactile moving canvas, inviting the eye to shift back and forth between surfaces and textures. Eventually, the figurative contours of the trees—the indexical traces of reality—give way to what resemble painterly brushstrokes, blurring the boundary between objective and subjective impressions (Fig. 3.11).

Rode Molen (Red Mill) (2013) extends this exploration of colour, drawing inspiration from the Dutch painter Piet Mondrian and his series of works depicting windmills. In his post-impressionistic *Red Mill* of 1911, Mondrian employs bold, solid colours—the deep red structure floats against a bright blue background, creating a sombre yet vibrant scene where spatial and contextual markers are conspicuously absent. The images of Urlus's film take on a strikingly similar quality, as though breathing life into Mondrian's image. Exploding the boundary between film and painting, the windmill of the film's title is manually reworked with the use of masks that allow colour to be added to different parts of the image through repetitive printing procedures. Depending on the developing process used—positive or negative—the colours manifest differently from one sequence to the next, thrown across the screen through the sweeping movement of the windmill's arms. *Rode Molen* is a study of perception through the deconstruction of movement—slowing down, speeding up and changing perspective, with the intensive work on the surface of the film appearing to melt the solid structure into the material substrate. However, as the film progresses, Urlus's skilful printing of positive and negative layers produces relief effects that seem to reverse this impression. At points, the windmill appears to rise out of the film surface in ways not dissimilar to Guy Sherwin's *At the Academy* (1974), where negative and positive layers of academy leader are contact printed with a slight displacement that creates depth from a flat plane. The process relies, of course, on what might otherwise be considered a technical aberration—as a result of the slight misalignment of the layered positive and negative versions, the image becomes unstable, shaking its way back out of the material and taking on a new perceptual resonance.

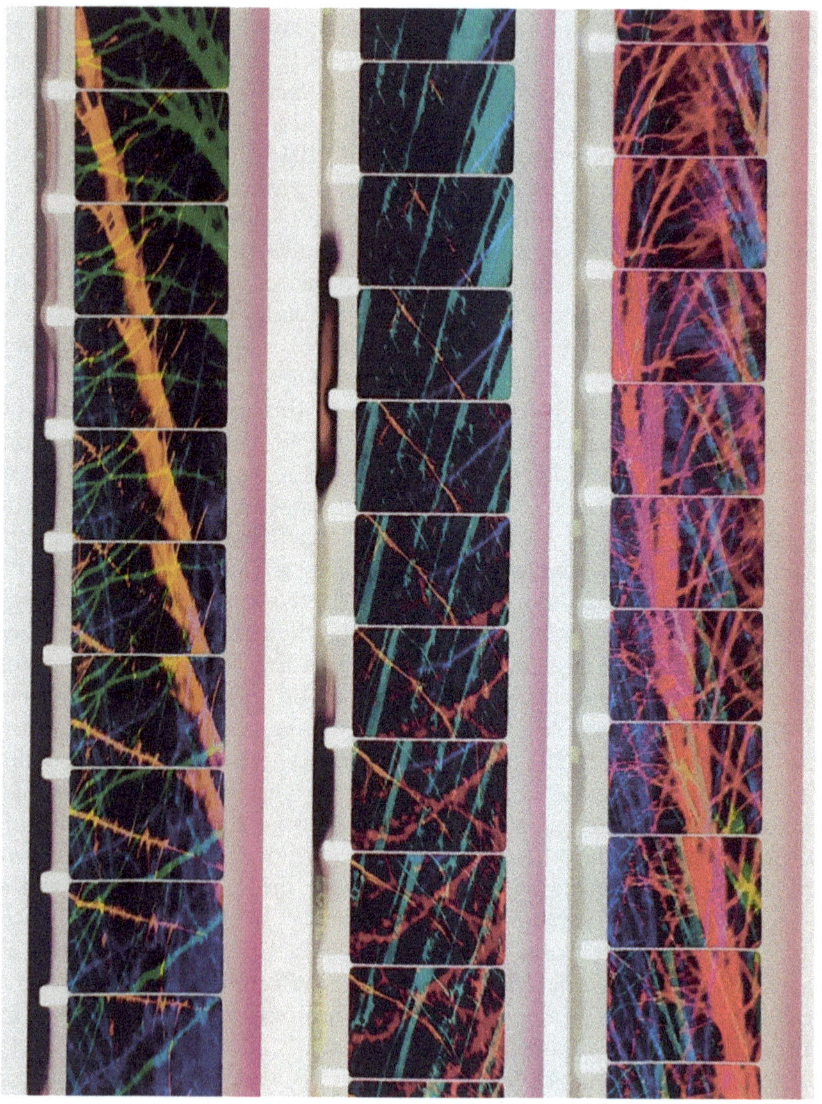

Fig. 3.11 Film strips from *Deep Red*, Esther Urlus, 2012 (Image courtesy of the artist)

Describing her relationship with moving images, Urlus refers to a desire to access what she terms the 'dinosaur brain', a pre-cognitive form of understanding that appeals to the senses rather than the intellect.[73] In an echo of Brakhage's 'untutored vision', she relates her films to a primal form of experience, where an instinctive bodily response replaces intellectual reasoning. Colour is therefore used, as Janis Crystal Lipzin explains in relation to her own darkroom working methods, to *allude* to the world rather than simply describing it, wrapping the image of things into an exploration of internal landscapes. Not surprisingly then, Urlus often works with specific places or landmarks that are already inscribed with a certain historical resonance that cannot be represented via traditional visual means. To make *Deletion* (2017), for example, the filmmaker visited six notorious locations in the Netherlands, all of them associated with what she describes as horrific or disturbing crimes. Instead of the actual location, the viewer is presented with a swarming sea of colour, out of which periodically emerges a barely legible outline or shape—a swaying leaf, a piece of fabric, a plastic bag—all the more terrifying for its refusal to be pulled out of this blurry in between-ness. In fact, Urlus seems to revel as much in the existential anxiety produced through visual blur as in the colour process itself. Like *Chrome* (2013), a work created specifically for the Vertical Cinema project, *Deletion* resurrects the autochrome technique, a method of colouring black and white photographs invented in 1903 by the Lumière brothers.[74] In this process, 'microscopic grains of potato starch dyed red-orange, green and blue-violet act as colour filters. At normal viewing distances, the light coming through the individual grains blends together in the eye, reconstructing the colour of the light photographed through the filter grains'.[75] The effects, in both *Chrome* and *Deletion*, are both compelling and unsettling, producing an overwhelming sense of dissolution.

In *Elli* (2016), this takes the form of a series of static images looking out to the sea, an outwardly indifferent portrait of a place, but one imbued with history and violence. The specific location in Tinos, where Urlus was undertaking a residency, relates to the fate of the Greek cruiser Elli, which was hit by an Italian torpedo on 15 August 1940 during an annual Catholic pilgrimage. The ship caught fire and sank, killing several people and signalling the start of Greece's involvement in World War II. As with *Konrad & Kurfurst*, Urlus uses the material reactions of photochemical interventions, and their physiological effects in the viewing process, to allude to historical reverberations:

> I'm using [the] flicker effect to evoke an oppressive feeling, the opposite of the exhibited calmness of the sea. I interfered in the 24-images per second experience [of motion picture film] as strong sequential changes in the frames-per-second series can cause physical reactions and the beholder will sense seeing colours and shapes.[76]

The initial moments hover between serenity and anxiety as the deep blue colour applied to the image of ripping water frequently soaks out the division between sea and sky, figure and ground, the eye struggling to make out the details. The clear horizon returns again, only to be violently interrupted by the sudden fleeting image of a ship—the imagined ghost of Elli that conflates past and present.[77] Something appears to be moving in the water, and as the eye strains a second time to make out the human form, a flickering force takes over the screen, alternating different colours and disrupting any attempt at figurative identification. From between the throbbing frames we make out images of the ship and traces of people standing and swimming in the water. Urlus's technique is similar to that of Paul Sharits, who used the rapid alternation of coloured frames and figurative images to stimulate altered consciousness through a stroboscopic effect. Like Sharits, Urlus is interested in how the retinal processing of visual information delivered too quickly to be parsed produces a residual afterimage, effectively leading spectators to experience colours that are not really there. What manifests *between* the images is as important as what exists within them. The texture of the film is tangibly present in the surface movement of the grain brought out by colour processes, as well as the visible traces and stains of chemical intervention. Enhanced by a soundtrack created from the optical noise of the film grain, the images in *Elli* are grounded in the sensuous materiality of perception (Fig. 3.12).

In Richard Tuohy's films, handmade colour inventions are developed alongside extensive optical and contact printing, moving the original image further and further from its basis in reality. Often made in collaboration with Diana Barrie, Tuohy's work is a tireless exploration of the outside world, a traveller's quest for new formal languages of each new encounter with a place. His earlier output displays a clear interest in natural environments, using film to draw out the formal qualities and material texture of trees in *Twisty* (2005), *Ironwood* (2009), *Tree Lines* (2009) and *Trees Breathing* (2009), to examine the visual details of plants and weeds in *Bristle* (2005), *Pear Shapes* (2006) and *Mallee Stretching* (2007) and

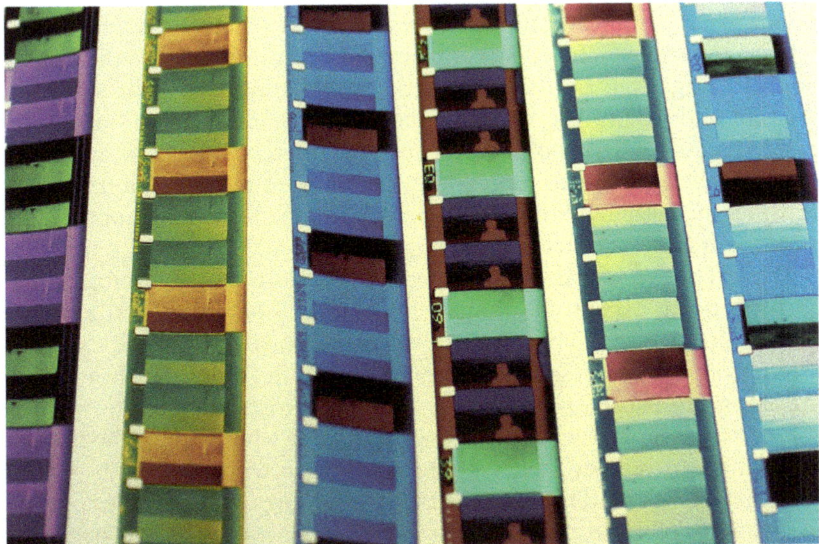

Fig. 3.12 Film strips from *Elli*, Esther Urlus, 2016 photographed on a light (Image courtesy of the artist)

to reimagine landscape in *Ripple* (2005), *Centre Spot* (2008) and *Landscape Rippled and Rifted* (2009). More recently, however, largely due to a shift in the rhythm of his own life, attention has tended to focus on the deconstruction of cityscapes, using repetition as a key device in eliciting both visual excitement and sensory overload. Central figures in the artisanal film 'movement', and widely recognised for facilitating the establishment and development of several artist-run film labs, Tuohy and Barrie seem to be in perpetual motion, reflected in the aesthetic of the films themselves.[78]

Seoul Electric (2012), as the title suggests, uses the thick, draping electrical wires that adorn the streets of Seoul as the starting point for an exploration of material processes. Extending the black and white sequences into a tapestry of temporal echoes and spatial multiplications with the use of an optical printer, Tuohy then transferred the footage to colour print stock using a contact printer, creating a new canvas on which to play out a further series of manipulations. During the hand-processing stage, the footage was solarised using bursts of coloured light from a torch, an intervention that creates an uneven halo-like glow across parts of the image. The effect is one in which the colours give the impression of being lifted out of the material, undulating across the surface of the film and licking the edges of the electric lines and contours of the buildings. As the layers of imagery drift in different directions and as the voice on the soundtrack repeats the same phrase over and over again, it becomes increasingly difficult to differentiate one form from another, one impression from another, with seeing gradually giving way to sensing.

What Tuohy's artistic practice teaches us more than anything is that, far from being exhausted, photochemical film is still only in the process of being discovered. There are still so many possibilities to be explored. The chromaflex processing technique, on which Tuohy has been working alongside Barrie, is evidence of this. The procedure effectively allows colour negative, colour positive and black and white to exist within the same image by masking off sections of the film with Vaseline or tape so that they resist the different processing chemistry. One is able to selectively apply colour to certain sections, creating a collage of photochemical interpretations of the same scene. Shot in Tokyo, *Ginza Strip* (2014) was the first film to be created in this way. Here, Tuohy uses the technique to literally slice open the representation of a place, creating ruptures and dislocations that resemble a cut-up collage, similar to Annabel Nicolson's *Slides* (1976) or the work of Frédérique Devaux in *Fils d'image* (1999), *Ellipses* (1999), *F(ilm)* (2001) and the *'K'* series (2001–2008), where fragments of film are reassembled through either optical or contact printing. Tuohy creates a kaleidoscopic depiction of the already visually dense cityscape, with the colourful neon lights creating a starting point for a vibrant reinterpretation that refuses traditional spatial cues (Fig. 3.13).

The screen is a bustling site of perpetual movement, a space of sensory stimulation and embodied encounter that continually shifts the eye back and forth between surface and depth. The chromaflex technique is combined with image compositing through contact printing, where two strips of film are brought together in the final print. As Tuohy explains in relation to specific sections of the film:

> I punched out a lot of triangles of masking tape using a triangle hole punch. These triangles were stuck roughly in the centre of the images on each frame on two strips of film. One strip was chromaflex developed such that the area outside the triangles would become completely black. The other was chromaflex developed such that where the triangle was would

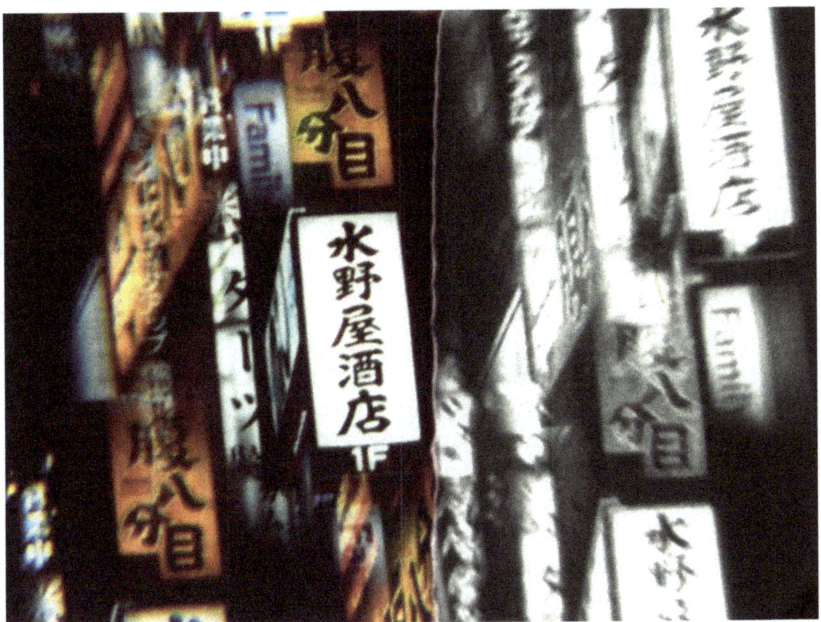

Fig. 3.13 The chromaflex technique in *Ginza Strip*, Richard Tuohy, 2014 (Image courtesy of the artist)

> itself become completely black, while everything outside the triangle would have image. Incorporate these two strips into the two master positive rolls for the film, then print each master roll onto the same print stock one after the other, and now on the print you have images inside and images outside the triangle shapes.[79]

In this way, the shapes quiver with their own internal energy, creating a form of surface tension that communicates the dynamic pace of the urban environment. Depicted in a washed-out negative image against the saturated colours of the city, the anonymous bodies that move en masse towards unknown destinations appear as somnambulists, detached and drifting as though not really there. Through extensive material manipulation in the printing and processing stages, Tuohy is able to produce layers, juxtapositions and movements both within and across frames that translate the frenetic activity and visual overstimulation of the city. Representation is thus both destabilised and reinvented, as the images are reworked over and over again, releasing the medium's chemical potential to elicit sensations as well as sights.

Tuohy is realistic about the possibilities and parameters of artisanal practice, emphasising the importance of darkroom experimentation as a way of creating alternative pathways and not reproducing industry-standard techniques. 'Basically, it's impossible to make colour film,' he admits. 'The idea of suggesting than an artist or group of artists can get together and make colour film that was remotely recognisable as colour film, let alone film that was comparable to Kodak, it could never happen'.[80] Likewise, the potential for homemade film emulsion becoming a viable alternative to commercially manufactured film stock is, at least for the moment, quite low, and it seems more realistic to predict that a home-brewed option will sit alongside more conventional stocks, 'perfected' to the extent that it can achieve a particular aesthetic. What is clear, however, is that explorations into chemistry are giving rise to a new photochemical film aesthetic that foregrounds process, highlights the physical gestures of handling and privileges the haptic as a site of visual resistance and reinvention. Home-brewed DIY methods stake out alternative pathways for film—they are playful, irreverent, imaginative and pioneering; but they are also grounded in a material awareness and ecological sensibility that extends beyond the images to address their frequently environmentally un-friendly coming into being.

Given the centrality of hand-processing (either in buckets or dedicated Lomo tanks) to practices of photochemical film—due largely to factors of creative freedom, autonomy and immediacy—it is not surprising that the last decade has seen a surge in the search for alternative forms of film processing to those that require the use of toxic chemicals.[81] For we cannot get away from the fact that, whilst film has been celebrated for its innate ability to explore and communicate with the natural world in radical new ways, it remains an industrial art form that, like analogue still photography, relies heavily on a whole range of substances that are harmful to the environment. Some artists, such as Vicky Smith, embrace a back-to-basics approach that removes the need for processing in the first place, using direct-on-film processes of mark-marking such as scratching, painting and drawing. For those invested in the chemical transformations that awaken a latent image from the celluloid emulsion, however, a number of options present themselves through the field of eco hand-processing. As Kathryn Ramey admits, '[f]ilm developing is never completely environmentally friendly, but you can minimise the risk to yourself and the environment' through recipes circulating online, during dedicated workshops or in books such as Ramey's own invaluable *Experimental Filmmaking: Break the Machine.*[82] It is, in fact, possible to replace traditional film developers with a combination of household substances such as coffee, wine or beer combined with vitamin C (the combination is called caffenol) and washing soda (sodium carbonate). The active ingredient in this solution is phenol, the acidic chemical required to oxidise (turn black) the silver particles in the celluloid that have been exposed to light. Since phenol is also found in varying strengths in many plants, flowers and herbs—from rhododendron to rosemary—the possibilities of ecologically—aware film processing become almost limitless.

Through the dedicated chemical explorations and educational initiatives of Dagie Brundert in Germany, Lisa Marr and Paolo Davanzo of the Echo Park Film Center in Los Angeles, and countless others, the field of eco-processing has progressed to the extent that it is now widely practiced and taught in workshops throughout the world. The flowers must first be selected and foraged, encouraging a form of wandering, close looking and touching that seems particularly in tune with the kind of tactile artisanal practices I have been discussing in this chapter. This is followed by a process of chopping, crushing and squeezing in order to release the chemicals, with the mixture then being soaked in boiling water and the remaining ingredients later added to the cooled solution and employed in much the same way as standard developer to produce a negative image. Eco-processing has become popular in recent years not simply because it provides an alternative to the use of traditional chemicals, but because it extends darkroom processes into a chain of material gestures and engagements that awaken a heightened sensitivity to natural surroundings. For those that choose the path of eco-processing, a whole new world of artisanal practice opens up, where chemistry and botany come together in a creative journey of discovery.

Many films are now created from entirely plant-based developers, often giving the image a distinctive tone that derives from natural dyes in particular species of flower. This is the case in Terra Long's *Horses in the Year of the Dog* (2018), processed in hibiscus and lavender, or Philip Hoffman's *vulture* (discussed in more detail in the following chapter), in which the artist developed, tinted and toned with some twenty different plants, flowers and trees that happened to be in blossom at the time of filming. Hoffman discovered that by harvesting walnuts and soaking them over the course of a year, a most effective toner could be fabricated that imbues the image with a silky brown colour. In addition to environmentally friendly developers and toners, explorations into alternatives to photographer fixer are also underway, with seawater offering some future potential.

A very recent example of how film processes are evolving through an intensified ecological awareness is the phytogram method, 'a technique that uses the internal chemistry of plants for the creation of images on photographic emulsion'.[83] Developed by the Dutch filmmaker Karel Doing, the process modifies the rayogram camera-less approach, where images are created by placing objects directly onto the filmstrip, leaving an imprint or trace of their presence. The process emerged, as Doing explains, through an interest in the generative possibilities of the film emulsion:

> I wanted to look at how notions of green and ecological awareness could be connected to media and filmmaking. I got this idea of growing things on film. A lot of experimental film that works with the emulsion is about destroying it in one way or another. I wanted to approach it from the idea of growing something and so I started to experiment with different organic materials. I did lots of experiments and there were some interesting images but no actual growth. I soaked a leaf in the caffenol solution and realised that since plants also contain phenol, I could use the leaf to both create an image and act as developer.[84]

Doing has emphasised the element of playful discovery that emerges through this process, connecting people to plants in new ways and providing a means for the natural world to 'speak' through the medium in much the same way as the buried and submerged films discussed earlier. Like Brakhage's *The Garden of Earthly Delights* (1981), in which plant matter is placed directly onto the celluloid in a technique that echoes the earlier *Mothlight*, the viewer is brought into an uncanny proximity to matter in order to see into and through it. In Brakhage's film, blades of grass, leaves, petals, seeds and other natural debris are carefully arranged between two strips of clear 35mm film, which are then optically printed to produce a single image. On projection, the light glides through these veiny forms, giving life to the fragile magnified membranes—a moment arrested before inevitable death and decay. The phytogram method involves a slightly different approach: whilst we are still presented with imprints and traces of the original plants, the images are more amorphous—a result of the liquid solution seeping outwards as it makes contact with the film. The flower or plant registers its physical presence on the material surface, whilst also using its own internal chemistry to render the image legible. No darkroom is required, only bright sunlight and the passing of time. Doing's film *The Mulch Spider's Dream* (2018) was created in this way, using plants and weeds on expired 16mm stock. Inspired by Thomas Nagel's 1974 essay 'What is it Like to Be a Bat?', the film explores the potential of material contact for opening up an experience of non-human consciousness through organic shapes and forms.[85]

In Francisca Duran's *It Matters What* (2019), the phytogram method is woven into a visually dense reflection on human–non-human relations, using Donna Haraway's *Staying with the Trouble* as a conceptual starting point. Produced at the Independent Imaging Retreat in 2018, where Doing was artist-in-residence, Duran's phytograms add experiential weight to a section of Haraway's text that is both spoken on the soundtrack and imprinted directly on to the film: 'It matters what thoughts think thoughts. It matters what knowledges know knowledges. It matters what relations relate relations. It matters what worlds world worlds. It matters what stories tell stories'.[86] Letters flutter by, interspersed with a shimmering black and white image of a corn spurry plant (Spergula arvensis) shot with a macro lens one frame at a time over a period of about an hour.[87] The technique seems to bestow on the plant an inner life that animates its delicate stems, buds and flowers, whilst the traces of hand-processing that register on the surface of the film merge with the natural forms and invite a tactile reading. This opening passage gives way to an archival image from the 1920s or 1930s of a woman proudly holding open the wings of an owl, the dead animal's head hanging lifeless below her smiling face. As an ambiguous emblem of human superiority and conquest, the image resonates with Haraway's text, which highlights the importance not only of actions but also of deeply embedded and normalised patterns of thinking and perceiving that structure human behaviour. Language, discourse, knowledge and power are tightly interwoven and must be deconstructed and reconstructed to release what Haraway terms 'response-ability'.

Duran's systematic analysis of this unidentified fragment of time allows us to dwell on the wider consequences and implications of what might otherwise be seen as a banal gesture. By zooming in and slowing down the footage with the use of an optical printer, latent meanings are brought to the surface—guilt, denial and the repression of a fundamental connection to other living beings. As we break through the veneer of the image, Duran takes us further into Haraway's text, again both spoken on the soundtrack and presented as fragments of contact printed text:

> What is it to surrender the capacity to think? These times called the Anthropocene are times of multispecies, including human, urgency: of great mass death and extinction; of onrushing disasters, whose unpredictable specificities are foolishly taken as unknowability itself; of refusing to know and cultivate the capacity of response-ability; of refusing to be present in and to onrushing catastrophe in time; of unprecedented looking away.[88]

Echoing the concept of ecological thinking that Timothy Morton believes is capable of negotiating and overcoming the invisible 'hyperobject' of climate change, Haraway issues an urgent wake-up call in the face of society's collective apathy. It is at this midway point that the film moves into an extended phytogram sequence, countering the act of looking away suggested in the text with an intensely intimate confrontation with plant matter. The screen becomes a forceful expression of non-human interiority, an insistent articulation of material presence that refuses representational distance in favour of sensory immersion. As a site of struggle between abstraction and figuration, the phytogram imagery pulls the eye in multiple directions, in a haptic rediscovery of the natural world. What is particularly striking about this technique—and what distinguishes it from the rayogram process—is the impression of seeing into soul of the plant, creating a trace that is both familiar and strange (Fig. 3.14).

Reworking the phytograms digitally, Duran harnesses the visual impact of the colourful formless stains. The 16mm images were scanned to high resolution 5k, which allowed the artist to zoom into and extend the range of the colours. Resisting medium-specificity and artistic purity, this flexibility of approach allows the striking effects of the artisanal method to be

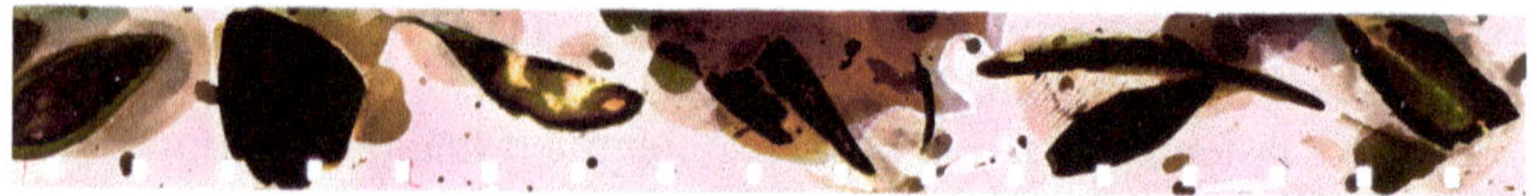

Fig. 3.14 A strip of phytogram imagery from *It Matters What*, Francisca Duran, 2019 Image courtesy of the artist

accentuated without compromising their textured and tactile quality. The digital translation of the analogue image draws out the ethereal quality of the indexical trace, rendering the colours more vibrant and creating a complex visual palette that invites a sustained reflection on process. It is in giving visual form to Haraway's polemical text that these chemical and material interventions take on a political resonance. They demonstrate ways in which response-ability as a mode of 'thinking-with' might be elicited through direct physical engagement and processes of working through material realities from new perspectives. These are small gestures, but they generate to a certain extent what Haraway refers to as 'a collective knowing and doing, an ecology of practices'.[89] What does it mean to apply these theoretical concepts to forms of art making? How can alternative modes of representation give rise to new forms of thinking and relating? It is perhaps in the embrace of processes that implicate the natural world on a very physical level that we can begin to unravel the sensitivities and sensibilities—the new modes of thinking, feeling and knowing—that characterise Haraway's imagining of a more ethical earthly cohabitation.

Materialist Action Films

Whilst many of the works discussed in this chapter play with the tension between abstraction and figuration, implicating the surface of the filmstrip in the process of (re)visioning the world, a number of artists have taken a different approach to the material specificities of photochemical film. In the work of British artists Bea Haut and Jenny Baines, performance comes to play a pivotal role in teasing out parallels between the material constraints of the Bolex camera and the limitations of the physical body. As I have already discussed, performativity is inscribed into materialist filmmaking, be it through repetitive mark-making, gestures of burying or submerging, or other forms of tactile intervention. Here, I would like to explore the relationship between the human body and filmic spaces and surfaces from the perspective of a self-conscious staging of process. Re-appropriating the term 'action film' and liberating it from its association with the male-dominated, excessively violent and adrenaline-fuelled context of mainstream cinema allows us to think about these female interventions in both public and private space as a form of materially engaged resistance to traditional representations. This brings our consideration of photochemical film practice into a more direct focus on the body as the site of political struggle. Although their films might not be considered political in an explicit sense, it is possible to detect an implicit oppositional force in their very unique form of what Baines describes as 'serious play'.[90]

Long-time friends and collaborators, Haut and Baines demonstrate shared thematic interests and a similar creative approach, but with ultimately quite distinct formal qualities.[91] Both artists work predominantly with the 28-second wind of a Bolex camera, filming from a fixed position and in continuous takes that allow actions to be unfolded in a predetermined space and time-frame. For Baines, these actions frequently take the form of absurd physical feats, such as swimming against a tide, climbing a lamppost, wrapping a rope around a tree, balancing on a tightrope or blowing a ping pong ball in the air. The seemingly pointless gestures are performed repeatedly, eliciting laughter not only from the audience, but often from the performer herself, cognisant of the ultimate futility of the action and, in the case of the lamppost in *Untitled (Victoria Park)* (2007), the obvious impossibility of its accomplishment. Hope and failure circle around each other as each new wind of the camera opens up a space of possibility, just like the video game that allows the turn to be replayed, over and over again.

Whilst the actions in Baines's films gesture towards specific goals, however pointless or unachievable, this is not always the case with Haut, whose industrious comings and goings lead only to a sense of confusion. In *I Saw, I See, I Look* (2013), for example, the filmmaker manoeuvres a large white cube through an empty room that contains only a wooden door propped against the wall in the background, entering the frame on the right and leaving it again on the left. Mimicking classical continuity editing, the action is repeated in exactly the same space, only with the door repositioned to give a false sense of distance travelled. Climbing onto the top of the cube with the help of a wooden step ladder, she then proceeds to saw the ladder apart in line with the edge of the cube. The baffling randomness of the gesture is heightened by the need to continually interrupt the action each time the camera stops, with each new iteration beginning with the filmmaker appearing from behind the camera and climbing back onto the cube to continue the task. Rather than provide context and meaning to this introductory sequence, the rest of the film serves only to heighten the puzzlement. The next section sees Haut opening out her studio doors to reveal an exterior location and then proceeding to walk foreground to background and right to left, in and out of the frame. She appears with a short step ladder, which she places in the middle of the frame, climbs, and then inexplicably empties a bucket of water onto the ground, before closing the doors of the studio. The film ends in what appears to be a woodland setting, with a path receding into the background. Haut runs along it and then carries a wooden door from the first section and places it in different parts of the frame. On the surface, *I Saw, I See, I Look* might seem to resist any attempt at interpretation, but behind its simple form and nonsensical nature lies an interest in the reconciliation of filmic space with its material foundation. In each section of the film, the represented space *within* the frame refers to the material space *of* the frame, as well as the temporal and spatial limitations of the shot (Fig. 3.15).

This becomes more explicit in Haut's *Abject Noise* (2014). Here, perspective is reduced to a tight framing with few identifiable coordinates, emphasised by the grainy high contrast black and white image that obscures vision and brings attention to the material surface. Hands

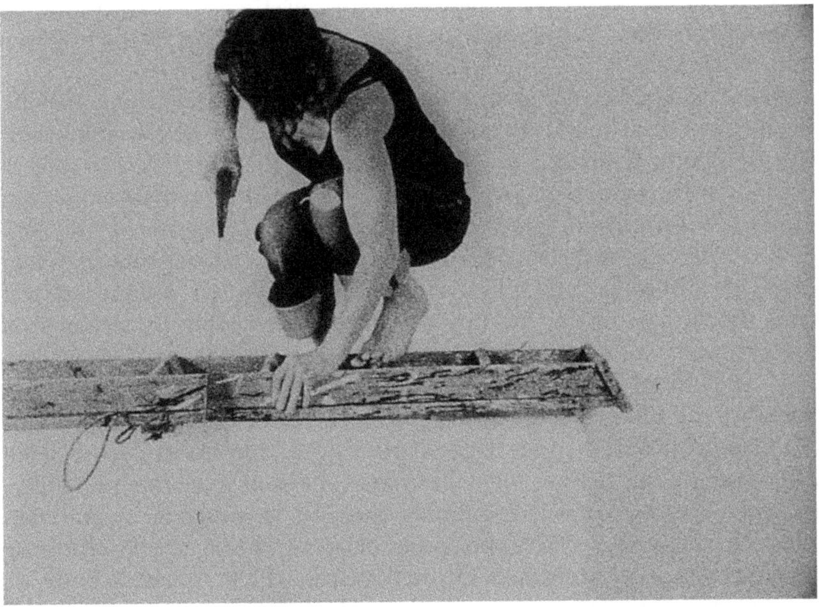

Fig. 3.15 Sawing a ladder whilst standing on a white cube in the middle of an empty room in *I Saw, I See, I Look*, Bea Haut, 2013 (Image courtesy of Light Cone)

are seen tearing pages from a scrapbook and discarding them into off-screen space to a corresponding buzz on the soundtrack. As the action is repeated with different textures and dimensions of paper, it becomes clear that the buzz refers to a direct manipulation of the optical soundtrack, as though the paper, as it passes across the threshold of on and off-screen space, were registering its physical presence on this part of the filmstrip (as the early direct animators discovered, the size and density of the object or mark on the optical area creates a different kind of sound). Juxtaposing the material contours of the film frame with the recorded image it holds produces a humorous discord that is both spatial and temporal, since whilst Haut conflates the outer limit of the screen space with the edge of the actual film, she also confuses the 'then' of the pro-filmic action with the 'now' of the material intervention. A similar relationship plays out in *Gravure* (2013), where Haut, again in a tight framing that removes spatial context, draws black lines on a papered wall with the aid of a ruler. As each line registers, a corresponding vertical black mark or white scratch appears on the film itself, inviting the viewer to shift attention between surface and depth, physical gesture and tactile intervention (Fig. 3.16).

These works enact a unique form of materialist filmmaking that ties engagement with the filmic substrate to an awareness of the filmmaker's onscreen body. Corporeal implication is central to handmade and cameraless film, with artists such as Vicky Smith (*sobbingspittingscratching*; *Noisy Licking Dribbling and Spitting*), Thorsten Fleisch (*Bloodlust*, 1998; *Skinflick*, 2002), Emma Hart (*Skin Film*, 2004) and Louise Bourque (*Jours en fleurs*, 2003) placing their own bodily fluids and residues directly onto the surface of the filmstrip in what Gregory Zinman describes as 'a very specific mode of auto-portraiture or autobiography'.[92] As we have seen, scratching, drawing and other forms of material contact also carry traces of the filmmaker's body in the form of compressed actions that can channel physical—and, it could be argued, emotional—states. Haut extends these associations by embracing at the same time the body's photographic representation, specifically through its onscreen negotiations with other objects, surfaces and spaces between. If Smith's *Primal* brings together the material surfaces of the film strip, the filmmaker's body and the wooden structures of her studio through abstract traces, Haut finds a corresponding language of contact that cleverly moves across different material registers.

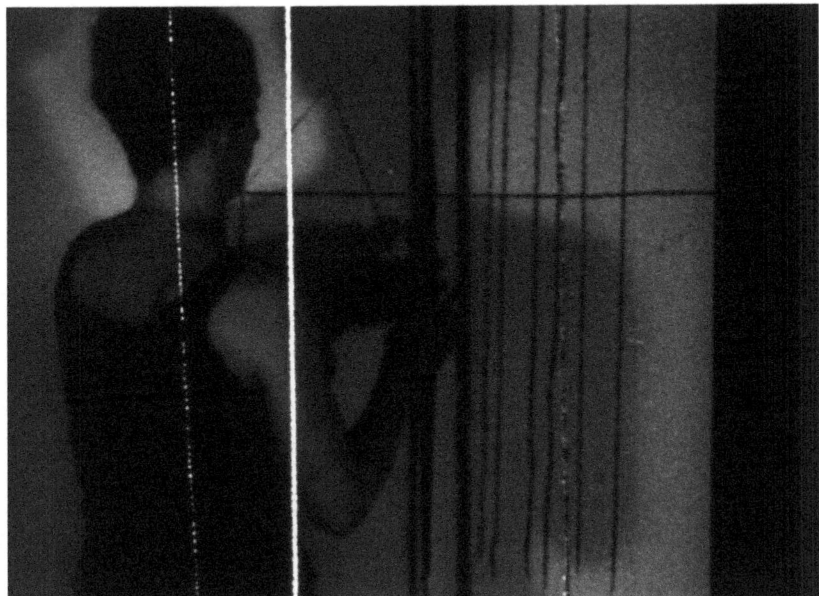

Fig. 3.16 *Gravure*, Bea Haut, 2013 (Image courtesy of Light Cone)

The two films *Bush* (2011) and *Defenestration* (2015) draw on the passage from interior and exterior as a way to explore the relationship between onscreen and offscreen space. Again, the viewer is faced with physical gestures that seem to suggest, but ultimately resist, logical narrative resolution. In the former, Haut chops down an overgrown bush outside her house and proceeds to push it indoors, whilst the latter sees her exiting (or escaping?) the same house from everywhere but the front door, repetitively climbing through the windows and skylight of different rooms. In *Defenestration*, these frames clearly function as a metaphor for the film frame (a frame within a frame), which Haut disappears out of and reappears into as though on a loop. Marks made directly onto the sound area with Letraset transfers serve to draw attention to the physicality of the material as the rhythmic buzz and the occasional trace of the dots in the image track draw attention to the edge of the frame. By mapping the physical contours of the house through its passageways to the outside world, the filmmaker also manages to traverse all four edges of the film frame, subverting the classical emphasis on the vertical extremities as entry and exit points. This is humorously accentuated when Haut, jumping downwards from the living room window onto the street outside, is then seen running in and out of the frame, left to right and right to left, with no evident motivation beyond a form of physical rebellion against spatial constraints. The gesture of escape is therefore also related to the representational confines of film itself, with its cultural tendency to fix and objectify, particularly women. There are echoes, here, of Maya Deren's treatment of domestic space in *Meshes of the Afternoon* (1943) as something physically and emotionally constraining, a feeling that is heightened by the fact that Haut always finds herself back indoors. But we might also look to the element of ritual and the choreography of everyday movements and gestures that characterises Deren's *Ritual in Transfigured Time* (1946).

Haut presents the spectator with a sense of material struggle that takes a number of forms; in *Defenestration*, each window passage is preceded by an increasingly protracted undoing of locks and mechanisms, turning escape into a mundane domestic ritual of repetitive actions. At the beginning of *Bush*, she climbs a metal ladder and disappears out of the upper limit of the frame, her chopping down of a bush represented only by the shuddering of the ladder and then a scattering of leaves. As the mass of foliage descends, the wind of the Bolex runs out and the next shot sees the filmmaker walking into the frame to continue the action, the bush suspended half-way down the ladder. In a similar way to *I Saw, I See, I Look*, Haut invites contemplation of the inherent absurdity of cinematic realism and the trickery of continuity editing by staging a one-woman show of both camera operator and performer. But the film has further significance in its representation of nature as something to be tamed and contained, domesticated and controlled. The battle of human and non-human forces plays out partly as a slapstick performance, as the unwieldy vegetation resists its indoor relocation and the filmmaker has to repeatedly restart the camera in between attempts to force it through the door. Behind the comical scenario lies a serious commentary on our relationship with the material world and the long-standing human desire to dominate.

The absurdity of the human condition is similarly staged through material encounters in Baines's work. Whilst Haut frequently focuses on interior locations to draw attention to the contours of the film frame, Baines carries out her actions in open spaces such as parks, often retaining a single static camera position. In *Untitled (Victoria Park)* the filmmaker repeatedly runs into the frame and tries, unsuccessfully, to climb a lamppost. Each failed attempt is punctuated by a brief flash of light on the surface of the film, marking the exhaustion of the camera wind, as well as, increasingly, the filmmaker/performer herself. As this very brief film progresses through each subsequent climb, the viewer comes to realise that the physical challenge is not simply the lamppost but also the material and temporal constraints of the Bolex camera, wound only enough to release roughly three to seven seconds of film. Sometimes the wind runs out mid-climb, sometimes mid-run, with the body appearing to magically disappear from the picture in a passing nod to the early film illusionist George Méliès.[93] Failure is thus pre-programmed into the actions, creating a dual effect of staging the material and mechanical foundations of photochemical film on the one hand and drawing attention to human/non-human interactions on the other. Although it is the camera mechanism that determines the futility of the gesture, the repetition inadvertently bestows on the lamppost a kind of magnetic agency, both attracting and repelling the strangely insistent human force. The fact that Baines frames the image to include a nearby tree adds weight to this significance, as well as comic juxtaposition through inversion (it is the tree and not the lamppost that one normally associates with climbing). It witnesses the absurdity of the scene with indifference (Fig. 3.17).

Visual composition comes to play a key role in Baines's series of double projections, where carefully choreographed movements from one adjacent screen to another again draw attention to the material confines of the film frame. *Untitled (insertional)* (2014), *Untitled (#1 25/25 x 10/4)* (2016) and *Untitled (slackline)* (2018) all use ropes of different sorts to create an illusory impression of spatial continuity. Actions that begin in one screen appear to cross the threshold into the other, carrying echoes of Deren's linking of disparate spaces in *Meshes of the Afternoon*, *At Land* (1944) and *A Study in Choreography for Camera* (1945). In those films, seemingly fluid and unbroken movements 'transcend geography' through the use of matches on action, illustrating film's inherent ability to manipulate space and time for poetic effect—what Deren refers to as the 'creative use of reality'.[94] In *A Study in Choreography for Camera,* Talley Beatty raises his foot in the forest in one shot and in the subsequent shot places it down in a domestic interior, whilst the famous sequence of *Meshes of the Afternoon* sees Deren traverse multiple spaces in only five steps. However, in a slightly different vein, Baines transcends not the imagined space

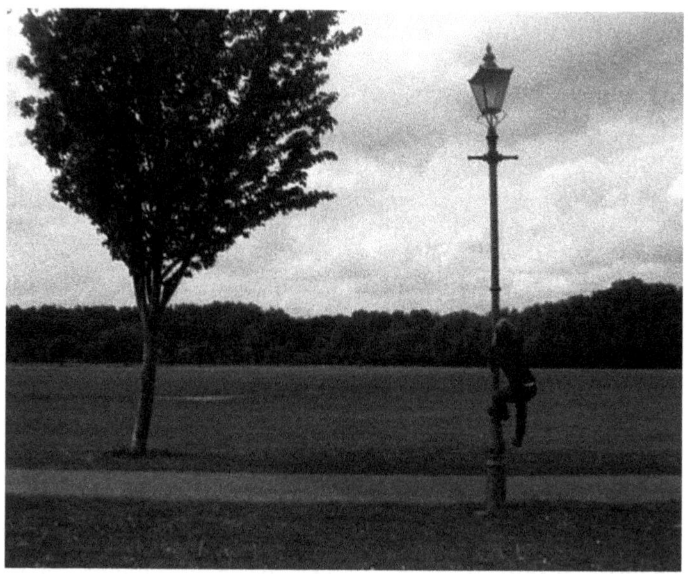

Fig. 3.17 Climbing a lamppost in *Untitled (Victoria Park)*, Jenny Baines, 2007 (Image courtesy of the artist)

within the shot but the material space of the frame. In each case, two 16mm Bolex cameras are placed side-by-side and angled in such a way that the same action is filmed simultaneously with a slight overlap. The tightrope of *Untitled (slackline)* stretches across the two images, with the filmmaker-performer appearing to step literally across the divide that separates them, transgressing representational boundaries and creating a dynamic tension between onscreen and offscreen space (Fig. 3.18).

Baines has described herself as a structural filmmaker, and her stripped-back approach, fixed camera position, emphasis on duration and extended use of repetition certainly resonate with key examples of this tradition (Michael Snow and Hollis Frampton in particular). Content is anchored to an emphasis on formal structure, with the actions only really making sense in relation to this meta-reflection on the spatial limits of the film frame. But these films, like those of Haut, are also imbued with a sensitivity to material textures, the grain of the film and the relationship between the filmmaker's body and the world through which it moves. Both artists use their own physical presence as a rebellious force, occupying space in

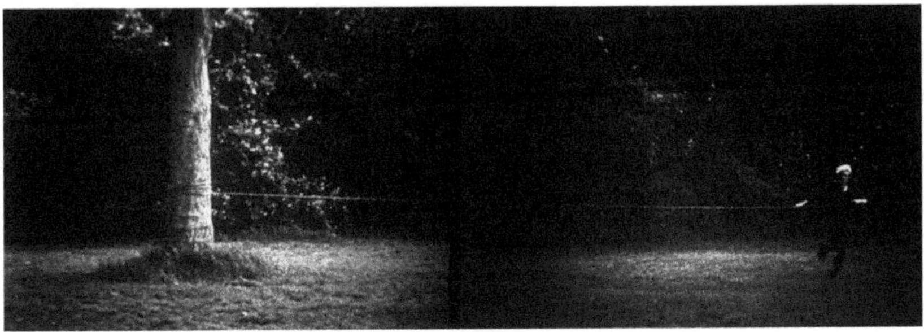

Fig. 3.18 Double screen actions in *Untitled (#1 25/25 x 10/4)*, Jenny Baines, 2016 (Image courtesy of the artist)

resistant ways and interacting with objects in a manner that questions normative relations. There are feminist undertones to this staging of the female body as producer of situations, intervening in social space and redefining its fundamentally gendered dynamic on different terms. As a signifier of predominantly male manual labour, the ladder that reappears in different forms across Haut's films is radically re-gendered as an object with fluid roles and diverse performative possibilities. It frequently fails to operate in a conventional way, leading nowhere or disappearing out of the frame, and several gestures explicitly release it from its own physical conformism—it is sawn apart (castrated?) in *I Saw, I See, I Look* and, in the live performance *Pending* (2016), held in the air in every possible alternative to its habitual vertical position. In this live piece, 100ft of film is unspooled into the audience, who hold it in the air in a 'living loop' before it is taken up and played out by the projector. The various hands through which it passes leave marks and traces of fingerprints, adding a further layer of physicality to the one presented in the image. Extending the feminist liberation of the ladder to the projection event, Haut effectively deconstructs and reconstructs multiple material relations, bringing into the viewing situation a level of physical empathy—arms raised, the audience gradually begins to experience the weight of the onscreen ladder.

Similarly, Baines finds in the material specificities of the Bolex camera a language of bodily endurance and perseverance. Running, swimming, climbing, jumping, blowing and balancing, the female body is, in these films, an active body, engaged in material negotiations with no narrative resolution. The duration of the action corresponds to the length of the camera wind, and the mistakes, failures, inconsistencies and anomalies become part of the film, which is always edited in-camera. The female body is therefore, like the film itself, also an imperfect body, susceptible to malfunction and never airbrushed or packaged to convince otherwise. Finally, the female body is an androgynous body. Often turning their backs to the camera, both filmmakers refuse the spectacular and objectifying frontal view of mainstream cinema. Walking into the frame from behind the camera draws attention to the dual role of filmmaker-filmed whilst de-emphasising the traditional facial perspective. The body, in this way, is reduced to the essence of the gesture, allowing other objects, surfaces and spaces to take on an expressive role. In *Untitled (Victoria Park)*, this leads to a kind of vibrant energy that resonates between the tree, the lamppost and the incessant human body that hurtles towards the inanimate but increasingly charged object.

Materialist film is thus reconceptualised in the work of these two contemporary filmmakers, and I have extended the term beyond a concentration on the celluloid surface in order to consider other forms of material awareness. Whilst Haut incorporates photographic representation and material intervention as a way to shift between pro-filmic space, screen space and frame space, Baines works within a more conceptual mode, not touching the material as such, but using the wind of the camera to establish physical limits. Certain characteristics of the photochemical material are central to their working practices. In Haut's case, the use of high contrast print stock flattens the space of the screen and brings attention to the surface texture, giving the image a raw and tangible quality. Baines also works with the performative nature of the film grain, but prefers a finer, more even palette in the construction of the image. As we have seen, the physicality of the film becomes a way of reflecting on different aspects of the material world. In *Drag* (2017), Haut ties an abandoned sofa to a van and surfs it around an industrial estate in London, directing both the camera operator (Baines) and the driver from her anti-domestic position. Lines scratched frame-by-frame into the sound area of the individual release prints create a unique sonic equivalent to the image of the sofa scraping (nosily, we imagine) along the city streets. She waves at an overtaking driver, laughing cheekily as she gestures full steam ahead. This comical and defiant act of collaborative civil disobedience in many ways characterises the work of both filmmakers, whose interest in peripheries, extremities and spaces between takes on a political charge. Momentarily rescuing this abandoned object from the rubbish tip and giving it a heady second life, they enact a form of creative recycling that reimagines place, highlights the power of objects to elicit new relationships and, importantly, stages a form of playful protest against a wasteful consumer society. As Adam Krause states:

> We see ourselves acting upon the world. There is subject and object. Action upon. Separation. We do things to things. But this view obscures the active role of the non-human. The world also acts. And the boundary between that active world is porous and fluid.[95]

In bringing together actions and materials, Haut and Baines engage in a powerful form of social critique that ties the possibilities of photochemical film to a much-needed reworking of material relationships (Fig. 3.19).

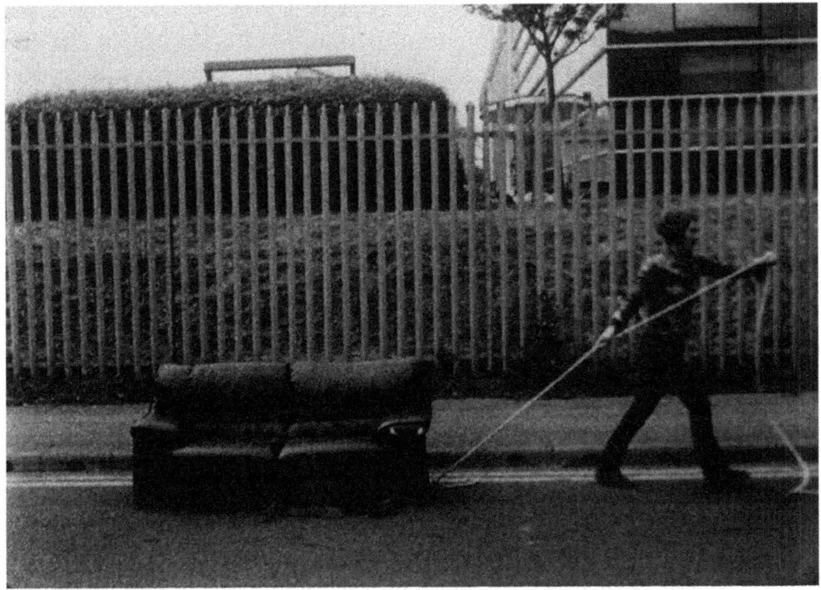

Fig. 3.19 Acts of civil disobedience in *Drag*, Bea Haut, 2017 (Image courtesy of Light Cone)

Despite the challenges of working with an ostensibly 'outdated' medium, the rise of digital technology has arguably given the artisanal film movement new momentum. As we will see in the following chapters, this is sustained to a large extent by a vibrant network of interconnected communities, where resource and skills sharing comes to replace the logic of the market. Although it would be misleading to present contemporary photochemical film practice of the past twenty years as resembling anything like a homogenous field, what I have attempted to unravel in this chapter are the various ways in which the staging of process comes to play a key role in the continuous reinvention of the medium. The gestures of material intervention that draw attention to the physical substrate both revive and reinvigorate techniques from the historical avant-garde, bringing the present into a dynamic dialogue with the past in the quest for new formal languages of political significance. Far from representing a Greenbergian modernist self-searching, the films discussed in this chapter both revel in the creative possibilities of film and pursue tactile modes of communication capable of negotiating and articulating the complex entanglements that make up our physical existence. The surface of the film substrate becomes a site of multiple material transformations that challenge perceptual stabilities and representational certainties, encouraging a heightened awareness of how matter comes to matter.

Notes

1. Chris Gehman, 'Toward Artisanal Cinema: A Filmmaker's Movement', in Scott MacKenzie and Janine Marchessault (eds.), *Process Cinema: Handmade Film in the Digital Age* (Montreal: McGill-Queens University, 2019), p. 178.
2. Ibid., p. 172.
3. See Tess Takahashi, 'After the Death of Film: Writing the Natural World in the Digital Age', *Visible Language*, Vo. 42, No. 1, 2008, and 'Meticulously, Recklessly Worked Up: Direct Animation, the Auratic and the Index, in Chris Gehman and Steve Reinke (eds.), *The Sharpest Point; Animation at End of Cinema* (Toronto: YYZ Books, 2005), pp. 166–178. I have also made similar arguments about the significance of artisanal practice in the digital era. See Kim Knowles, '(Re)visioning Celluloid: Aesthetics of Contact in Materialist Film', in Martine Beugnet, Allan Cameron, and Arild Fetveit (eds.), *Indefinite Visions: Cinema and the Attractions of Uncertainty* (Edinburgh: Edinburgh University Press, 2017), pp. 257–272, and 'Slow, Methodical, and Mulled Over: Analog Practice in the Age

of the Digital', *Cinema Journal*, Vol. 55, No. 2, Winter 2016, pp. 146–151.

4. Janis Crystal Lipzin, 'A Materialist Film Practice in the Digital Age', *Millennium Film Journal*, Vol. 56, Fall 2012, p. 50.
5. Pip Chodorov, 'The Artist-Run Film Labs', *Millennium Film Journal*, Vol. 60, Fall 2014, p. 36.
6. Paula Willoquet-Maricondi, 'Introduction: From Literary Criticism to Ecocriticism', in Willoquet-Maricondi (ed.), *Framing the World: Explorations in Ecocriticism and Film* (Charlottesville and London: University of Virginia Press, 2010), p. 2.
7. Lawrence Buell, 'The Ecocritical Insurgency', *New Literary History*, Vol. 30, Summer 1999, p. 699.
8. For an overview of cinema's uneasy relationship with the environment, see Nadia Bozak, *The Cinematic Footprint: Lights, Camera, Natural Resources* (New Brunswick: Rutgers University Press, 2012).
9. Pat Brereton, *Environmental Ethics and Film* (London and New York: Routledge, 2016), p. 2.
10. Paula Willoquet-Maricondi, 'Shifting Paradigms: From Environmentalist Films to Ecocinema', in Willoquet-Maricondi (ed.), *Framing the World: Explorations in Ecocriticism and Film*, p. 50.
11. Scott MacDonald, 'Toward an Eco-Cinema', *Interdisciplinary Studies in Literature and Environment*, Vol. 15, No. 2, Summer 2004, p. 108.
12. Paula Willoquet-Maricondi, 'Introduction: From Literary Criticism to Ecocriticism', in Willoquet-Maricondi (ed.), *Framing the World: Explorations in Ecocriticism and Film*, p. 7.
13. See, in this respect, Derek Bousé's discussion of how classical narrative conventions, such as close-ups and cross-cutting, are employed in wildlife films to fabricate tense interactions. Bousé, 'False Intimacy: Close-Ups and Viewer Involvement in Wildlife Films', *Visual Studies*, Vol. 18, No. 2, 2003, pp. 123–132.
14. Guinevere Narraway, 'Strange Seeing: Re-viewing Nature in the Films of Rose Lowder', in Anat Pick and Guinevere Narraway (eds.), *Screening Nature: Cinema Beyond the Human* (New York: Berghahn Books, 2013), p. 215.
15. Deke Dusinberre, 'On British Avant-Garde Landscape Films', *Undercut*, Vol. 7/8, 1983, p. 49.
16. Peter Wollen, 'Chris Welsby', in David Curtis (ed.), *A Directory of British Film and Video Artists* (Luton: The Arts Council of Wales, 1996), p. 199.
17. Tess Takahashi, 'After the Death of Film: Writing the Natural World in the Digital Age', *Visible Language* Vol. 42, No. 1, 2008, p. 48.
18. Gregory Zinman, 'Echoes of the Earth: Handmade Film Ecologies', in Scott MacKenzie and Janine Marchessault (eds.), *Process Cinema: Handmade Film in the Digital Age*, p. 110.

19. Ibid.
20. Jürgen Reble, 'Chemistry and the Alchemy of Colour', *Millennium Film Journal*, Vol. 30/31, Fall 1997: http://mfj-online.org/journalPages/MFJ30%2C31/JRebleChemistry.html (accessed 10 August 2019).
21. See also Jennifer Reeves's, *Landfill 16* (2011) and Louise Bourque's, *Self Portrait Post Mortem* (2002). In the former, Reeves recycled outtakes from a previous double-projection work *When It Was Blue* (2008) by burying them in the ground to create new layers of imagery from the enzymes in the soil. The unearthed results were then hand-painted and optically printed. Bourque's film involves a similar process—outtakes from the filmmaker's first three films containing images of her younger self were buried in the back garden of her family home. Both films work through issues of waste, time and decay.
22. Canyon Cinema catalogue entry: http://canyoncinema50.org/collection/films/QuarryMovie1537225104973.
23. Ibid.
24. See Martine Beugnet and Kim Knowles, 'The Aesthetics and Politics of Obsolescence: Handmade Film in the Digital Era', *Moving Image Review and Art Journal*, Vol. 2, No. 1, 2013, pp. 55–65; Kim Knowles, 'Slow, Methodical, and Mulled Over: Analog Practice in the Age of the Digital'; Kim Knowles, '(Re)visioning Celluloid: Aesthetics of Contact in Materialist Film'.
25. Beugnet and Knowles, 'The Aesthetics and Politics of Obsolescence: Handmade Film in the Digital Era', p. 60.
26. Artist's talk: 'Conversation Pieces: Alia Syed', Tate Britain, 21 May 2010.
27. Laura U. Marks, *The Skin of the Film: Intercultural Cinema, Embodiment, and the Senses* (Durham and London: Duke University Press, 2000), p. 1.
28. David Gatten's unique engagements with photochemical film have greatly inspired my research into this field and I have discussed *What the Water Said* in several previous articles. However, his work has been a central focus of several recent accounts of camera-less film by Takahashi and Zinman and I have therefore refrained from repeating these arguments here (see note 3 for references). See also, Kim Knowles, 'Fragments of Memory: Personal Dialogue with the Films of David Gatten', in Edgar Lissel, Gabriele Jutz, and Nina Jučik (eds.), *Reset the Apparatus! A Survey of the Photographic and the Filmic in Contemporary Art* (Vienna: De Gruyter, 2019), pp. 134–137.
29. https://lightcone.org/en/film-2853-underground.
30. Maurice Merleau-Ponty, *The Visible and the Invisible* (Evanston: Northwest University Press, 1968).
31. Ibid., p. 3.
32. Ibid., p. 133.

33. http://lightcone.org/en/film-5833-parties-visible-et-invisible-d-un-ensemble-sous-tension.
34. Personal interview with the artist, 12 September 2019.
35. See Günter Anders, *L'Obsolesence de l'homme: Sur l'âme à l'époque de la deuxième révolution industrielle* (Paris: NUISANCES, 2002).
36. Günter Anders, 'Commandments in the Atomic Age', in Claude Eatherly and Günter Anders (eds.), *Burning Conscience: The Case of the Hiroshima Pilot, Claude Eatherly* (New York: Monthly Review Press, 1957), p. 12.
37. Scott MacDonald, *The Garden in the Machine: A Field Guide to Independent Films About Place* (Berkeley: University of California Press, 2001), p. 3.
38. Federico Windhausen, 'Conducting Light: Remarks on Two Argentine Films, Sergio Subero's *Espectro* and Pablo Mazzolo's *Fotooxidación*', La Furia Umana, Vol. 36, 2019: http://www.lafuriaumana.it/index.php/69-archive/lfu-36/866-federico-windhausen-conducting-light-remarks-on-two-argentine-films-sergio-subero-s-espectro-and-pablo-mazzolo-s-fotooxidacion (accessed 14 September 2019).
39. Erin Brannigan, 'Micro-Choreographies: The Close-Up in Dancefilm', *International Journal of Performance Arts and Digital Media*, Vol. 5, Nos. 2–3, 2009, p. 123. See also Erin Brannigan, *Dancefilm: Choreography and the Moving Image* (New York: Oxford University Press, 2011).
40. Gilles Deleuze, *Cinema 1: The Movement Image* (Minneapolis: University of Minnesota Press, 1986), p. 87.
41. Béla Balázs, *Theory of the Film: Character and Growth of a New Art* (New York: Arno Press, 1972), p. 65.
42. Jean Epstein, 'Magnification and Other Writings', translated by Stuart Liebman, *October*, Vol. 3, 1977, p. 9.
43. For a fuller discussion of this film and other experimental works using bodily excretions, see Kim Knowles, 'Blood, Sweat and Tears: Bodily Inscriptions in Contemporary Experimental Film', *NECSUS: European Journal of Media Studies*, Vol. 2, No. 2, Autumn 2013, pp. 447–463.
44. Walter Benjamin, 'The Work of Art in the Age of Mechanical Reproduction', in *Illuminations*, translated by Harry Zohn (New York: Schocken Books, 2007), p. 236.
45. Charlotte Pryce in discussion with Elena Duque following the screening 'The Heart of the Matter' at the Rotterdam International Film Festival, 24 January 2019. Vicky Smith has related her practice to *arte povera* ('poor art'), an Italian art movement of the 1960s and '70s that drew on basic, everyday materials in a challenge to the commercialisation of art.
46. See earlier discussion of women in the London Filmmakers' Co-op in Chapter 2. Smith's early films include *Rash* (1997), *Fixation* (2002) and *Stacking* (2006).

47. Smith's studio at the time was based in the Portland Square residence of the artists' collective Bristol Experimental and Expanded Film (BEEF), referred to in Chapter 5. The location is important given its transient nature at the time: the building is located in the St Pauls area of Bristol, an inner suburb that, at the time of writing, is in the grip of gentrification. The run-down former office suite, which was rented out to BEEF on a temporary basis, and which for that short time hosted screenings, installations, workshops and talks, was eventually bought by a property developer and turned into a luxury apartment block. Smith's material gestures can be read as a form of preservation—a document of site that for a fleeting moment was a space of radical artistic creation and collaboration.
48. In one of his last interviews, Brakhage described his minimalist working method and the relationship between the material of the film and his own body: 'I spit upon this and loosen the emulsion and that gives me just enough so I can get in there with the fingernails and usually, with my eyes closed feeling, feeling what I'm shaping. Knowing very well that it's nicely delineated, the individual frames. Knowing the frame very clearly, I can get in there, and I can work from my meat out, to what this is. So in one sense you could say, "This is the spit of the poet!" The spit of the filmmaker, as I won't fancy myself a poet, nope. And it's made from the nails themselves, feeling, pressing, making an impress of whatever feelings there are to them in space and shape and so on. So maybe a little film is being born, maybe not, who knows. But I'm trying, I'm trying. [*laughs*] I'm trying from this sickbed to sing a song.' https://brooklynrail.org/2008/03/express/stan-brakhage-with-pip-chodorov (accessed 12 August 2019).
49. Personal interview with the artist, 7 August 2019.
50. Len Lye, quoted in Roger Horrocks, *Len Lye: A Biography* (Aukland: Aukland University Press, 2001), p. 40.
51. Marina Estela Graça, 'Handmade Films: Questioning and Integrating Cinematic Technology', *International Journal of the Humanities*, Vol. 3, No. 3, 2005/2006, p. 103.
52. Ibid., p. 104.
53. Sean Cubitt, 'Ecocritique and the Materialities of Animation', in Suzanne Buchan (ed.), *Pervasive Animation* (New York: Routledge, 2013), pp. 105–106.
54. Hans Richter, 'The Badly Trained Sensibility', in P. Adams Sitney (ed.), *The Avant-Garde Film: A Reader of Theory and Criticism* (New York: Anthology Film Archives, 1978), p. 22.
55. These sounds are slightly reminiscent of Chris Marker's *La Jetée* (1962), where the whispered commands and observations of the team of scientists are only barely audible but they succeed in communicating a strange atmosphere of urgency.

56. *Noisy Licking Dribbing and Spitting* continues the themes of the earlier film, concentrating exclusively on dribbling coloured saliva directly onto the film. Smith had wanted to use the natural dye of berries that she would chew and spit out but found that the colours were not deep enough to register on the film. Food colouring was used as an alternative.
57. *Not (a) Part* emerged out of an interdisciplinary research project funded by The Brigstow Institute at the University of Bristol. Geographer Merle Pratchett (University of Bristol), literary scholar Rachel Murray (Loughborough University and Smith collaborated over the course of a year to bring together apiculture, modernist language and filmic practice in an examination of how animated film might engage with the issue of environmental decline and its impact on flying insect populations. See Vicky Smith, 'Not (a) Part: Handmade Animation, Materialism and the Photogram Film', *The International Journal of Creative Media Research*, Issue 2, September 2019: https://www.creativemediaresearch.org/post/not-a-part-handmade-animation-materialism-and-the-photogram-film (accessed 11 March 2020).
58. Brakhage described *Mothlight* as 'What a moth might see from birth to death if black were white and white were black.'
59. Personal interview with the artist, 29 July 2019.
60. Virginia Woolf, *The Death of the Moth, and Other Essays* (London: Harcourt Publishers, 1974), p. 4.
61. The importance of phenomenology to understanding Woolf's writings has also attracted a considerable amount of scholarship. See Ariane Mildenberg, 'Virginia Woolf's Interworld: Folds, Waves, Gazes', in *Modernism and Phenomenology: Literature, Philosophy, Art* (London: Palgrave Macmillan, 2017); Suzette A. Henke, 'Virginia Woolf's *The Waves*: A Phenomenological Reading', *Neophilologus*, Vol. 73, No. 3, 1989.
62. Kelly Elizabeth Sultzbach, 'The Phenomenological Whole: Virginia Woolf', in *Ecocriticism in the Modernist Imagination: Forster, Woolf, and Auden* (Cambridge: Cambridge University Press, 2016), p. 81.
63. Opal Whiteley, *The Singing Creek Where the Willows Grow: The Mystical Nature Diary of Opal Whiteley* (New York: Penguin Books, 1994), p. 7. As Benjamin Hoff explains in his extensive biographical preface, the publication received an enthusiastic response and became an immediate bestseller. However, it soon fell into disgrace, with accusations that the diary was not, as the author claimed, the result of a child's innocent yet perceptive observations about nature, but an adult-written hoax. Hoff's detailed examination of the original text within the context of Whiteley's biographical history leads him to conclude that the diary is indeed an authentic account.
64. Personal interview with the artist, 29 July 2019.

65. Ibid. The 7285 Ektachrome colour reversal film stock, on which Pryce shot a previous film *Curious Light* (2011), was discontinued by Kodak in 2012 due to 'lower sales and limited customer usage, combined with highly complex product formulation and manufacturing processes.' https://www.super8.nl/file/Kodak-discontinue-E100d.pdf (accessed 21 August 2019). Long favoured by experimental filmmakers due to its fine grain, sharp detail and saturated colours and, the discontinuation of Ektachrome dealt a harsh blow to the photochemical film community. However, Kodak have recently announced the reintroduction of Super 8 Ektachrome, with 16mm possibly to follow.
66. Charlotte Pryce in discussion with Elena Duque following the screening The Heart of the Matter at the Rotterdam International Film Festival, 24 January 2019.
67. Esther Urlus, *Re:inventing the Pioneers: Film Experiments on Handmade Silver Gelatin Emulsion and Color Methods* (Rotterdam: Self Published, 2013), p. 2.
68. Daïchi Saïto, *Moving the Sleeping images of Things Towards the Light* (Montréal: Les éditions Le Laps, 2013), pp. 58–59.
69. Scott MacKenzie and Janine Marchessault, 'Introduction: Process Cinema: Handmade Film in the Digital Age', in MacKenzie and Marchessault (eds.), *Process Cinema: Handmade Film in the Digital Age*, p. 3.
70. Esther Urlus, *Re:inventing the Pioneers*, p. 2
71. Robert Schaller, 'Thoughts on Handmade Film Emulsion Versus Commercial Filmstock', Handmade Film Institute, 10 March 2012: https://www.handmadefilm.org/writings/emulsionThoughts.html (accessed 10 September 2019).
72. For full details of the project, see: http://www.re-mi.eu/.
73. Personal interview with the artist, 3 June 2019.
74. *Chrome* was one of the ten films commissioned for the *Vertical Cinema* project that premiered at the Kontraste *Dark As Light* Festival in October 2013 and went on to feature at the International Film Festival Rotterdam in 2014.
75. Mirna Belina (ed.), *Vertical Cinema* (Amsterdam: Sonic Acts Press, 2013), p. 42.
76. Esther Urlus, *Elli* online film description on Vimeo: https://vimeo.com/159693531 (accessed 1 October 2019).
77. Urlus's residency in Tinos coincided with the annual commemoration event on the island, where a battleship sails to the port. She describes the unease she felt at seeing the menacing form of the ship against the stillness and serenity of the sea, a feeling that initiated the making of the film. Interview with the artist, 3 October 2019.

78. As well as running the Nanolab Super 8 film processing centre in Daylesforld, the pair are also actively involved in Melbourne's Artist Film Workshop, a collectively run space for the production and exhibition of 16mm experimental film. The have assisted a number of labs with setting up or modifying processing and printing machines, such as Lab Laba Laba in Indonesia, Crater Lab in Spain, Baltic Analog Lab in Latvia, and are regularly invited to run film workshops around the world.
79. Richard Tuohy, email correspondence, 5 October 2019.
80. Richard Tuohy, quoted in Lauren Bliss, 'Second Nature: On the Experimental Work of Richard Tuohy', *Senses of Cinema*, Vol. 78, 2016: http://sensesofcinema.com/2016/feature-articles/richard-tuohy/#fnref-26262-1 (accessed 20 September 2019).
81. The processing tank is an indispensable tool for many contemporary photochemical film practitioners since, once the spiral is loaded with the exposed film in the dark, the processing can effectively be done without the need for a darkroom. Designed for small-scale processing, a number of tanks were manufactured in the Soviet Union (Lomo) and the USA (Morse). The tanks differ in size, but they generally hold up to either 50ft or 100ft of film and some can be used for Super 8, 8mm, 16mm and 35mm.
82. Kathryn Ramey, *Experimental Filmmaking: Break the Machine* (London and New York: Routledge, 2016), p. 197. Paolo Davanzo and Lisa Marr of the Echo Park Film Center in Los Angeles have been particularly instrumental in the sharing of eco-processing skills through workshops across the world.
83. Karel Doing Phytogram blog: https://phytogram.blog/ (accessed 26 June 2019).
84. Personal interview with the artist, 26 July 2019.
85. Thomas Nagel, 'What Is It Like to Be a Bat', *The Philosophical Review*, Vol. 83, No. 4, 1974, pp. 435–450.
86. Donna Haraway, 'Tentacular Thinking: Anthropocene, Capitalocene, Chtulucene', in *Staying with the Trouble: Making Kin in the Chthulucene* (Durham and London: Duke University Press, 2016), p. 35.
87. 'The time increments were irregular. I might shoot a couple of frames or four or seven or one, then have a conversation with someone, then shoot a few more. In addition, for some of the exposures, I kept the shutter open longer, also for variable amounts of time. That and the variation in daylight during the time I shot in created a pulsating white light'. Email correspondence with the artist, 11 October 2019.
88. Haraaway, 'Tentacular Thinking: Anthropocene, Capitalocene, Chtulucene', p. 35.
89. Ibid.
90. Personal interview with Jenny Baines, 20 August 2019.

91. Haut and Baines shared a studio in London between 2014 and 2016 and have worked as camera operators on each other's films since 2014.
92. Gregory Zinman, *Making Images Move*, p. 108.
93. According to Méliès, the stop trick effect was discovered when his film accidentally jammed in the camera causing the shot to abruptly end and objects and persons appearing to vanish. In this way, 'a Madeleine-Bastille bus changed into a hearse and women changed into men.' Georges Sadoul, *Georges Méliès* (Paris: Seghers, 1970), pp. 106–107.
94. Maya Deren, 'Cinematography: The Creative Use of Reality', in P. Adams Sitney (ed.), *The Avant-Garde Film: A Reader of Theory and Criticism* (New York: Anthology Film Archives, 1978), pp. 60–73.
95. Adam Krause, 'Toward an Economy of Repair', in Eirik Eiglad (ed.), *Social Ecology and Social Change* (Porsgrunn: New Compass Press, 2015), p. 83.

CHAPTER 4

From Film Labs to Film Farm: Alternative Communities and Eco-Sensibilities

A marginal practice existing outside the well-oiled machine of the mainstream film industry, experimental cinema has always to some extent been facilitated and communicated through the existence of alternative infrastructures and communities. From cine clubs and film societies to independent distribution centres and co-operatives, not forgetting the important contribution of specialist film criticism, the history of oppositional and resistant forms of filmmaking could not be told outside of the broader film culture in which it circulates.[1] In the case of photochemical film, this relates specifically to various DIY practices, which includes, but is certainly not limited to, the worldwide network of artist-run film labs. As this scene grows in size and importance, a corresponding scholarly discourse is developing around it, with several studies now devoted to documenting, mapping and assessing its wider relevance in the context of technological transition, media archaeology and community-based forms of resistance.[2]

It is beyond the scope of this chapter to provide a historical overview of the artist-run labs and DIY practices, which are less of a unified movement than a disparate assortment of localised activities and informally connected international communities. Whilst it is perhaps possible in some respects to speak of a 'photochemical film scene', it would be misleading to suggest that this is in any way stable or coherent. It would also be difficult to present any account as exhaustive or historically accurate, given the necessarily subjective nature of any form of historical mapping. For these reasons, this chapter assesses several key characteristics and pivotal moments

K. Knowles, *Experimental Film and Photochemical Practices*, Experimental Film and Artists' Moving Image,
https://doi.org/10.1007/978-3-030-44309-2_4

before moving onto a case study approach that folds subjective experience into a broader theoretical reflection on alternative communities and practices.

DIY Film Culture

As digital technology has superseded celluloid film as the industry standard for moving image production, professional film labs throughout the world have been forced to close their doors. Film manufacturers—Kodak, Fuji, Agfa, Ferrania—have similarly either ceased to operate or have adapted their commercial operations to more profitable endeavours. Although Kodak continues to produce motion picture film stock, it now supplies a limited range of products to a dwindling market, the future of which seems dependent on business decisions that often have little to do with creative integrity. Paradoxically, however, the dismantling of the commercial photochemical industry has facilitated the establishment of independent labs run by artists with a passionate investment in keeping film alive. These production centres acquire specialist film equipment such as optical printers, contact printers, black and white and colour developing machines, flatbed editing tables, animation stands, scanners, cameras and projectors. Over the past few decades, film schools, archives, cinemas and art centres have also discarded their analogue machines, often on the grounds that there is not enough room for both film *and* digital technology. These once-valuable objects are willingly saved from the scrap heap and given a (re)new(ed) status through a culture of recuperation, recycling and repurposing that, in a capitalist economy 'utterly dependent on disposability', takes on a distinctive critical edge.[3] Marcy Saude perfectly captures this alternative economy of use:

> The objects and machines that form node points around which the artist labs are organized [...] have moved from the realm of commercial production into a de-commodified state where they are collectively owned and put to use making films that themselves are objects that stubbornly resist the logic of the market.[4]

The artist-run film labs are modelled to a large extent on the London Filmmakers' Co-op, where artistic control over the means of production had intense political relevance in an intellectual climate permeated by Marxist ideology. Access to printing and developing processes that had traditionally been controlled by professional technicians opened up a new way of working and experimenting with films that included a range of tactile interventions. Machines were interrogated, repurposed and intentionally mis-used, and 'mistakes' that were shunned by the commercial labs now became part of the alternative language of experimental film. Within this context, artists embraced artisanal approaches to filmmaking that both highlighted the physicality of the material and exposed the illusionistic workings of the apparatus. But equally central to the Co-op was its collaborative ethos and sense of shared ownership, not to mention the enabling effects of technological demystification, particularly for women.

There are important parallels between the case of the LFMC and the current climate of artist-run film labs in terms of their non-hierarchical organisational structure, creative inventiveness and opposition to industrial conventions, but the contemporary situation is characterised by a spirit of resistance to market-driven technological obsolescence and a desire to stake out alternatives to the all-encompassing digital norm. This is not to suggest that photochemical film culture rejects the digital outright, since there are many innovative examples of digital technology being used to repurpose analogue equipment.[5] The lab movement is certainly not an anti-digital movement and it would be a mistake to present it solely in these terms. It is, rather, an opposition to the standard narratives of technological replacement that, as I have argued in previous chapters, is driven by largely financial rather than artistic interests. Whilst the LFMC sought to bring film technology into the hands of artists, the contemporary labs strive for both creative autonomy *and* creative diversity, where photochemical film continues to remain a choice for artists whose practice is anchored in the kinds of physical engagement that the medium allows.[6]

At the time of writing, there are roughly fifty independent film labs, operating, in most cases, on a model of collectivity and a desire to share knowledge, skills and innovative new practice. Differing in size and structure, they are united in their grassroots embrace of alternative ways of working and collaborating, often alongside other forms of political engagement and ecological awareness.[7] As Pip Chodorov states, 'We are not in an economy but an ecology, a grassroots network, filmmakers helping each other, outside the capitalist system'.[8] The labs range from large-scale state-funded institutions with several paid employees, such as the Liaison of Independent Filmmakers of Toronto (LIFT)—which runs residency and educational programmes, rents out equipment, sells film stock and houses both analogue and digital post-production studios—to much smaller and far more precarious operations, such as the Baltic Analogue Lab in Riga or AgX in Boston. In these more modest set-ups, artists tend to work on a voluntary basis, with income generated from membership fees, workshops, screening events and occasional arts grants. With a large majority of the labs situated in cities, stability is a rare luxury, and several have been forced to relocate at least once during their existence as a result of rising rent or sudden eviction—Crater Lab, Barcelona; LaborBerlin; L'Abominable, Paris (Fig. 4.1).

The London context, in particular, has its own history of precarity and instability. According to Patti Gaal Holmes, 'the LFMC's survival was plagued by lack of finances, having an itinerant existence in various sites across north London', and although it consolidated its activities in the Gloucester Road site for some 20 years, it relocated in a merger with London Electronic Arts (LEA) in 1997, before eventually closing in 2001.[9] Some of the original equipment from the LFMC formed the

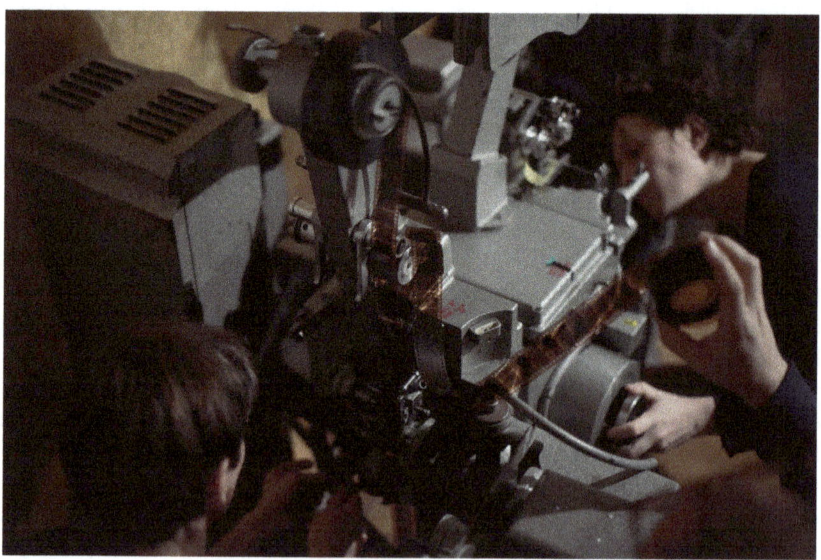

Fig. 4.1 First workshop on the newly built Debrie Contact Printer by Sophie Watzlawick at LaborBerlin. Participants learn how to blow 35mm down to 16mm (Photo: Laurence Favre. Image courtesy of LaborBerlin)

basis of no.w.here, established in 2004 by Karen Mirza and Brad Butler, with James Holcombe overseeing the day-to-day management of the photochemical resources and running its various activities. Based in Bethnal Green in East London, the lab was a vibrant site of experimental film production, providing technical support and access to film equipment, hosting workshops, critical discussions, screenings, performances and residencies, as well as selling film stock and offering services such as film developing and digital scanning. Between 2013 and 2016 it also published *Sequence*, a journal dedicated to artists' film practice.[10] With the expanding gentrification of the city and the prospect of a lucrative sale for the landlord, the organisation was threatened with eviction in 2015, which it fought with the help of a public campaign but ultimately lost, closing its doors in 2018. The cessation of activities at no.w.here led to the formation of a new co-operative called Not/nowhere and then—following Holcombe's relocation to Frome in Somerset—a garage conversion lab called erehwon.

In the 2010 issue of *Sequence*, Maxa Zoller employed the term 'radicant' to describe the structure and activities of no.w.here and I extend it here to encompass the film lab and DIY scene more generally.[11] Coined by Nicolas Bourriaud in 2009, the radicant is the contemporary answer to modernist radicalism, where the search for artistic and subjective essences is replaced with a responsive fluidity. The radicant is a product of precarity, of wandering bodies and shifting identities, of the need to adapt to changing times and circumstances by building networks and non-hierarchical structures, finding sustainable alternatives to normative patterns and transgressing boundaries and borders. Radicant is the botanical term for a plant whose roots extend outwards for the purpose of climbing, creeping or crawling in different directions, and, thus, for Bourriaud:

> [t]o be radicant means setting one's roots in motion, staging them in heterogeneous contexts and formats, denying them the power to completely define one's identity, translating ideas, transcoding images, transplanting behaviours, exchanging rather than imposing.[12]

The botanical origin is appropriate for a field so invested in exploring new ways of representing and engaging with the natural world, but this notion of the radicant also places DIY film practice within a broader anti-capitalist sensibility that includes the slow food movement, secondhand culture, and more recently, the Commons movement.[13] These networks function on the basis of both contribution and exchange, making use of what is available and finding creative solutions to what isn't. Similar to Charles Leadbeater's 'frugal innovator', 'they put down roots, draw in and create the resources to sustain themselves as they grow'.[14]

Whilst many of the labs are concentrated in Europe, particularly in France, Germany and the UK, the network stretches to the USA, Canada, Colombia, Uruguay, Mexico, Australia, Indonesia and South Korea.[15] A rudimentary historical lineage takes us from the LFMC to Karel Doing in the Netherlands who, keen to explore the medium of Super 8 film during a period when art schools were moving to video, was able to establish a lab with equipment that was no longer used by the Arnhem Academy of Art, as well as a printing lab that was closing. 'We thought a lot about DIY as a kind of parallel economy, a parallel society', remembers Doing. As soon as Studio Één was established it rapidly gained international attention.[16] While printing labs closed down, DIY labs became a viable alternative, triggering a domino effect that led to the opening of MTK lab in Grenoble in 1992, followed by L'Abominable in Paris in 1996, no.w.here in London in 2004 and a flurry of other labs in cities across Europe.[17] Studio Één moved to Rotterdam in 1995 and was instrumental in the setting up of what is now one of the most important labs in the world—Filmwerkplaats (Fig. 4.2).

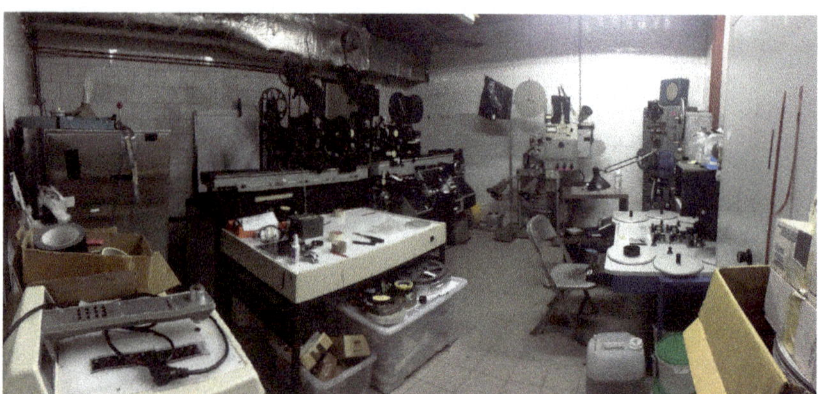

Fig. 4.2 The workspace at Filmwerkplaats, Rotterdam (Photo: Esther Urlus)

The lab circuit is only one part of a bourgeoning DIY film culture, where skillsharing takes a variety of forms and circulates through multiple channels. Rather than adhere to industry specifications, experimental film has a long history of innovative and playful rule-breaking, where doing things 'wrong' opens up a whole new field of creative possibility. As we have seen, Filmwerkplaats founder Esther Urlus belongs to a network of artists interested in returning to primitive techniques in order to map out alternative trajectories, particularly in the field of homemade emulsion production. The self-published booklet *Re:inventing the Pioneers: film experiments on handmade silver gelatin emulsion and color methods* is part of a growing number of recipes and instructions appearing in both print and online, which includes Steven Woloshen's *Recipes for Reconstruction: The Cookbook for the Frugal Filmmaker* and *Scratch, Crackle and Pop*, as well as Kathryn Ramey's recent *Experimental Filmmaking: Break the Machine*.[18] One of the first of these to appear was Helen Hill's fanzine *Recipes for Disaster: A Handcrafted Film Cookbooklet*, a compilation of typed and hand-written notes, recipes, handouts and drawings put together with the intention of sharing and facilitating further experimentation.[19] These publications are crucial not only in the sharing of information but also in establishing alternative channels of film education outside the mainstream. It is this educational impulse, as well as the importance of community building that sits at the heart of photochemical film culture.

Film Farm—The Independent Imaging Retreat

Established in 1994 by Canadian filmmakers Philip Hoffman and Marian McMahon, the Independent Imaging Retreat in Mount Forest, Ontario is one of the most enduring examples of a community-based celebration of handmade film processes. Not a film lab as such, and operating differently to the examples discussed above, it provides the opportunity for small groups of artists and filmmakers to spend a week immersed in craft-based 16mm film production in the Canadian countryside, two hours outside of Toronto. Participants with differing art practices and varying levels of expertise in photochemical film come together for what might be described as an intensive residency, where workshops on basic Bolex camera operation, hand-processing, tinting and toning, underwater filming and editing quickly give way to a concentration on individual practice. Although few participants complete a film in this short period of time, the works in progress are screened on the final day of the workshop, with many continuing to work on the footage in the months and years that follow. To date, the retreat has hosted some 300 participants and over 100 films bear the Film Farm stamp.

The history of Hoffman's utopic endeavour coincides with the emergence of the independent lab scene in the 1990s and overlaps in many ways with the contemporary development of these creative hubs as important sites of artisanal film practice. Hoffman and McMahon purchased the former farm and associated 50 acres of land in 1992 and, with the help of students Rob Butterworth and Tracy German, began running film workshops out of the barn two years later. Hoffman was then a teacher at Sheridan College but had spent a period of time in Finland, where he had developed a more personal approach to teaching. 'It seemed easier to set up an alternative teaching space away from home with these pragmatic and inventive Fins!' he remembers. 'So when I returned I had the idea of making a school of image-making, using similar methods we were developing in Finland'.[20] One of the defining features of the retreat has been the facilitating of a space of production for women within a more diverse and inclusive environment. 'Instead of the urban, male dominated and technology heavy atmosphere' of traditional film schools, this new space emphasised accessibility through artisanal modes of practice similar to those being developed in labs such as Studio Één and Atelier MTK.[21]

The key factor here is the embrace of DIY hand-processing technique, incorporating a greater level of artistic autonomy and control over the image than the traditional reliance on commercial film labs.[22] Removing technological barriers and employing basic means, participants are able to move freely and quickly between shooting, processing and projecting, opening up a more liberated form of practice and a new language of immediacy. Cara Morton, a participant in the Farm's early days in 1994, captures the essence of this artistic freedom in a short article published shortly after her visit. In one section she states:

> At the workshop it becomes clear to me that I had been missing that sense of wonder about film – that sense of playing an important role in a magical process. Thank's [sic] to Phil's workshop I got that feeling back. How? Hand Processing! It's better than polaroids! You can control the process in the development! You can develop your film as negative or reversal you can solarize (a personal fave), you can under develop over develop – anything you want – in minutes. Imagine – you wander around

> the countryside shooting to your heart's (and wallet's) content and then run back to the barn where the darkroom is set up and process your film. It's hard to describe the feeling you get when you hang your film out to dry. It's a mixture of wonder, accomplishment and connection to the medium.[23]

Foregrounding both artistic and personal discovery as interconnected and equally vital, the workshop stands in opposition to the purely skills-based emphasis of many filmmaking courses. As Scott MacKenzie highlights, Film Farm privileges 'a labor-intensive artisanal form of filmmaking that is also a conscious rejection of the model of industrial-based filmmaking that now dominates North American universities'.[24] We might extend this observation to a large number of universities across the world, given the increasing 'marketisation agenda and neoliberal policymaking in higher education', particularly in countries such as the United Kingdom.[25] Rosi Braidotti, in particular, raises concerns about an academic context where '"excellence" is indexed on money, markets' demands and consumers' satisfaction'.[26] However, she also expresses hope about the 'possibility of new spaces' opening up as the 'rationalist tradition' of Humanities research—based on white, male, Eurocentric models of truth and objective reality—is thrown into question. Although the small-scale rural setting of Film Farm seems a universe away from Braidotti's 'globalised, technologically mediated "multi-versity"', the environmentally conscious modes of being and radical forms of material thinking that the retreat elicits loop back into the more traditional university contexts in myriad ways.[27]

Underpinning the Film Farm approach is the pedagogy of what Hoffman describes as 'process cinema'—drawing attention away from the final product and emphasising a more mindful practice of observation, reflection, being in the moment and responding instinctively to one's surroundings. The work emerges through an organic relationship between different material elements that make up each individual experience of the workshop—the body and mind of the participant, the landscape, the physical properties of the camera, celluloid and chemistry, as well as the unique social setting. Traditionally distributed to participants on arrival, the 'manifesto' outlines the philosophy of the workshop:

> Enter through the big barn doors, without sketches, scripts, props, actors, or cell phones. Your films will surface through the relationship between

> your camera and what passes in front. It may take the whole of the workshop for you to shake away the habit of planning, what has become the guiding light of the profit-driven film world. Without the blanket of preconception, the processes of collect, reflect, revise mirror the underpinnings of your formation.
>
> Dive deep to encounter those strange fish who stare without seeing.[28] Mental processes effect the physical when the mind is open to what appears in front of you. These images you make will be charged with your inner architecture. Don't be surprised if a person, animal, place or thing shows you a way to go. These pathways can be provocative, treacherous joyful. They are places you have to go to, one way or another, so you might as well start your trip.[29]

Spontaneity, chance, freedom and discovery are guiding factors, replacing technical mastery and artistic perfection. Key to this philosophy is the rejection of standard ways of thinking about images in terms of 'success' or 'failure'; once these are revealed to be arbitrary criteria, the creative process opens up to more instinctive modes of inquiry, where both the imagination and the material possibilities of the medium are given free reign. What would, in the conventional sense, be considered the 'wrong' aperture setting, for example, might in a different context draw out the latent qualities of an object or create a dream-like atmosphere. Under-exposure and over-exposure, aberrations produced in the camera or mistakes created in the darkroom can be harnessed for specific artistic effects. Let us not forget that some of the most famous photographic techniques were discovered by accident and then intentionally reproduced for their unique visual qualities.[30] In fact, the history of experimental cinema could be told as history of 'failure' and 'imperfection' being embraced as a journey of visual discovery, with many filmmakers wilfully doing things the 'wrong' way to explore alternative ways of seeing the world.[31] Sometimes, as in *Kokoro is For Heart* (Hoffman, 1999), it is the (ghost in the) machine that makes this decision for the filmmaker, introducing a glitch into the material that can either be rejected as a mistake or accepted as part of the process. As Hoffman describes in relation to this particular film: 'When I got the footage back from the lab I was disappointed because of the periodic flipping of the image. After screening the footage several times I realized that the malfunctioning camera rendered the filmed nature unnatural … and this poses questions: what is nature? What is natural?'[32]

This questioning of representational clarity is central to materialist film aesthetics, particularly when the surface of the celluloid is brought into relief. Participants at the Independent Imaging Retreat are invited to explore the specificities of photochemical film through extensive handling of the material, changing the shape of the images with each gesture. Hand-processing not only gives the filmmaker control over a key stage of the production process traditionally dealt with by commercial lab, it also introduces an element of chance that to a large extent determines the visual palette. To control and at the same time be out of control—this is the beauty of handmade cinema, yielding results that would be almost impossible to reproduce, so connected are they to specific material conditions. Additionally, as soon as one plunges into the vast sea of tinting and toning—the former acting as a dye across the lighter parts of the image, with the latter adding colour to the emulsion—a whole new world of serendipity opens up. Used primarily in the early cinematic period as a way of adding colour to black and white film stock by hand, these older techniques have been revived as a way to reintroduce craft-based experimentation, in much the same way as the DIY emulsion production of Kevin Rice, Esther Urlus and Robert Schaller.[33]

A factor that is perhaps underplayed in some accounts of the workshop is the extent to which it has developed as a collective endeavour, shaped by the many people that have contributed to the team over the years. Often referred to as 'Phil's Film Farm', the key to its success is the combined energy of several people working largely voluntarily in a non-hierarchical structure.[34] The list of contributors has shifted over the years, with the involvement of Rob Butterworth, Chris Harrison and Deirdre Logue spanning over two decades. Scott Miller Berry took part in the retreat in 2003 and 2004 and joined the workshop team in 2010, and Terra Long was a participant in 2013 and also came on board as staff in 2015.[35] The educational philosophy is similar to the many projects mentioned above, which tend to operate on passion, goodwill and a desire to share skills, knowledge, laughter and experiences, often with little financial recompense. Whilst Hoffman's quietly brilliant creative spirit and endlessly generous personality holds things together in the background, it is the sense of shared and equal responsibility that allows the retreat to function in the way it does. Interconnectedness is the very essence of the workshop, with the films emerging from a context of communal living and thinking. Participants are invited to reflect on their surroundings through the materiality of process, but this is greatly facilitated by a pedagogical infrastructure based on care and collectivity.

From this perspective, given the importance of lived experience and the centrality of a particular space, Film Farm presents a challenge to the academic researcher. It resists commentary from the outside, unless it is to provide historical facts, details and prosaic accounts of when, what and why. Accessing the spirit of process cinema—the 'how'—requires active participation and physical immersion. It demands that one plunge in with a spirit of discovery in order to 'encounter those strange fish' and to bring thoughtful and embodied reflections to theoretical articulations. Film Farm offers an antidote to institutionalised modes of instruction and, by extension, questions the adequacy of a writing style that eradicates the self. Only an autoethnographic account—one that embraces the personal and translates lived experience—can therefore do justice to what has always been a celebration of self-discovery in proximity to nature (Fig. 4.3).

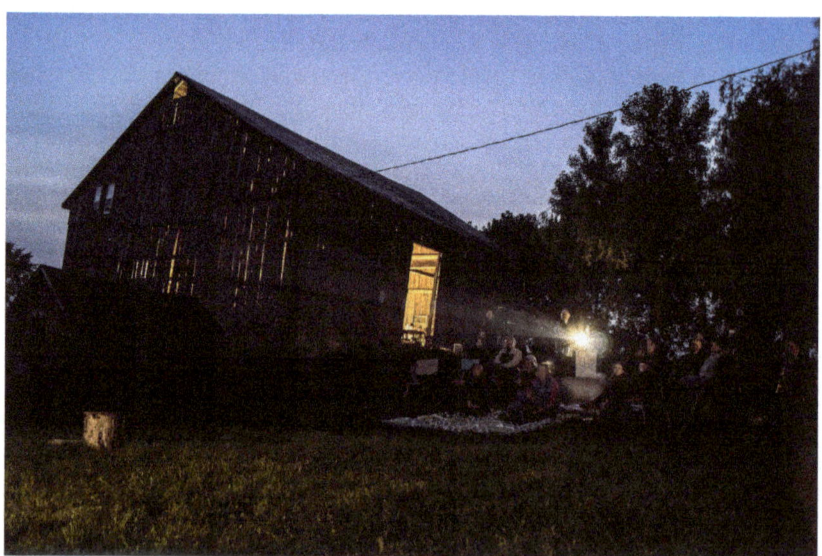

Fig. 4.3 Barn screening at the Independent Imaging Retreat (Photo: Marcel Beltran. Image courtesy of Philip Hoffman)

A Personal Journey to Mount Forest

Having met Hoffman at the (S8) festival in A Coruña in May 2018,[36] a series of exchanges and collaborations unfolded and ultimately led to me taking part in the 25th edition of Film Farm in July 2019.[37] During this time, I moved from my habitual position of academic researcher and objective commentator to the relatively uncertain role of participant-observer, actively involved in the filmmaking processes that have fascinated me for so long. This was to be my first real experience of photochemical filmmaking, following several years of writing on the topic and watching thousands of works as both an academic and curator. In some ways, taking part in the retreat felt like the natural progression of a building passion for the medium of film and a growing personal investment in its material properties. I packed a notebook, a recently acquired Bolex, several books and enough clothes for a countryside retreat with changeable weather and set off on my journey. The Bolex attracted some fascinated stares at the airport. 'That's old school!' said the man at security, turning it over carefully with his gloved hands. 'Depends how you frame it', I replied. 'What a beautiful object!' offered a fellow traveller. 'Thanks', I beamed proudly, not knowing if that was the appropriate response. I did feel quite protective of my precious hand luggage—it felt both fragile and tenacious, standing proudly but awkwardly amongst a sea of iPads, laptops and mobile phones.

Hoffman had hired a school bus to transport a handful of the participants from the city centre to Mount Forest. As we sipped our takeaway coffees in the morning sun, full of expectation and excitement, the trip facilitator attempted to explain Hoffman's hand-written directions to the confused driver. No postcode, no GPS—this was the first step in the analogue adventure that would involve several anxious roadside stops. The wind whipped through the windows making conversation difficult, and so, still suffering from jetlag, I settled into my seat with Bruno Latour's *Down to Earth: Politics in the New Climactic Regime*, a book I'd been revisiting all year. I noted one paragraph in particular, in which Latour suggests '*two directions* of politics':

> one that defines social questions in a restrictive manner, and other that defines the stakes of survival without introducing a priori differences between humans and non-humans. The choice to be made is between

> a narrow definition of the social ties making up a society, and a wider definition of associations that make up what have been called collectives.[38]

I wondered about the extent to which it is possible to unravel this kind of theoretical discourse about the world in practical quotidian contexts. Does Film Farm, with its rural setting and proximity to nature, provide the conditions for exploring the interconnected threads of our worldly existence, where a collective politics means that 'we don't have to choose between workers' wages and the fate of some little birds, but between two types of worlds in which there are *both* workers' salaries and little birds, but associated differently in the two contexts?'[39] We were about to close ourselves off from one kind of world, where the contentious politics of Trump and Brexit (still too fresh in my mind) were raging, in order to immerse our bodies and minds in a kind of physically engaged art-making that might be considered by some as escapist, frivolous even. I grappled with these thoughts throughout the journey, trying to make sense of the relationship between art and politics, and reflecting on how an attentiveness to this interconnection of micro and macro politics might be elicited through my own practice. What kind of film would I make and how might my experience inflect the arguments I've been developing about the relationship between materialist (or handmade) film, the ethics of vision and eco-awareness?

Occasionally I glanced into the driver's rearview mirror, subtly scanning my co-travellers for signs of what the week ahead would hold. Some were exchanging polite words, but most were gazing dreamily out of the window, on their own secret inner journey. As the bustling city streets gradually gave way to open fields, I sensed a physical easing—a collective bodily sigh that brought us together as we moved closer and closer to the 'Farm'. We tumbled out of the bus, greeted by Hoffman's partner Janine Marchessault and their canine companion Astrid, followed by the rest of the crew and the other six participants. We were an eclectic bunch, with an age range of 25–60, originating from Britain, Finland, Austria, Iran, Canada and the USA. We all carried the look of eager anticipation, fresh from the city and ready for our countryside 'film camp', as Helen Hill liked to refer to it.[40]

Walking into the barn, I am overcome by the sight of so many objects, signs, relics, souvenirs and leftovers from the past twenty-five years that carry the aura of previous workshops. I can almost sense the trace of the many participants who have moved through these spaces. The place is perfectly equipped and impeccably thought-through but also reassuringly chaotic, as any handmade film retreat with such a long history should be. 'Hey Stranger, Look Danger!' says a hand-written sign on the stairs leading down to the barn's darkrooms. Outside the upper darkrooms sits an Eiki projector, apparently mid-autopsy. In the corner, below an opening in the barn that resembles the 4:3 aspect ratio of 16mm is a makeshift screening area with old cinema seats and beat-up sofas. Wandering around, I feel instantly at home.

Over the next few days, our world reduces to the contours of this barn and the surrounding fields, but I feel my mind expanding into new terrain. We are taught how to operate the Bolex camera, how to hand-process in negative and reversal with traditional chemistry, as well as eco-friendly formulas with local flowers and plants. We immerse ourselves in the colourful world of tinting and toning, the handmade and largely unpredictable processes that define such films as Jennifer Reeves' *We Are Going Home* (1998), Eve Heller's *Behind This Soft Eclipse* (2004) and Penny McCann's *Crashing Skies* (2002). We experiment with solarisation in the darkroom, each of us secretly hoping to get results as striking as Chris Chong's *Minus* (1999), an uncut stream of superimposed movements on a single roll of film that was apparently produced in one sleepless night at the barn.

Most of my efforts during the first few days are focused on working with the macro extension tubes that I'd acquired several years earlier. Adding a 40mm tube to a 25mm lens reduces my visual field substantially and, squatting awkwardly, I point the camera at a flower. Nothing. Or, rather, a colourful blur that gathers on the surface of the viewfinder and draws attention to the grainy glass between me and my subject. It makes me think that few theoretical accounts of haptic visuality address the stage of image creation, concentrating rather on how the body is implicated in the viewing process. I think back to the influential scholarship of Laura Marks and Vivian Sobchack. In an essay that has always resonated with me—'What My Fingers Knew: The Cinesthetic Subject, or Vision in the Flesh'—Sobchack describes her encounter with the opening moments of Jane Campion's *The Piano* (1993), where the world is seen through the fingers of the central character Ada:

> Despite my "almost blindness," the "unrecognizable blur," and resistance of the image to my eyes, my fingers knew what I was looking at – and this before the objective reverse shot that followed to put those fingers in their

> proper place (that is, to put them where they could be seen objectively rather than subjectively "looked through").[41]

These words rush back to me as I struggle to find that sweet spot, where the unrecognisable blur gives way to an image so sharp and close that it takes my breath away. I'm fascinated by the world of small things that opens up before me, but I'm equally compelled by that space between legibility and illegibility. The tiny gestures I have to make in order to shift from one visual plane to the other makes me intensely aware of my own body; my breathing becomes softer and shallower, my movements more delicate and considered. This kind of filming requires such an intimate encounter for an image to appear that the lens has to almost touch the object. I remember my good friend Vicky Smith describing this as 'grazing not gazing'—a form of representation, she argued, that does not objectify, but enters into a physical dialogue with the world in a more ethical form of 'being with'.[42] However, I can't help but feel that this lengthened vision machine, poking intrusively into a world that I am too big to see properly with my naked eye, represents some kind of anthropocentric phallus. My body suddenly feels awkward and I'm unsettled by my voyeurism.

On the second day, after torrential rainstorms, the sky clears and a brilliant light bestows poetry upon everything. I notice tiny raindrops on leaves shot through with the evening sunlight and I rush to find my camera again. The pleasurable intensity of rocking back and forth with the whirring machine, letting the drops move in and out of focus, restores my connection with the macro extension and I sense that this will sustain me for several more days at least. My body settles into the rhythmic movement and I feel like I am dancing with the world. We watch the sun go down as it spreads pink rays across the sky, some capturing it on iPhones, others on Super 8 cameras—we're here to work with film, but no technology is excluded, and anyway, in this sublime moment, no one really cares.

What strikes me about the hand-cranked Bolex camera is that, unlike digital cameras and smartphones, it is heavy, noisy and initially quite awkward to work with. Its mechanical knobs, levers and various adjustments take some getting used to and it demands a significant amount of bodily investment. As Joel Schlemowitz puts it:

> Working with 16mm film, one shoots not just with one's eyes but also with one's hands. The hands hold the camera, manipulate the controls, turn the rings on the lenses, and push the button to release the spring. Shooting film (especially with a camera like the Bolex), one can be physically aware of the momentum of the film through the camera, the release of the camera's spring tension, the machine subtly trembling in one's hands. The film camera's subtle shuddering energy can affect one, as if transferring the spring's energy to the act of filmmaking – what the experimental filmmaker Marie Menken referred to as 'the twitters of the machine.'[43]

Under the heat of the summer sun and the constant menace of various blood-sucking critters, the sublime gives way to a kind of material struggle. A tripod would make my life much easier, especially for the kind of close-up work I've committed myself to, but I resist it for most of the week. I want to feel this trembling of the camera in my hands, the frenzied activity of its mechanisms and the passing of film through the gate. I spend a lot of time crouched uncomfortably in long grasses, straining to fix a tiny creature that catches my eye. I'm so drawn into this miniature world that I often forget to wind the camera, meaning that many beautiful shots exist only in my head and I quickly learn that frustration and loss are an inevitable part of the process. As the week progresses, my movements become more fluid, my reactions sharper; I am attentive and responsive. The series of gestures that the Bolex requires become second nature and certain parts of my body begin to take the role of the tripod. I start to see everything as a potential cinematic image and the scurrying and fluttering of insects sparks my attention so much more than before.

But it is in the darkroom that the real magic happens. We use the 3378 high contrast black and white film stock manufactured by Kodak for sound recording. It is cheap and easily processed as either negative (develop-wash-fix) or reversal (develop-wash-bleach-expose to light-develop). With a low light sensitivity of 12 ASA it can be processed with a red darkroom light, allowing a kind of fuzzy half-vision. Plunged into the not-quite-darkness, my movements are once again modified. Every gesture is premeditated, and every object has a special role to play in the series of actions I am about to carry out. I'm apron-clad, goggled and gloved, my feet shuffling tentatively from one tub of chemicals to another; only my nose seems to operate freely, inhaling the damp and cool atmosphere—a welcome momentary respite from the heat outside. Nowhere has Bruno Latour's actor–network theory or Graham Harman's object-oriented ontology resonated so much for me than in the barn's basement darkrooms. As I slide my hands into the still warm and damp gloves, I feel the absent presence of my co-workers, sensing in some way a trace of their own excited anticipation as I dip the exposed frames into the chemicals that will reveal the very landscapes we're standing in. Nor has time ever felt so precious, represented by the darkroom clock in the corner that marks each faintly glowing second spatially and screams out when the minutes are up. Here, I discover a different kind of material connection—the very unique experience of hand-processing the images that I have captured just moments, hours or days before and being physically part of their coming into being.

We hand-process in buckets—there is no aspiration for perfect images. The unspooled film is gathered spaghetti-like, submerged by hand and agitated for several minutes. It splish-splashes around in the tub, the surfaces and edges of the celluloid crunching against each other. It's a distinct and unforgettable sound—a symphony of artisanal film production that will translate into physical traces of the process. Lifting the dripping bundle, holding it high to release the liquid, then plunging it once more into the wash feels like a baptism. The metaphors are endless, and there is certainly time to give imaginative life to them in this obscure space of waiting. In fact, my mind drifts in many directions, but I think mostly about the images that I hope will appear, squinting to make out frame-lines and the tiny contours of life arrested, soon to be reanimated. It's hard not to feel spiritual about the 'final bath' situated at the back of the barn. It's where we congregate, peering excitedly at our own and each other's images—'did you get good results?' Just beside us, pegged in suspended loops, several hundred feet of drying film flap gracefully in the wind. Over and over, on and on. I imagine us in time-lapse, running in and out of the barn like ants.

By the third day, I have been the target of countless hungry mosquitoes. I've been bitten by spiders and stung by a bee. I have bumps, rashes and allergies that make me painfully aware of my fleshy and vulnerable existence and I can't help feeling that the creatures are trying to tell me something about my voyeuristic tendencies. Our coexistence does not feel particularly harmonious to me at this point and getting close to nature loses its appeal. I spend the morning filming a tree in the distance, alternating between a 10mm and a 75mm lens and experimenting with single frame exposures and the variable shutter. I get some interesting results, but something is lacking. I resort back to the extension tubes, only this time I turn the camera on myself, pushing my hands, fingers, feet and toes into the lens. I think of Willard Maas' *Geography of the Body* (1943) as I film the hairs on my legs and the textures of my skin. The difference is, of course, that Maas captures the surfaces of other bodies, not his own, resulting in carefully choreographed movements that glide smoothly and consistently, tracing individual parts and forms that ultimately create a whole. There is beauty in those images and a sense of compositional balance, but I am not searching for beauty when I point the camera towards my own body. I'm trying to come to terms with the itching, throbbing, sweaty and bruised physical container that feels as cumbersome as the camera I'm operating. Considered alongside the microscopic world I've been fixing, it takes up too much space and I want to expose its ugliness. What can I learn about my own body through this process?

I haven't yet experimented with eco-processing so a couple of us decide to spend the rest of the day foraging for flowers and making up the mixture. We journey down to the pond at the hottest part of the day, gathering the most colourful specimens, pointing out interesting critters, laughing about events of the past few days and talking about higher education. I've been blissfully removed from the pressures of my everyday academic life and it occurs to me more than once that I am living an extremely privileged existence, floating around the farm filming bugs. I came here to research photochemical processes and communities, but I find more and more with each day that various strands of politics are aligning in the way that Latour describes. Do the things for which we strive as human beings actually lead to spiritual entrapment rather than emancipation? I understand more than ever that politics can *only* be approached from the perspective of material entanglements, and this heightened awareness of my own body is a key part of the process. Back at the barn, we chop the flowers and notice a tiny caterpillar poking its face out the bundle. The camera! It looks magnificent under the macro lens, straining its body upwards, and in the process of filming I spot a spider. I'm giddy with excitement and angle my lens straight at it. It turns and gazes right at me—a perfect shot! However, the materiality of the medium comes racing back at me as I realise that there is no film in the camera.

Failure continues when I find that the images of my body, eco-processed as negative, do not come out as expected. Everything is too dark, and I can barely make out the textures. On the other hand, the flower mixture—to which we added a generous amount of oregano—smells like a most delicious herbal tea and our chatting continues in the darkroom. Somehow, the process seems more important than the images themselves, and when we project our results, I find myself drawn to the scratches, marks and traces of material contact that play out on the surface. I'm told that a bleach bath or some heavy toning might tease out my latent images. Maybe I'll revisit them at some point, but there is something oddly compelling about the shadowy forms that never quite materialise in the traditional sense. I wonder if the act of filming my body was more important than seeing it—I don't actually care so much about the images themselves and there might as well have been no film in the camera. The process was an embodied one—a way for me to think through the relationship between my corporeal existence and the insects I was gradually forming bonds with, and this ultimately makes me more comfortable with the macro work.

I continue in this vein, thinking all the while about Paul Clipson's series of macro studies—*Moth and Moon* (2008), *Compound Eyes* (2011), *Odonata* (2011), *Diptera and Lepidoptera* (2011)—all inspirational works for me. Clipson was a San Francisco-based filmmaker who worked primarily in Super 8 but had embraced 16mm towards the end of his life. His tragic passing in February 2018, followed closely by that of another poet of the natural world, Robert Todd, in August 2018, was a great loss to the experimental film world. Both filmmakers accompany me in spirit on this, my first creative journey into film practice. But I find it hard to fix these critters in the same way as Clipson. They move quickly, pause, then just as I have got the lens in exactly the right position, go busily on their way again. 'Film at 48 frames per second', suggests Terra Long. 'Insects experience time differently, so you need to reflect that in your filming'. This makes sense, and I think for a while about the constructed nature of human time under capitalism, explored particularly in the writings of Mary Ann Doane, Jonathan Crary and Paul Virilio, as well as recent scholarship on slow living. Wendy Parkins and Geoffrey Craig, for instance, argue that 'slow living is a process whereby everyday life [...] is approached with care and attention as subjects attempt to negotiate the different temporalities that they daily experience'.[44] Through my desire to connect with other life on a much smaller scale than my own, I am drawn into a different temporality, which requires, paradoxically, running the camera at a faster speed. Going faster to perceive more attentively feels slightly ironic and, as a result, opens up for me a new dimension of slow living. My mind concentrates, my breathing slows, but the camera whirs noisily, sending the film hurtling through its mechanisms.

On the final afternoon we screen our works in progress to the other participants and workshop leaders. It is striking to see how, despite spending a week in exactly the same location, we have all created very different representations of the place, filtered through our own subjective experience and personal concerns. This is one of the great achievements of the workshop: although it is possible to detect a Film Farm aesthetic across the years, each work displays a unique creative voice. The films are poetic, performative, humorous, rigorous, playful and inventive. Rapid in-camera editing and single-frame exposures sit alongside long contemplative takes (facilitated by Phil's electric Bolex) and flowing underwater movements. My close-up critters send shocks through the room. 'Wow!' shouts the group, almost in unison, as a tiny body with twitching antennae fills the screen. 'Call National Geographic!' jokes Deirdre Logue with her characteristically dry wit. It hadn't been my intention to create the kinds of spectacular images of nature that one finds in glossy magazines and impeccably produced television programmes. These representations have always made me uncomfortable for their othering tendencies—the transformation of nature into something to be gazed at and consumed, not truly felt. But how could I really be sure that I was doing anything different? Perhaps because my images were anything but impeccable. They were shaky, jerky, uncertain and de-centred. The bodies of those little creatures, with all their different temporalities, are filtered through several other bodies that make their presence felt on the screen: my body, the body of the camera and the body of the film strip, marked and scratched. Multiple materialities overlap and intertwine. The traces of process are as fascinating to me as the images themselves, and they become an equal part of the visual field.

When I'd projected the results of one of my first processing sessions, I'd been surprised to see a line of sprockets glide across the screen. Having been immersed in contemporary handmade practices for so long as a viewer/commentator, I'm familiar with this sight—the self-reflexive staging of film's material properties. I've written about it from a distance, objectively commenting upon its aesthetic significance and wider ontological bearing on the tension between image and support. Now, however, confronted with my own images, this theoretical scaffolding falls away and I'm confused. I have a very distinctive bodily reaction to this sight that might approximate in some way Sobchack's corporeal response to the blurry fingers of Campion's Ada in *The Piano*. There is a flash of material recognition that shifts my perception from seeing to feeling, all the more visceral because I had not expected it. That is to say that I had not intentionally produced it, this brazen flicker of film, bursting onto the stage unannounced like a drunken actor breaking the fourth wall. It was an aberration of the process, an 'accident' of developing that had allowed a part of one strip to register on the surface of another. I think of Jane Bennett's *Vibrant Matter*, and her argument that inanimate objects have agency. This kind of hand-processing in buckets opens up to chance in a relinquishing of artistic control. I am only one part of an assemblage of things—chemicals, gloves, the film emulsion and the units of time—each of which is an 'actant', to quote Latour, in its own right. The fact that these theoretical formulations do not always sit harmoniously together matters little in a practical sense, because I am able to appreciate individual aspects of each position and approach them from an experiential rather than a purely intellectual standpoint.

None of this is entirely exclusive to film, however, as other art practices and creative processes clearly open themselves up to chance and contingency. What made this a unique experience were the layers of material connection that extended to the social infrastructure and the sense of community. Thrown together in this space, each participant was required to communicate, negotiate and collaborate in either direct or indirect ways. Some films were made collectively, creating bodily unions across the landscape, whilst others were the result of a very solitary process, a psychic working through of a particular issue or a concentrated focus on a specific detail or form. Regardless of the approach, we were held in this space by each other, and, importantly, by the workshop leaders who were always somewhere in the background, ready to offer help if needed but equally happy to stand back and let the work unfold. We shared meals, jokes, anxieties and hopes. We passed around insect repellent and sun cream, exchanged lenses, light metres and tripods, bartered for time on the viewing stations. Certain phrases echoed like mantras—'Is anyone using this splicer?' 'Is that darkroom free?' Gradually people begin to leave—heartfelt goodbyes, promises to stay in touch. I'm still there the following day. The place is empty, echoey. I find what I guess is about 50 feet of exposed but unprocessed film in my drawer and decide to end my experience with a last session in the only darkroom that hasn't been cleared out and cleaned up. I miss the buzz, the excited and industrious to-ings and fro-ings in and out of the barn, the sight of bodies transporting buckets of water back and forth. I process the film as reversal and to my surprise I see floating in the final bath the sharp contours of my toes and the clear lines of my skin.

Back in Toronto, I visit the exhibition at TIFF Bell Lightbox celebrating Film Farm's 25th anniversary. It's strange to see objects similar to those that I have been using just days ago presented in glass boxes and displayed on the walls. I recognise instantly the rectangular piece of wood with hand-written instructions for developing film as reversal. There is one in each darkroom and I have squinted at it so many times over the past week that it feels odd to see it now, slightly out of context in the full light of the gallery space. Just underneath this is a viewing station with rewind arms, a Moviscop machine and an invite to visitors to try it out for themselves. It's the exact set-up I struggled over on the last morning in the barn, anxiously putting together my final screening reel and trying to construct some sort of rhythm from a shot here, a sequence there. It's where I got frustrated at the stubborn film splicer that didn't cut properly (just how many films has it spliced?). I remember secretly admiring its refusal to conform, forcing me to resort to a splicer-scissor combination. The three of us danced around the film strip in some awkward choreography that made me aware of my movements and my negotiation with material surfaces, edges and in-betweens. All this comes back as I watch someone moving the film backwards and forwards on the viewer. He stays there for a while, as though transfixed by the physical connection with the images and the uncanny life-giving force of those simple mechanisms. It reminds me of pre-cinematic optical devices—the Zoetrope, the Praxinoscope, the Phenakistoscope—and the fascination that they would have elicited at the time. The circularity of technological development, I think, always comes back to a sense of visual, but also material, wonderment.

Similarly transfixed, but for different reasons, I sit for hours watching the projected loop of video diaries and works in progress, compiled out of years of home movie footage shot by participants and workshop staff. I'm fascinated by the sight of these ghosts from the pasts engaging in the same activities and having similar conversations in those very spaces that I occupied just days ago. Our feet have walked the same floorboards, our hands have struggled with the same splicers, perhaps our bodies have followed similar trajectories, thought the same thoughts, experienced the same anxieties, felt the same excitement to arrive and then reluctance to leave. 'There's something profound about a space that has ghosts that are continuously present', Terra Long tells me. Moments that are years apart come together in a dense multiple superimposition, and I wonder if the complex set of emotions I felt during my time at Film Farm were in some way the processing of feelings that were not entirely my own, a lingering residue of all the bodies and minds that have been part of its history.[45]

That evening, my last before I return to the UK, I introduce the second Film Farm screening. I have been invited by Janine Marchessault and Scott MacKenzie, editors of the *Process Cinema* book that will have its launch after this event.[46] Many people in the packed auditorium have been involved in the Independent Imaging Retreat in some way over the years, and as I get up to fold my experience into the theoretical and curatorial work I've been involved in, I realise that the room is already alive with memories and experiences. In the post-screening Q&A, Karyn Sandlos, who helped run the workshop from 1998 to 2008, talks passionately about being 'immersed in the intensity of the experience'. The wider significance of the workshop, she states, is 'being able to go somewhere and get a little closer to what's hard to feel or think about'. She speaks about loss, about how the Film Farm acts as a connecting point between the present and the people who have passed away—Marian McMahon, Cara Morton, Helen Hill. I've never met any of the people she mentions but I understand quite intensely the feelings she describes. During the workshop, Phil had screened Hill's *The Florestine Collection* (2010), posthumously completed by her partner Paul Gailiunas following her tragic death in 2007. It affected all of us in very profound ways. We'd also seen the delightfully irreverent *Your New Pig Is Down the Road* (1999), a film that Hill had made during her participation in the workshop that year. Displaying all the landmarks and hallmarks of a Film Farm film, Hill draws out a delicate relationship between material things. Stop-motion animation produces a flutter of bodies through the landscape, whilst superimpositions, tinting and toning and mark-making on the surface of the celluloid (often traces of hand-processing), create a thick, pulsating image that constantly shifts between legibility and blur. The new pig in question, which we see towards the end of the film, was indeed bought from a neighbouring farm down the road—a potbellied present to Paul, to whom the film is a sort of love letter. Hill's playful spirit is everywhere at Film Farm and her name comes up in relation to several anecdotes. In one of the video diaries we see her making cotton candy with a machine that she transported by car from Halifax. 'It's too damp', she says to Phil as she pours in the sugar to make him a batch. It has to be dry for it to catch, but she perseveres anyway and it's touching to watch, not just because of Hill's backstory, but because this memory fragment captures so poignantly the spirit of the place—the importance of the *spaces between* the creative work, those moments of communality, exchange, playfulness and being outside of prescribed normative social structures. This is not separate from the process of art making, but actually feeds into alternative representations through an embrace of otherness.

In fact, what resonated particularly in Sandlos's short speech during that Q&A was her celebration of perceptual renewal—a form of seeing that comes about through an instinctive sensitivity to the world. 'The experience of the Farm shaped my ways of seeing everything', she stated. '[L]ook around you, notice what's immediately around you, notice yourself noticing and just capture that. That's the starting point. And that filters out into everything'.[47] This perfectly encapsulates the spirit of process cinema, which refers both to a way of working and a way of being, and it's probably fair to say that most, if not all, of the films to emerge from Film Farm express this attitude, each in its unique way.

Crashing Skies and Falling Bodies: Twenty-Five Years of Film Farm Aesthetics

It gradually became apparent at the two TIFF screenings that it would be hard to find a body of work with such a consistent aesthetic across a twenty-five-year period. Not all the films produced in this context display the recognisable traces of hand-processing, tinting and toning, solarisation and other forms of material intervention, nor do they necessarily depict the flora and fauna that surround the barn. However, several dominant themes and techniques resonate across the years in different constellations, demonstrating distinctive approaches to body, identity, memory, landscape, and, importantly, the relationship between humans and nonhumans. Nowhere else could one find such a sustained concentration on a particular place and the psychic associations to which it gives rise. At the first TIFF screening, Scott MacKenzie referred to Film Farm as 'one of the world's smallest movie sets', placing emphasis on the enabling qualities of creative constraints and conjuring up a parallel universe to the star- and money-driven industry which, for many, is synonymous with the art form. The films that have emerged from the retreat over the years present a stark alternative to this world, reminding us that film exists also a craft, a deeply personal and physical form of expression that is capable of bringing together the internal and external world without conforming to traditional formulas and tropes. Here, the spectacular is replaced with the sensuous, and a different kind of wonderment accompanies the images, associated not with an objectifying gaze, but with a curiosity about the world and our place within it.

In *Markings 1-3* (2011), Eva Kolcze draws on handmade techniques to express a tactile sensibility that translates an intensely physical connection to the surrounding environment. Feet shifting tentatively over a barely perceptible terrain are superimposed onto images of the different natural surfaces found around the barn—grass, daisies, stones, water, foliage, flowers and the branches and trunk of a tree. The slow and delicate movements suggest a journey that is not pre-determined, but exploratory and curious, feeling for a direction, sensing the way—a body receptive to the energies of the land and listening intently. The second section reveals an open field with a sparse scattering of trees in the distance. A finger enters the frame in the foreground and traces a line along the horizon, hand-scratching directly into the emulsion in a playful manipulation of proximity and distance. These performative gestures continue, sometimes scratching, sometimes placing small dots of tint on the image and then across the whole frame. The uncanny fusion of this seemingly giant hand and the landscape appears as a spark of contact, perhaps a visual representation through the surface of the material of the kinds of psychic bonds we form with a place. Physical connection becomes a more explicit idea as hands reach out and rest on a bale of hay, a wooden gate, a stone wall, a metal fence, each object emitting an energy or life force through a combination of scratching, tinting and the crackle of static on the soundtrack. As a finger delicately removes the drops of water from a pair of plastic gloves pegged out on the line, it becomes clear that Kolcze is directly referencing the inseparability of the process from the physical experience of the landscape (Fig. 4.4).

'What first struck me about so many of the films coming out the workshop', says Janine Marchessault in her overview of several Film Farm works by women, 'is the tension between female self/body and nature; each film is in some way an exploration of the filmmaker's relation to the land as space'.[48] Unsurprisingly, the relationship between landscape and the female body has been a consistent theme across the years. The workshop, as mentioned earlier, has always been conceived as a place where women could regain a sense of agency and ownership over the filmmaking process, freed from the pressures and prejudices of both film schools and the film industry more generally. But there is also something

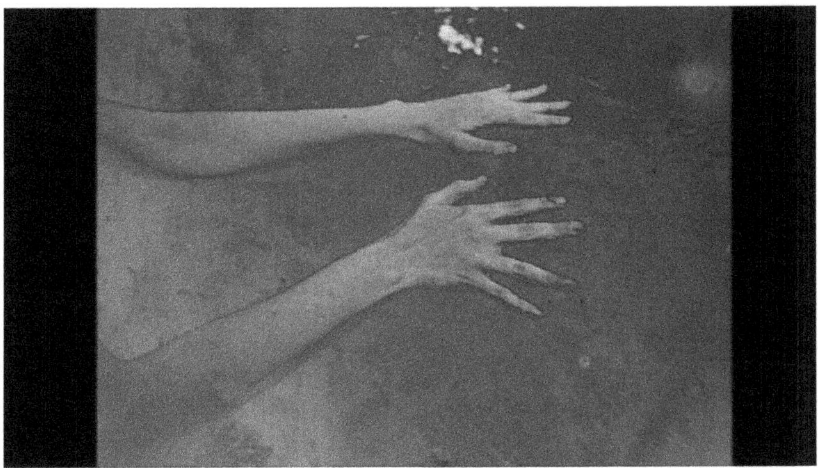

Fig. 4.4 *Markings 1-3*, Eva Kolcze, 2011 (Image courtesy of the artist)

freeing about the geographical location of the retreat and the fact of being constantly outdoors in nature. It is a liberation of both body and mind, and ultimately a way of working through the relationship between interior and exterior space in an environment that is far removed from the often alienating urban centres that have traditionally been the main sites of artistic activity. No wonder, then, that so many filmmakers use the retreat to explore questions of identity, memory and what it means to co-exist with the natural world. Marchessault relates this artisanal approach to a politically engaged interrogation of body, materials and environments that can be traced back to the feminist filmmaker Joyce Wieland, 'who famously made films on her kitchen table'. In *Water Sark* (1965), for example, Wieland employs creative playfulness to transform her habitual surroundings, turning the domestic setting of the kitchen into a kaleidoscope of visual effects that render the familiar strange. Water, mirrors, glass surfaces, a medley of household objects, the family cat and Wieland's own body are brought together in an exploration of light, depth and texture. Stephen Broomer has described the film as 'torn between an interior experience that shirks dimension and perspective, that uses the "water dress" of its title to distort the image, and an exteriority that reveals the depth and dimensions of this domicile, its contents and inhabitants'.[49] The self-reflexive staging of the process plays a central role in this tightrope walk between interior and exterior spaces, with the reflected image of Wieland's Super 8 camera acting as a constant reminder of film as a mediating portal.

Wieland's interest in the materiality of things is expressed through the malleability of the cinematic image—its ability to bring to the surface the latent qualities of everyday objects. Pushing the limits of legibility, the camera searches for a tactile form of representation that is able to communicate the essence of a moment and the relationship with the physical world as constantly in flux rather than fixed or fix*able*. Although Broomer argues that this is what makes *Water Sark* 'less an environmental portrait or performance' and 'more a work of introspection', I would suggest that Wieland is interested precisely in challenging these strict demarcations.[50] What is nature? What is interior and what is exterior? These questions, inherent in Wieland's oeuvre, resonate throughout many of the films from the Independent Imaging retreat.

Speaking about the work of Deirdre Logue, Cara Morton, Dawn Wilkinson, Carolynne Hew, Sarah Abbott and Jennifer Reeves, Marchessault observes that:

> Like Wieland, this new generation of filmmakers is exploring the relationship between bodies, the materiality of film stocks and the artifacts of the world around them. The simple images of nature (daisies, fields, frogs, trees, rivers, clouds, and so on) and rural architectures (bridges, barns, roads, etc.) are exquisite in their different cinematic manifestations. This is not idealized or essentialist nature, rather the landscapes are grounded in an experience of place.[51]

In the two films by Jennifer Reeves—*We Are Going Home* (1998) and *Strawberries in the Summertime* (2013)—one finds very different subjective approaches to landscape. A strong Surrealist sensibility permeates the images and sounds of the earlier film, with its wandering protagonists, spatial and temporal dislocations and erotically charged encounters displaying the legacy of both Luis Buñuel and Maya Deren.[52] An otherworldly atmosphere is produced through the combination of a dream-like structure and layers of formal intervention—double exposure, tinting and toning (including split toning), solarisation and, later, optical printing. Unlike Buñuel, who avoided any self-reflexive staging of the medium in order to plunge the viewer into a recognisable and believable 'reality', Reeves maintains a dynamic suspension between psychological depth and material surface.[53] Chemical alterations play a key role in expressing character psychology—desire seems to ooze out of the on-screen bodies and onto the surface of the film strip as internal energies erupt in explosions of colour. The landscape appears not as an indifferent backdrop but as a mediating force, an amalgamation of porous substances that channel and transform desire into something visible and tangible. This gesture of folding nature into a representation of the human psyche through handmade film techniques is one of the most compelling examples of re-visioning and revisiting; that is, returning to a narrative structure so familiar from earlier forms of avant-garde cinema with a haptic awareness rooted in the materiality of the world demonstrates both a historical continuum and a radical reworking of artistic traditions.

Reeves returned to Film Farm in 2011 as a Marian McMahon Award Recipient, this time with her partner and two-year-old son.[54] *Strawberries in the Summertime* is a sensitive record of their collective exploration of the landscape, moving between the child's tentative discoveries and the mother's visual reveries. As with Kolcze's *Markings 1-3* (which happens to have been filmed during the same workshop), Reeves emphasises touch from the very beginning of the film. Images of a hand brushing the wooden slats of a bridge that crosses the river communicate feelings of carefree abandon, tactile pleasure and physical union with a place. The restless camera searches out hidden mysteries of the landscape, alternating between wide perspectives of distant fields and close-up images of plant and animal life—a spider's web here, a dead bird there. A combination of rapid editing, fast-motion, close-ups and constant camera movement means that focal points sometimes shift too quickly for the eye to follow and much time is spent in the blurred spaces between. This feeling of indeterminacy is enhanced through a tension between surface and depth, with the material presence of the film strip turning optical certainties into embodied fumblings. Whilst in *We Are Going Home*, this perceptual variation contributes to the expression of psychic states, *Strawberries in the Summertime* seems to relate it to a deeper form of material questioning (Fig. 4.5).

The alternation between positive and negative imagery, as well as the extensive use of tinting and toning, brings out different material textures and contributes to the sense of sensory stimulation from the child's perspective. Split toning, in particular—where the film is treated with two different colours that work on the same areas of the image—creates the impression of a physical world constantly shifting before our eyes. It acts

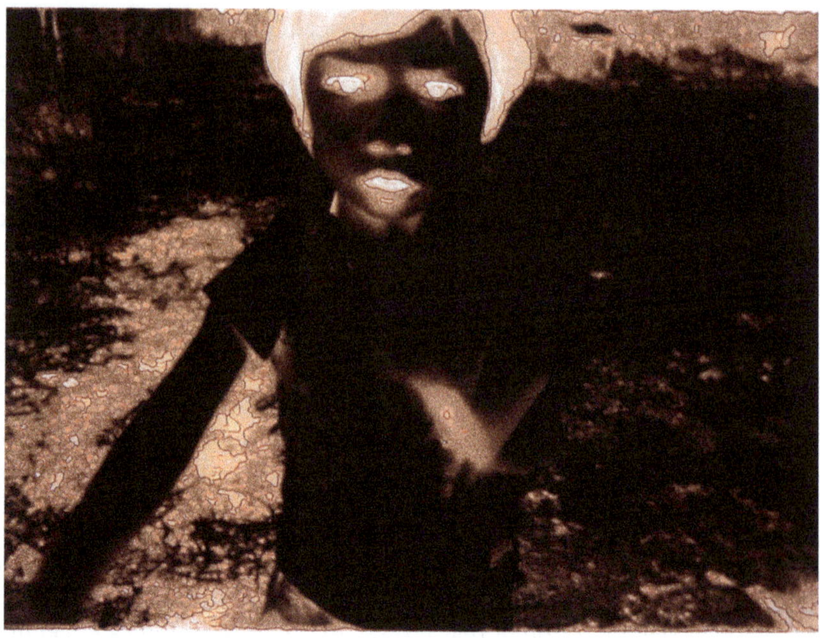

Fig. 4.5 Negative imagery in *Strawberries in the Summertime*, Jennifer Reeves, 2013 (Image courtesy of the artist)

as a form of animation, bestowing movement and visible change on inanimate objects and surfaces, and, in this sense, it seems to literalise Jane Bennett's challenge to the association of matter with passivity in many philosophical accounts. 'Does life only make sense as one side of a life-matter binary', she asks, 'or is there such a thing as mineral or metallic life?'[55] Looking at the world through these handmade practices, where chemical intervention seems to activate the inner life of things, we are drawn to affirm the latter. To Hoffman's 'what is nature?' we might add, then, 'what is life?': a question that seems pertinent to a child's vision of the world. This brings us back to the relationship between perception and ethics, and the urgent need for alternative languages—both visual and linguistic—for representing the physical world. Challenging photographic realism through the manipulation of surfaces, handmade film practices are capable of uprooting material certainties. The vibrating textures of solid objects that we see in hand-processed, solarised, tinted and toned films are certainly not *proof* that inanimate things have a 'life', but the radical shift in the perceptual register moves us closer to an understanding that they might. What if our habitual ways of seeing the world are conditioned by the long-standing belief in human superiority and the domination of all things, both animate and inanimate? What if we relinquish this position and start to see 'life' as a complex concept that perhaps exceeds the capacities of human understanding? How might this be represented visually, materially, with the body, through the body, folding other bodies—human and non-human—into the process? (Fig. 4.6).

Penny McCann's *Crashing Skies* (2012) is a further example of how artisanal techniques of material intervention can elicit an alternative visual language of things. In the opening moments of the film, solarisation and copper toning activate the surface of the celluloid, inviting us into a vibrant and constantly shifting relationship with the landscape. The

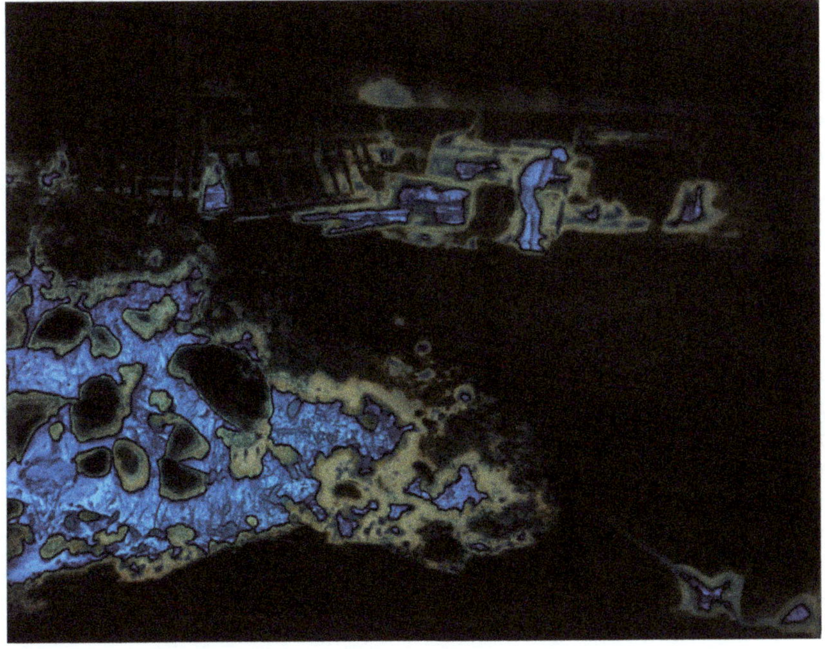

Fig. 4.6 Split toning in *Strawberries in the Summertime*, Jennifer Reeves, 2013 (Image courtesy of the artist)

ground seems to light up and trees pulsate in the background. The split-toned bodies of grazing horses in shimmering blue stimulate a renewed perceptive attentiveness, drawing the curious eye of the spectator into colours and textures that depart so dramatically from 'realistic' representations of the landscape that the experience could be described as learning to see again. This is the magic of tinting and toning techniques: they bestow on the images an otherworldly feeling that adds mystery and intrigue to the most mundane scenes. A barn in the distance is glimpsed through a field of long grasses gently swaying in the wind. Although there is nothing particularly remarkable about this image, its contemplative stillness is mesmerising, and it resonates with a temporality that is slightly out of kilter with the real world. The viewer is lured into a dreamy in-between space, a state of reverie that is heightened by the earthy brown shade of the copper toning. The aleatory nature of the tinting and toning process—since it is not an exact science, one can never be entirely sure of how particular images will respond to the dyes—translates into a viewing experience defined by anticipation and surprise, with each frame of the film telling a different story of physical contact. As the eye shifts continuously from the photographic image to the traces of hand-processing and colouring on the surface of the film, it becomes clear that a stable reference point is impossible. *Crashing Skies*, like many of the works emerging from the Independent Imaging Retreat, represents the physical world as being in a constant state of becoming (Fig. 4.7).

If material questioning is at the heart of the Film Farm output, it is certainly not the case that these films all share the same interest in coexistence and harmony with nature. In contrast to some of the works described above, Deirdre Logue's series of films made at the retreat self-consciously rejects the poetic and imaginative possibilities of the countryside setting, using it instead as a backdrop for an exploration of physical difficulty, isolation and anxiety. In *Tape* (2000), Logue, positioned uncomfortably close to the camera, wraps her head in sticky tape as though packaging herself off for shipment to an unknown destination, an indirect reference, perhaps, to the physical and psychic journeys that feature so heavily in the Film Farm back catalogue. Instead of an imaginative release, Logue emphasises physical entrapment, with the landscape existing as a silent and indifferent witness to the material struggle being played out in front of it. The repetitive scratch on the soundtrack marks out each gesture as an accumulation of tape, but it also points to the materiality of the film itself, which is always present in the image, be it through the grain of

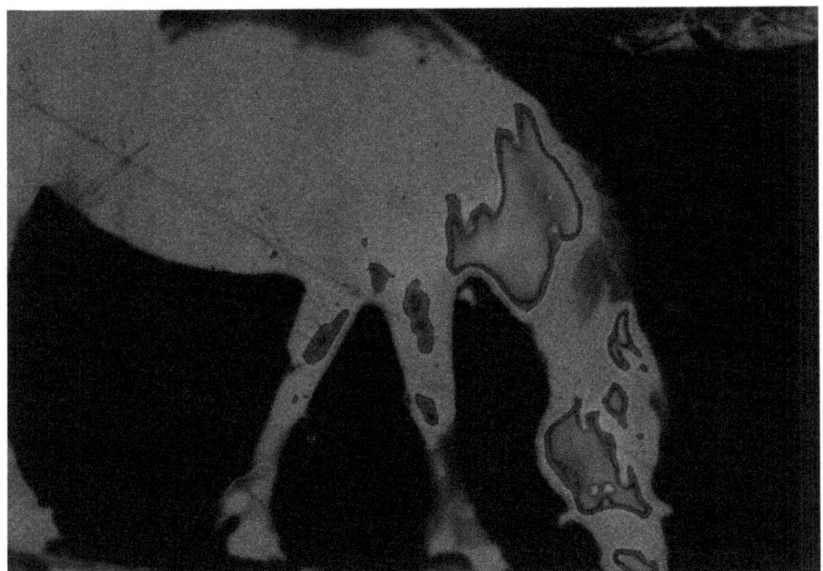

Fig. 4.7 Split toning in *Crashing Skies*, Penny McCann, 2012 (Image courtesy of the artist)

the high contrast stock or the visible traces of hand-processing. In this sense, Logue's films resonate with the early performative works of Mara Mattuschka, whose 'smeared and choppy' aesthetic in films such as *Nabel Fabel* (1984), *Cerolax II* (1985) *Kugelkopf* (*Ballhead*, 1985), *Parasympathica* (1986) and *Kaiserschnitt* (*Caesarean Section*, 1987) 'emphasizes the physical body, both human and filmic'.[56] In *Nabel Fabel*, Mattushcka's pained and distorted face frees itself from the constraining material of tights, whilst in *Kugelkopf* she appears to cut her own head with a razor.

Self-inflicted discomfort is indeed a central part of Logue's oeuvre, which also looks back to the pioneers of feminist video art—Yoko Ono, Carolee Schneemann and Joan Jonas, for example. Yet whilst Logue's aesthetic approximates in some way the body politics of video art in the 1960s and 1970s, it lacks the temporal immediacy, the simultaneous feedback loop, that led Rosalind Krauss to describe narcissism as *the* psychological condition of the video medium.[57] Like the British artists Bea Haut and Jenny Baines, discussed in Chapter 3, Logue instead highlights a different kind of temporality that is tied to the ontological specificities of film, humorously incorporating the repetitive actions required by the spring-wound clockwork Bolex camera into a commentary on the absurdity of the human condition. Whilst in the work of Baines, the repeated acts of endurance often push the filmmaker-performer to laughter, in Logue's *Fall* (1997) and *Moohead* (1999) we are offered no such cathartic release. Body and landscape are brought together, here, in a deadpan exploration of painful memories and physical challenges. The queer body does not find quietude in this rural utopia—it falls, faints and collapses painfully into the grass. It is hit on the head with a basketball, over and over again. 'My path is deliberately difficult' a hand-written text tells us at the beginning of *Scratch* (1998), before revealing a series of breakages and ruptures—images and sounds taken from a 1950s instructional film combined with an audible crackle that serves to increase the sense of building tension and anxiety.

The bright thistles that surround the barn, and which form the basis of so many poetic explorations by Film Farm participants, are, in *Scratch*, related to female sexuality and bodily discomfort as Logue pushes them into her underwear and then reveals them to the camera in extreme close-up. In this association of nature with the wider concept of the 'natural', Logue questions culturally prescribed attitudes towards the body and brings the difficult relationship between nature and heteronormativity quite literally to the surface. We might look to the emerging field of queer ecology to uncover some key resonances between this aspect of Logue's work and the need for more ethical forms of relating to the world. Within this context, 'queer subjectivities contribute a more fluid and relational understanding of environmental stewardship', that resists traditional hierarchies and relationships of domination.[58] With its emphasis on 'affinity and solidarity over identity', queer theory offers a de-centred approach to ecological thinking that goes beyond sexuality in an embrace of other forms of otherness.[59]

In Hoffman's *vulture* (2019), this operates on the level of non-human bodies, through a gaze that is resolutely non-objectifying. Hoffman's work has followed a largely autobiographical path, exploring themes of time, memory and subjectivity—fleeting fragments of experience, moments captured, relationships remembered and relived. 'My work has always been process-based', he has stated, 'seeking rather than settling on something; the finished project has always been less important than the moments of epiphany that happen while I am collecting, processing, and digesting the materials'.[60] *Vulture* is, in many ways, a deeply personal film with an autobiographical focus, despite the fact that the camera almost never strays from a group of farm animals and their surrounding environment. The film was shot from the veranda of Hoffman's house in Mount Forest—the site of the Independent Imaging Retreat—over a two-year period, observing the various interactions that play out on the neighbouring farm. The filmmaker himself is absent from the frame, but this is far from an objective representation of the landscape. One senses acutely a certain familiarity, the kind of bond that one forms with a place over a long period of time and an eye trained in the particular movements, gestures, rhythms and routines of animals—horses, goats, cows, pigs and birds—that have become part of the filmmaker's own quotidian experience and visual frame of reference. Shooting with an electric Bolex (rather than the spring-wound models utilised by many experimental filmmakers), Hoffman is able to make extensive use of the long take to capture the minutiae of multispecies co-existence, oscillating between moments of stillness and sudden bursts of frenzied activity. As the image shifts from static extreme long shots to moving zooms, the filmmaker invites us to contemplate a spectrum of material relations: the textures of bodies, the affinities and conflicts that shape their daily existence, as well as the space that frames and contains them.

Occasionally the emphasis shifts to observe details of the environment—a row of trees on the horizon, majestic in their distant stillness; sunflowers standing proudly outside the barn; the hanging branches of the willow tree, behind which roam the chickens that would be a familiar sight to any previous Film Farm participant. In every corner, it seems, life is unfolding according to its own temporality. Brief glimpses of human activity (Phil's wife Janine cleaning the pond, farmers ploughing the fields, the workshop leaders preparing the site) are folded into the eclectic rituals of the natural world (a pig suckling on a cow, a bird of prey searching for food) in such a way that everything exists as though on the same level of significance and occupies a shared temporal continuum. Through this patient and non-objectifying gaze, Hoffman cultivates an ecological contemplation that resists the spectacular othering tendencies of mainstream nature documentaries. For sure, this film is a documentary, and it certainly takes nature as its subject, but its meandering form and dedramatised structure requires a level of thoughtful investment. Instead of the crisp, high definition images that reveal sights unseen and penetrate natural habitats under the guise of education, *vulture* is an uneven combination of 16mm film stocks of varying grain and speed and shifting between black and white and colour. For some shots, Hoffman used out of date film, giving the image a slightly washed out, ethereal feel, with particular colours (the yellow of the sunflowers, for example) not conforming to their 'true' appearance in nature. The marks and blemishes on the surface of the film that result from hand-processing draw attention to both the mediating presence of the material and the hand of the artist in crafting a visual record of the place (Fig. 4.8).

Sections of the film were processed and tinted with a variety of flowers, fruits and plants from around the farm—magnolia, hyacinth, hydrangea, daffodil, rhododendron, pond algae, lilac, oregano, comfrey, rose, mint, goldenrod, hosta buds, wild garlic seeds, tansy, aster, echinacea, sunflower

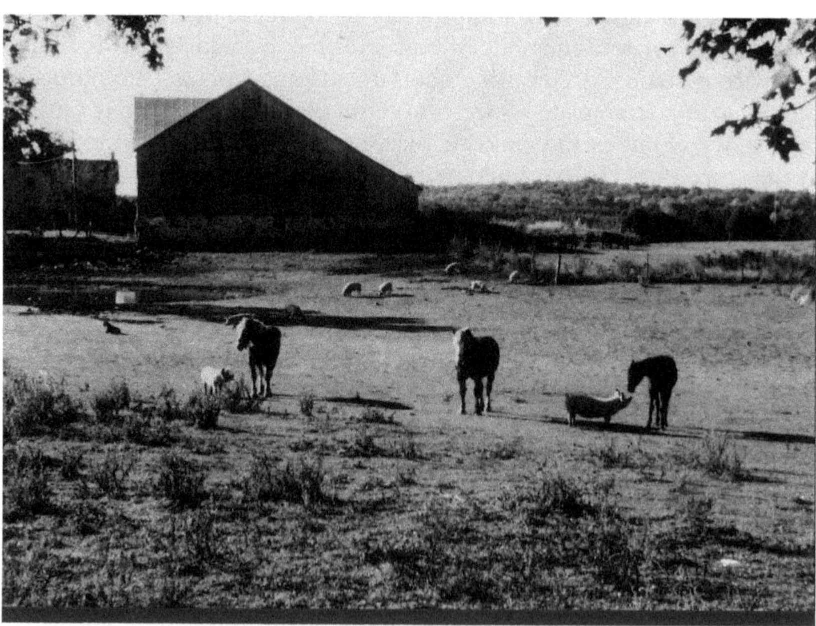

Fig. 4.8 Farm animals coexisting in *vulture*, Philip Hoffman, 2019 (Image courtesy of the artist)

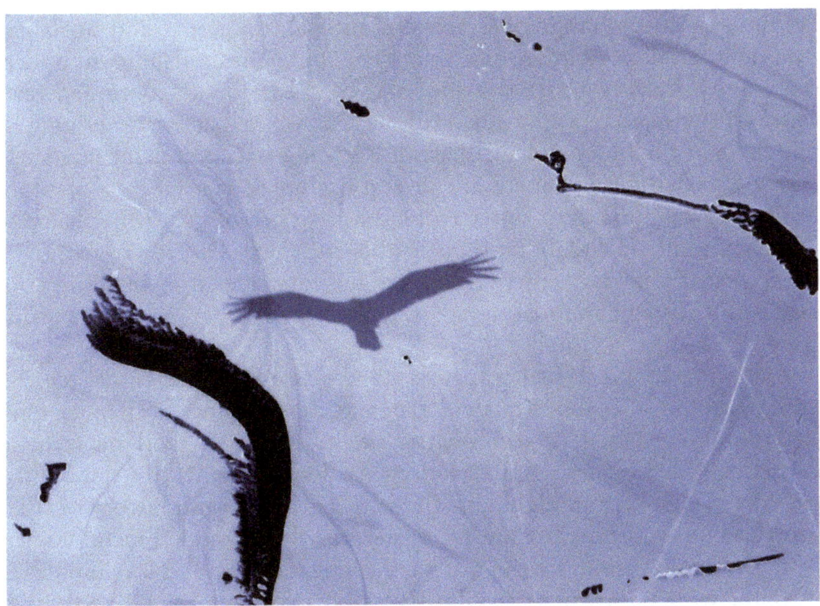

Fig. 4.9 Traces of hand-processing in *vulture*, Philip Hoffman, 2019 (Image courtesy of the artist)

and walnut. From this perspective, *vulture* is more than just a visual appreciation of the land; it is a complex material engagement with an ecosystem that draws out the expressive possibilities of living things beyond conventional forms of representation. Over a shot of a flying bird, we hear a child relating fragments of information about vultures and their hunting habits. 'Vultures live together, and they don't fight, they help each other', says the child. 'I didn't know that', replies Hoffman. Behind this simple exchange lie multiple layers of signification that testify to the intellectual and spiritual depth of the film, and, at the same time, point towards a philosophy of collective nurturing that quietly runs under the surface of the Independent Imaging Retreat (Fig. 4.9).

Social Ecology and Everyday Utopia

I have focused extensively in this chapter on one enduring example of community-based artisanal filmmaking, unearthing connections between photochemical film processes and engagements with the natural world.

Folding an autoethnographic account into a contextual and analytical overview has allowed me to open up some unique insights into an under-represented field of image-making, and to argue for its continued relevance in the contemporary era. However, as we saw at the beginning of this chapter, the Independent Imaging Retreat is part of much wider alternative film culture and there are several examples of projects that move beyond urban centres in order to establish spaces of creativity, dialogue and community in collaboration with the landscape. Directly or indirectly inspired by Film Farm, these initiatives take an interest in building connections with, and stimulating an awareness of, specific locations outside the city.

Mary Stark and David Chatton Barker, for instance, took part in Film Farm in the summer of 2016 and, soon after, created a similar community-based project on the site of a former working farm in Rossendale, Lancashire. Aptly named 'Analogue Farm', this new initiative 'draw[s] upon and highlights the nature, folklore and history of [the] surrounding landscape', connecting 'supposedly outmoded technologies' with the land through forms of tactile engagement.[61] Not limited to working with photochemical film, the duo organises events and workshops on topics that range from mud painting and stonewalling to tree planting and wand making, always with an educational agenda that promotes ecological awareness as much as the sharing of skills. The physical location in a particular geographical site determines the kinds of artisanal activities that participants engage in, with a view to stimulating an embodied thinking through our relationship with the land. Another example is the Allerdale Film Farm, a ten-day filmmaking event that took place in West Cumbria in the summer of 2017 and brought together eight artists from film labs around the UK.[62] The workshops were run out of a makeshift lab in Hayton Castle, with an emphasis on giving access to younger participants between the ages of 16 and 25, who may not previously have encountered analogue film equipment. Situated outside the main cultural centres in the UK, the project was also designed to shift attention to under-represented rural areas and to activate creative responses to the natural surroundings.

The Handmade Film Institute has, since 2005, run a series of outdoor film retreats in locations such as the Rocky Mountains, tying creativity to sustainability and emphasising physical, mental and material exploration. Like Film Farm, participants work in an artisanal mode in a rural setting, living together, sharing resources and drawing on the natural surroundings as a source of creative inspiration. The Wilderness Film Expedition, in particular, combines a high-altitude trek with 'zero emissions filmmaking', where the equipment is carried to the workshop location and the natural surroundings feed into the process as more than just subject matter. 'Once established', reads the workshop description, 'the base camp becomes a filmmaking studio en plein air – the streams hydrate our chemistry, the sun dries our film, and the darkness of the night provides the limitless darkroom in which we work'.[63] Such initiatives represent an attempt to further align photochemical film's culturally marginal position with an environmentally conscious one, weaving its organic needs—water, light and darkness—into a wider ecology. This resonates with Chodorov's statement, quoted in the previous chapter, that photochemical film artists work with 'organic, physical material that comes from the earth: salts, silvers, minerals'.[64] Although there are still issues of how to deal with the toxic residues that result from certain processing methods, the fact remains that many people involved in photochemical film practice are engaged not only in creating alternative communities and collective ways of working, but also in developing forms of environmental connectedness.

Are these rural utopias another kind of escapism? They clearly don't offer any immediate or outward solutions to the problem of overpopulated cities, expanding urbanisation, rising pollution, the reduction of green space, threats to wildlife, or the increasing corporatisation of public space and all the other negative impacts of a modern capitalist society whose primary agenda is economic growth. Where can these alternative communities and spaces lead us in the pursuit of a more ethical and egalitarian way of life? One could argue that they are, in the first instance, a way of (re)discovering an embodied relationship to the material world that filters through other interactions and encounters, both urban and rural. Stepping outside of our regular routines to embrace a slower rhythm and a more attentive engagement with our surroundings might sound like another 'wellness' trend, where spiritual enlightenment is co-opted by the lifestyle industry to sell yet more products for self-improvement with the promise of 'getting away from it all'. But the combination of a materially engaged art practice with environmentally conscious, non-hierarchical, community-based living can be understood from a social-ecological perspective.

In his essay on the relationship between social ecology and utopia, Dan Chodorkoff highlights utopia's fundamentally pejorative inflections, associated, as it so often is, with unrealistic and unfeasible desires and hopes. Returning to the original etymology of the term as relating, in Greek, to both 'no place' (*outopia*) and 'good place' (*eutopia*), he argues that it is important to embrace the latter as a way to think about, and ultimately move towards, what is possible. 'At its most profound', states Chodorkoff, 'utopia is an expression of real, existing potentialities in our own society', but these potentialities have been repressed by a system based on greed and individualism.[65] Imagining possible alternatives to an unjust and unequal society is thus a crucial part of contemporary political praxis, regardless of however unachievable it might seem on a large scale. From this perspective, the Independent Imaging Retreat and other similar projects based on collective experience and ecological responsibility *are* utopic, in the sense that they create a space of imaginative potential that taps into basic human values. As Chodorkoff puts it:

> Nurturing, caring, sharing, and mutualism; they are all part of our heritage, part of our common humanity. [...] Today, we are so limited in our ability to think about what we want by what is, that we often forget what could be. [...] we need to recapture an imaginary that can help to guide us toward a more ecological and just future.[66]

Of course, one does not have to embark on a high-altitude trek carrying photochemical film equipment to imagine other futures! And film is certainly not the only medium with which to explore alternative ways of being. But as it takes on a more marginal status in relation to mainstream practice, and as it increasingly becomes associated with cultures of recycling, recuperating, sharing and helping, photochemical film and the communities that emerge around it demonstrate a form of resistance that Davina Cooper describes in terms of 'everyday utopia':

> Everyday utopias don't focus on campaigning of advocacy. They don't place their energy on pressuring mainstream institutions on change, on winning votes, or on taking over dominant social structures. Rather they work by creating the change they wish to encounter, building and forging new ways of experiencing social and political life.[67]

Carving out oppositional technological trajectories, resisting capitalist 'progress', coming together to reinvent a medium deemed obsolete, 'cut[ting] against the narrative of disruption-worshipping techno-utopianism coming out of Silicon Valley',[68] finding ways to connect the materiality of film with an awareness of the environment, building communities and sharing knowledge—these are all gestures, I argue, of everyday utopia.

The interconnected networks, alternative communities and utopic spaces that I have discussed in this chapter are, like the film itself, in a continual state of flux. To be an artist in the current climate is to frequently find oneself in a situation of precarity, responding to personal circumstances, relocating to find paid work, moving from one city to another or sometimes from one country to another. A link may be broken in one location, but re-established somewhere else. A lab closes, another opens. Equipment travels or is left behind, finds itself in a new location or in different hands. A new technique or recipe is discovered and is communicated enthusiastically to others, who communicate it to others, who adapt it and pass it on, in an ongoing process of creative exchange and development. The continuation of photochemical film as an alternative, artisanal practice, is tied to these shifting infrastructures and collaborative endeavours. But it also requires financial support in order to flourish and pursue its utopic project. This is the ongoing conundrum of an art form still dependent to some extent on the commercial industry and state subsidy. It is an uneasy relationship, but there is no sign of giving up any time soon.

Notes

1. Overviews of these alternative networks can be found in Petra Bauer and Dan Kidner (eds.), *Working Together: Notes on British Film Collectives in the 1970s* (London: Focal Point Gallery, 2013); Sue Clayton and Laura Mulvey (eds.), *Other Cinemas: Politics, Culture and Experimental Film in the 1970s* (London and New York: I.B. Tauris, 2017); Duncan Reekie, *Subversion: The Definitive History of Underground Cinema* (London: Wallflower Press, 2007).
2. See, for instance, Pip Chodorov, 'The Artist-Run Film Labs', *Millennium Film Journal*, Vol. 60, Fall 2014, pp. 28–37; Elena Duque, 'Celluloid and Self-Sufficiency: Artist-Run Labs', *CCCB Lab Research and Innovation in the Cultural Sphere*, 23 February 2016: http://lab.cccb.org/en/celluloid-and-self-sufficiency-artist-run-labs/ (accessed 20 July 2019); Kim Knowles, 'Self-Skilling and Home Brewing: Some Reflections on Photochemical Film Culture', *Millennium Film Journal*, Vol. 60, Fall 2014, pp. 20–27; Noélie Martin, 'Pratique des émulsions artisanales', *La Furia Umana*, Vol. 33, 2018: http://www.lafuriaumana.it/index.php/

66-archive/lfu-33/767-noelie-martin-pratique-des-emulsions-artisanales (accessed 20 July 2019); Monise Nicodemos, 'Obolescence et reinvention du cinéma argentique à l'âge du numérique', Doctoral thesis, Université Sorbonne Nouvelle—Paris 3, 2019; Mariya Nikiforova, 'Laboratoires photochimiques indépendants: politique, technique, esthétique', Masters thesis, Université Sorbonne Nouvelle—Paris 3, 2016; Jussi Parikka and Rossella Catanese, 'Handmade Films and Artist-Run Labs: The Chemical Sites of Film's Counterculture', *NECSUS: European Journal of Media Studies*, Vol. 7, No. 2, 2018, pp. 43–63; Nicolas Rey, 'Contemporary Issues of Artist-Run Film Lab Practices', in Luisa Greenfield, Deborah S. Phillips, Kerstin Schroedinger, Björn Speidel, Philip Widmann (eds.), *Film in the Present Tense: Why Can't We Stop Talking about Analogue Film?* (Berlin: Archive Books, 2018), pp. 63–71; Mike Rollo, 'A Collective Charge: Collectif double négativ/Double Negative Collective', in Scott MacKenzie and Janine Marchessault (eds.), *Process Cinema: Handmade Film in the Digital Age* (Montreal: McGill-Queens University, 2019), pp. 214–230; Genevieve Yue, 'Kitchen Sink Cinema: Artist-Run Film Laboratories', *Film Comment*, 30 March 2015: https://www.filmcomment.com/blog/artist-run-film-laboratories/ (accessed 20 July 2019).

3. Gay Hawkins, *The Ethics of Waste: How We Relate to Rubbish* (Lanham: Rowman and Littlefield Publishers, 2006), p. 2.
4. Marcy Saude, 'Old Weird Materialism: Production and Distribution of Artist Film', paper given at the NECS Conference: Media Tactics and Engagement, Amsterdam, 29 June 2018.
5. Mono No Aware founder Steve Cossman, for instance, states: 'At some point, I'm going to be able to 3D scan my entire Bolex and print out a Bolex then shoot film with it! I can replicate almost any EIKI part I need; I'm going to be able to build an optical printer in Rhino. I'll be able to build custom gates and trick it out in any way I want. I think certain advancements in technology make it possible to sustain analog practices and improve upon them'. Tara D. Kelley, 'Is Film Really Dead? An Interview with Steve Cossman: http://reapmediazine.com/index.php/article-list/243-is-film-really-dead-an-interview-with-steve-cossman-2#.XWZ5jZNKgnU (accessed 28 August 2019).
6. Over the years, I have spoken with numerous artists who express frustration at the assumption that they should/could move their practice over to the digital because the industry tells them so. For many, the differences between the two technologies are so great that they appear as separate art forms, to the extent that should film cease to exist, they would continue their practice in painting, sculpture or other artisanal practices.
7. Although not a listed film lab, the itinerant collective Bristol Experimental and Expanded Film (BEEF) runs a range of analogue film and sound

workshops and organises screenings and events around the city. It has a radical and activist ethos, evidenced through its involvement in events such as Antiuniversity Now, a self-organised, anti-establishment learning project.

8. 'The Artist-Run Film Labs', *Millennium Film Journal*, p. 36.
9. Patti Gaal-Holmes, *A History of 1970s Experimental Film: Britain's Decade of Diversity* (London: Palgrave Macmillan, 2015), p. 139.
10. *Sequence* was edited by Simon Payne and was published in four issues in 2010, 2011, 2013 and 2016.
11. Zoller states: 'no.w.here is a radicant that roots its language in the present tense, and cultivates a discourse that can only grow in the unthreatening and intimate climate of no.w.here's spaces. no.w.here. speaks a kaleidoscopic and gestural language that plants new thoughts in the non-linear cybernetic condition of today's globalised living conditions. In its temporal and spatial disorientation it abandons hierarchies of knowledge in order to reconfigure the social'. Max Zoller, 'no.w.here, a Grass-Roots Radicant', *Sequence*, Vol. 1, 2010, p. 52.
12. Nicolas Bourriaud, *The Radicant* (New York: Lucas & Sternberg, 2009), p. 22.
13. According to Johannes Euler and Leslie Gauditz, 'the self-organising Commons point of view can be the foundation of a society beyond market economy and state. Core principles are: contribution instead of exchange; actual use instead of property; share all that you can […]; use all that you need'. 'Commons Movements: Self-organised (re)production as a social-ecological transformation', *Degrowth in Bewegung(En)* (blog), 13 December 2016: http://www.degrowth.de/en/dim (accessed 28 August 2019).
14. Charles Leadbeater, *The Frugal Innovator: Creating Change on a Shoestring Budget* (Basingstoke: Palgrave Macmillan, 2014), pp. 143–144.
15. For an up-to-date list of operating film labs see: http://www.filmlabs.org/ (accessed 1 August 2019).
16. Personal interview with Karel Doing, 26 July 2019.
17. For a more comprehensive overview of these historical origins see Pip Chodorov, 'The Artist-Run Film Labs'; Nicolas Rey, 'Contemporary Issues of Artist-Run Film Lab Practices'.
18. Esther Urlus, *Re:inventing the Pioneers: Film Experiments on Handmade Silver Gelatin Emulsion and Color Methods* (Rotterdam: self-published, 2013); Steven Woloshen, *Recipes for Reconstruction: The Cookbook for the Frugal Filmmaker* (Montreal: Scratchatopia Books, 2010); Steven Woloshen, *Scratch, Crackle & Pop: A Whole Grains Approach to Making Films Without a Camera* (Montreal: Scratchatopia Books, 2015); Kathryn Ramey, *Experimental Filmmaking: Break the Machine* (London and New York: Routledge, 2016).

19. Helen Hill, Recipes for Disaster: A Handcrafted Film Cookbooklet, 2005: http://www.filmlabs.org/docs/recipes_for_disaster_hill.pdf (accessed 20 July 2019).
20. James Holcombe, 'If There Is Life in the BARN: It Will Survive, Philip Hoffman interview, LUX, 22 January 2016: https://lux.org.uk/writing/james-holcombe-philip-hoffman-film-farm-interview (accessed 16 July 2019).
21. Janine Marchessault, 'Women, Nature, and Chemistry: Hand-Processed Films from the Film Farm', in Steve Reinke and Tom Taylor (eds.), *LUX: A Decade of Artists' Film and Video* (Toronto: YYZ Books/Pleasure Dome, 2000), p. 136.
22. Having initially worked with a processing machine, the retreat moved to hand-processing after Butterworth attended a workshop run by Karel Doing at Studio Één in the early 1990s. Doing had not been aware of the circularity of historical events until quite recently and had not himself visited Film Farm until 2018. Personal interview with Karel Doing, 26 July 2019.
23. Cara Morton, 'Films, Fairy Dust and other fucking cool shit (or "How I Found Myself on the Independent Imaging Retreat"), Liaison of Independent Filmmakers' (LIFT) Newsletter, Summer 1996, p. 18: https://philiphoffman.ca/films-and-fairy-dust/ (accessed 17 July 2019).
24. Scott MacKenzie, '"An Arrow, Not a Target": Film Process and Processing at the Independent Imaging Retreat', in Mette Hjort (ed.), *The Education of the Filmmaker in Africa, The Middle East, and the Americas* (New York: Palgrave Macmillan, 2013), p. 174.
25. David Yarrow, 'Lecturers Aren't to Blame for University Grade Inflation—The Government Is', *The Guardian*, 12 July 2019: https://www.theguardian.com/education/2019/jul/12/lecturers-arent-to-blame-for-university-grade-inflation-the-government-is (accessed 30 July 2019). See also Gary Hall, *The Uberification of the University* (Minneapolis: University of Minnesota Press, 2016).
26. Rosi Braidotti, *The Posthuman* (Cambridge: Polity Press, 2013), p. 174.
27. Braidotti, pp. 179–180. Many of the participants over the years have been involved in teaching film theory and practice in university contexts. In 2019, for example, over half of the group were employed in higher education. In May 2019, Phil Hoffman, Terra Long, Rob Butterworth and Deirdre Logue travelled to the UK to run a 'on the road' version of Film Farm at Aberystwyth University over three days.
28. This is a reference to David Lynch:

    'Ideas are like fish.

    If you want to catch little fish, you can stay in the shallow water. But if you want to catch the big fish, you've got to go deeper.

Down deep, the fish are more powerful and more pure. They're huge and abstract. And they're very beautiful.

I look for a certain kind of fish that is important to me, one that can translate to cinema. But there are all kinds of fish swimming down there. There are fish for business, fish for sports. There are fish for everything.

Everything, anything that is a thing, comes up from the deepest level. Modern physics calls that level the Unified Field. The more your consciousness – your awareness – is expanded, the deeper you go toward this source, and the bigger fish you can catch'. David Lynch, *Catching the Big Fish: Meditation, Consciousness, and Creativity* (London: Penguin Books, 2006), p. 1.

29. Philip Hoffman, 'Vulture Aesthetics: Process Cinema at the Film Farm', in Luisa Greenfield et al. (eds.), *Film in the Present Tense: Why Can't We Stop Talking about Analogue film?* p. 40.
30. If we are to believe Man Ray's accounts, for example, the techniques of rayography and solarisation were discovered in this way—the first by absent-mindedly placing objects onto photo-sensitive paper and the second by accidentally turning on the light during developing. See Man Ray, *Self-Portrait* (Boston: Bullfinch Press, 1999).
31. In his textbook on the motion picture camera, Joel Schlemowitz touches on many examples of filmmakers who have intentionally gone against the 'correct' way of producing images in order to bring forth poetic representations that challenge traditional ways of seeing and relating to the world around us. *Experimental Filmmaking and the Motion Picture Camera: An Introductory Guide for Artists and Filmmakers* (New York: Routledge, 2019).
32. https://philiphoffman.ca/filmography/kokoro-is-for-heart/ (accessed 10 July 2019).
33. For an historical overview of colour in film see Simon Brown, Sarah Street and Liz Watkins (eds.), *Colour and the Moving Image: History, Theory, Aesthetics, Archive* (New York and London: Routledge, 2013).
34. Janis Cole, 'The Harvest of Philip Hoffman', *POV*, No. 58, Summer 2005, pp. 4–8. The cover of this publication features the title 'Phil's Film Farm'.
35. The list of past contributors to the Independent Imaging Retreat can be found on the website: https://philiphoffman.ca/film-farm/retreat-participants-1994-2013/ (accessed 16 July 2019).
36. (S8): Mostra de Cinema Periférico was established in the Galician city of A Coruña in 2010 by Ángel Rueda, who also participated in the 2019 Film Farm.
37. In 2018, the Black Box experimental strand of Edinburgh International Film Festival featured a special focus on contemporary Canadian experimental film, curated in collaboration with Terra Jean Long. Attention was

given to handmade film processes and many of the works were created at the Independent Imaging Retreat.

38. Bruno Latour, *Down to Earth: Politics in the New Climactic Regime* (Cambridge: Polity Press, 2018), p. 57.
39. Ibid.
40. 'Helen Hill and I used to have a playful argument as she called it Film Camp, and though it may seem like that I always steered it away from camp […] in 1999 Helen Hill, Trixy Sweetvittles (Wattenbarger) and Amy Lockhart drove to the Film Farm all the way from Halifax, in an old car with Film Camp or Bust spray painted along the side of the car, and a candy floss machine in the back seat for all to enjoy!' Phil Hoffman in an interview with James Holcombe: https://lux.org.uk/james-holcombe-philip-hoffman-film-farm-interview (accessed 16 July 2019). Hill was a participant in Film Farm in 1999, 2000 and 2002.
41. Vivian Sobchack, 'What My Fingers Knew: The Cinesthetic Subject, or Vision in the Flesh', in *Carnal Thoughts: Embodiment and Moving Image Culture* (Berkeley: University of California Press, 2004), p. 63.
42. Much gratitude to Vicky Smith for this and many other enlightening conversations we have had over the years.
43. Joel Schlemowitz, *Experimental Filmmaking and the Motion Picture Camera: An Introductory Guide for Artists and Filmmakers*, p. 3.
44. Wendy Parkins and Geoffrey Craig, *Slow Living* (Oxford and New York: Berg, 2006), p. ix. See also, Mary Ann Doane, *The Emergence of Cinematic Time: Modernity, Contingency, the Archive* (Cambridge, MA and London: Harvard University Press, 2002); Jonathan Martineau, *Time, Capitalism and Alienation: A Socio-Historical Inquiry into the Making of Modern Time* (Boston: Brill, 2015); Paul Virilio, *Speed and Politics* (Cambridge, MA and London: MIT Press, 2006).
45. Thank you to Terra Long for this filmic metaphor, and for helping me to understand some of the personal context of Film Farm beyond static historical facts. Skype conversation with Terra Long, 24 July 2019.
46. Scott MacKenzie and Janine Marchessault (eds.), *Process Cinema: Handmade Film in the Digital Age*. The book launch was hosted by TIFF Bell Lightbox and organised to coincide with the Film Farm screenings.
47. Karyn Sandlos in the post-screening discussion of Film Farm: 25 Years of the Mount Forest Independent Imaging Retreat Programme 2, TIFF Bell Light Box, Toronto, 11 July 2009.
48. Janine Marchessault, 'Women, Nature, and Chemistry: Hand-Processed Films from the Film Farm', p. 138.
49. Stephen Broomer, *Codes for North: Foundations of the Canadian Avant-Garde Film* (Toronto: Canadian Filmmakers Distribution Centre, 2017), p. 140.
50. Ibid., p. 140.

51. Marchessault, 'Women, Nature, and Chemistry: Hand-Processed Films from the Film Farm', p. 136.
52. Several actions and motifs in *We Are Going Home* can be mapped across the films of Deren and Buñuel/Dalí. The legs buried in sand brings to mind the famous ending of *Un Chien andalou* (Luis Buñuel and Salvador Dalí, 1929), where the two characters are inexplicably buried up their waists on the beach, whilst the toe-sucking is a nod to the sequence in *L'Âge d'or* (Luis Buñuel and Salvador Dalí, 1930), where the female protagonist sucks suggestively on the toe of a statue. Furthermore, the trio of women in Reeves' film is reminiscent of the three-way identity struggle in Deren's *At Land* (1944), as well as the erotic exchange with the two women she encounters on the beach.
53. As Rudolf Kuenzli argues, early Surrealist film can be defined by its embrace of cinematographic realism, in contrast to dada film, which constantly draws attention to the image as a construct. 'Unlike Dada films, Surrealist movies do not use slow motion, they do not present the images produced by the cinematic apparatus as yet another illusion […] The incoherent, non-narrative, illogical nature of Dada films, which constantly defamiliarize the familiar world through cinematic manipulations, never let the viewer enter the world of the film'. Rudolf E. Kuenzli (ed.), *Dada and Surrealist Film* (Cambridge, MA: MIT Press, 1996), p. 10.
54. The Marian McMahon Award is a prize given annually by the Images Festival in Toronto to a female filmmaker working autobiographically. The award winner is invited to take part in the Independent Imaging Retreat free of charge.
55. Jane Bennett, *Vibrant Matter: A Political Ecology of Things* (Durham: Duke University Press, 2010), p. 53.
56. Christa Blümlinger, 'The Filmic Convulsions of Mara Mattuschka', in Peter Tscherkassky (ed.), *Film Unframed: The Austrian Avant-Garde Film* (Vienna: Austrian Film Museum, 2012), p. 230.
57. Rosalind Krauss, 'Video: The Aesthetics of Narcissism', *October*, Vol. 1, 1976, p. 50.
58. Jonathan M. Gray, 'Heteronormativity Without Nature: Toward a Queer Ecology', *QED: A Journal of GLBTQ Worldmaking*, Vol. 4, No. 2, 2017, p. 137.
59. Sharon Marcus, 'Queer Theory for Everyone: A Review Essay', *Signs*, Vol. 31, No. 1, Autumn 2005, p. 196.
60. Philip Hoffman in Jem Noble, 'As the Mind Tracks Shape … As the Mind Recalls Sound …', *LUMA*, Vol. 7, No. 2, Winter 2017: https://lumaquarterly.com/issues/volume-two/007-winter/as-the-mind-tracks-shape-as-the-mind-recalls-sound/ (accessed 26 July 2019).
61. https://www.analoguefarm.com/about (accessed 22 July 2019).

62. Julia Parks, James Holcombe, Jameela Khan, Marcy Saude, Leah E. Millar, Jaqui Knight, Martha Jurksaitis and Christo Wallers.
63. https://hmfi.handmadefilm.org/classes-2/.
64. Chodorov, 'The Artist-Run Film Labs', p. 36.
65. Dan Chodorkoff, 'Everything Depends on What People Are Capable of Wanting', in Eirik Eiglad (ed.), *Social Ecology and Social Change* (Porsgrunn: New Compass Press, 2015), p. 36.
66. Ibid., p. 37.
67. Davina Cooper, *Everyday Utopias: The Conceptual Life of Promising Spaces* (Durham and London: Duke University Press), p. 2.
68. David Sax, *The Revenge of Analog: Real Things and Why They Matter* (New York: Public Affairs, 2016), p. xvii.

CHAPTER 5

Projecting Film, Expanding Cinema

If alternative spaces of production and education have become central to photochemical film culture, ensuring the circulation of technical expertise and maintaining a continued interest in a now marginal art form, they are also closely connected to practices of film exhibition. Independently organised film screenings, small-scale festivals and dedicated platforms in larger events provide a context for radical and thoughtful programming outside the mainstream fare of commercial multiplexes and the taste-dictated content of repertory or arthouse cinemas. Like the London Film-maker's Co-op in the 1960s and 1970s, the majority of film labs host public screenings of work by members and visiting artists, as well as staging their own annual or biannual festivals.[1] In recent years, a number of international film festivals have placed emphasis on analogue film practice (the International Film Festival Rotterdam through the curatorial work of Erwin van 't Hart or my own Black Box strand at the Edinburgh International Film Festival), with the Oberhausen Film Festival introducing a 'Film Labs' section in 2017, curated by Vassily Bourikas.[2] These initiatives of varying size, scale and regularity play a vital role in disseminating photochemical film techniques, communicating the medium's ongoing artistic relevance, connecting practitioners and potentially reaching out to new audiences. Given the increasing scarcity of 16mm and 35mm film exhibition in cinemas, art centres, festivals and other cultural institutions, safeguarding and celebrating the projection event takes on particular significance. Discussions about the cultural status of photochemical film in

K. Knowles, *Experimental Film and Photochemical Practices*,
Experimental Film and Artists' Moving Image,
https://doi.org/10.1007/978-3-030-44309-2_5

the digital era have tended to emphasise production contexts and material practices, often neglecting to consider the physicality of the screening or performance environment. In this chapter, I will extend the discussion of institutional infrastructures and alternative communities to the sites and forms of embodied experience. I will outline some of the key contemporary concerns in relation to photochemical film exhibition, before moving on to assess the importance of expanded film performance, material presence and the live context. In many sections of this chapter, my position as an academic researcher and writer intersects with my activities as a curator, and the many years of presenting films to public audiences in a largely cinema-based setting significantly informs my reflections. Likewise, the examples of live film performance that I discuss are drawn from personal experience—they are amongst those that I have had the opportunity to witness physically and speak about directly with the artists. Like Catherine Elwes, who, in her book *Installation and the Moving Image*, 'nail[s] [her] colours to the mast', I privilege the embodied encounter as a source of knowledge and therefore embrace a subjective perspective in terms of the works included here.[3] What follows is not intended as any kind of overview of the field; rather I use particular examples to point to wider tendencies and developing concerns.[4] It should be seen as a montage of moments and intersecting activities that emerge from, feed into, overlap with and, to a large extent, determine the future of photochemical film.

The Death (and Rebirth) of Film Projection

It hardly needs spelling out: the projection of film as a physical object is a thing of the past, at least in mainstream cinemas and most cultural institutions. One need only compare two roundtable discussions published in the art journal *October*—the first, in 2002, on 'Obsolescence and American Avant-Garde Film', and the second, in 2011, entitled 'Digital Experimental Filmmaking'—for an illustration of how quickly the technological landscape changed in such a short period of time.[5] Whilst both debates, which took place between a small number of key figures in the experimental film world—filmmakers, critics and curators—acknowledged the changes, challenges and possibilities ushered in by new technologies, both in terms of filmmaking and film viewing, the former demonstrates the prevailing uncertainty around the real impact of digital technology on the future of the medium. A striking example of this is the filmmaker

Brian Frye's comment that, '[f]or all the talk about the imminent obsolescence of film, which may or may not take place [...] I have yet to see digital projection in a commercial theater. I'll believe it when I see it'.[6] Similarly, for John Belton, writing in the same 2002 issue of *October*, the 'so-called technological revolution' was a 'false revolution', one that was 'more clearly being driven by home theater and home entertainment software and hardware technologies [...] than by any desire [...] to revolutionize the *theatrical* moviegoing experience'.[7] 'In short', Belton confidently asserts, 'the digital revolution is part of a new corporate synergy within Hollywood, driven by the lucrative home entertainment market'.[8] In the nine years that separate the two publications, these uncertainties became realities, to such an extent that is now rare to find a theatrical projection that *isn't* digital. Furthermore, the majority of the viewing public neither notice nor care. At the same time, developments in technology have enabled the moving image to migrate to multiple sites and platforms, occupying screens of myriad sorts and shifting easily across geographical boundaries. As Janet Harbord observed over a decade ago, 'the designation "film" refers to multiple and proliferating objects'.[9] It mingles with other art forms, vies for our attention amongst a sea of other visual stimuli, resists a stable material reference point and thwarts notions of medium-specificity.

In their introduction to *Screen Dynamics: Mapping the Borders of Cinema*, Gertrude Koch, Volker Pantenberg and Simon Rothöhler emphasise the importance of looking positively into the future rather than lamenting a technological past. 'Rather than cultivating a narrative of decline and focusing exclusively on the dissolution of the film-celluloid-cinema nexus', they state, 'we are interested in the parallel process by which an extended and hugely productive field is opened up'.[10] A similar position is found in Janine Marchessault and Susan Lord's *Fluid Screens, Expanded Cinema*, whose main point of focus is 'the shift from traditional cinematic spectacles to works probing the frontiers of interactive, performative, and networked media'.[11] Interestingly, the term 'expanded cinema' is employed here, not in relation to the live performance of experimental film works, as it has come to be understood, but in its original formulation by Gene Youngblood, as 'an explosion of the frame outward towards immersive, interactive, and interconnected forms of culture'.[12] For Youngblood, expanded cinema relates to expanded forms of consciousness that exist at the intersection between different media.[13]

Whilst acknowledging the new creative directions that are made possible through the unmooring of the cinematic, I would like to dig deeper into what is at stake in this shift for those practices that do not align with digital 'fluidity', but which are anchored to the very specific material conditions of mechanical projection. For many of the artists discussed in the previous chapters, this form of presentation is central to the artistic process, rooted as it is in the distinct physical experience of the film strip and the emphasis on intermittence.[14] Unlike the digital projector, which emits a beam of uninterrupted light, opto-mechanical film functions on the basis of a constant opening and closing of the shutter as each frame of film is illuminated and then dragged away by the claw mechanism, to be replaced by the next frame, and so on, much in the same way as the exposure of film in the camera.[15] Against a backdrop of media convergence and digital plurality, however, arguing the case for what has rapidly become an antiquated mechanical technology is no easy task and few would take it on willingly. Such a pursuit would seem to fly in the face of technological progress and carry with it the negative associations of media fetishism and nostalgia mentioned in the introduction.[16] Yet the continuation of photochemical film projection is vital to sustaining a diversity of artistic practices and aesthetic experiences, and, as we shall see, has a key role to play in the reinvention of film spectatorship and embodied viewing, particularly in its pursuit of new sites and contexts.

Several recent accounts have pointed to the barely-hidden cultural and political agendas underpinning the rapid switch from film to digital in cinema projection and the consequences of this for both cinema history and artistic plurality. In her aptly titled article 'Who wanted the death of analogue projection? Not independent cinemas!' Katia Rossini states:

> By imposing a supposedly irrevocable end of the photochemical era – which is ultimately linked to the birth of cinema itself and its first century of existence – the film industry has decreed that there is now a 'past', a cinema which the industry wants to see relegated to museums, and a 'present', a 'new' cinema made with new technologies, which is allowed to be shown in film theaters equipped with state-of- the-art digital equipment.[17]

This cultural division relates especially to experimental cinema—a field in which 16mm has long been the medium of choice—and results in the further marginalisation of practices that do not conform to the demands of the market.[18] Indeed, as Rossini argues, the sweeping transition from film to digital technology has largely been driven by financial interests:

> let there be no mistake, the nature of the deals behind the extensive operation for replacing opto-mechanical projectors with digital ones had more to do with financial engineering than with any interest in the advancement of culture and the arts.[19]

In France, in particular, generous state subsidies that facilitated the purchase of digital projectors effectively hastened the demise of film projection, without much consideration for the cohabitation of the two technologies. Whilst the transition to digital distribution and exhibition has arguably facilitated increased access by allowing films to travel more easily, it has also led to a restriction in the way that both historical and contemporary avant-garde films circulate, since venues increasingly lack the means to project on film. Gerald Weber from Sixpack Film in Vienna,[20] a key distributor of Austrian experimental film, highlights this situation in plain terms:

> When it comes to distribution, what we realise is that it's more and more the venues and cinemas that can't screen 16mm. They always immediately ask if they can have a digital copy, which somehow always puts pressure on us, as well as the artist, to transfer all the films onto digital.[21]

For curators and exhibitors, this is also a question of cost and convenience—a digital file is clearly easier and cheaper to ship than a reel of film, cutting out the awkward business of coordinating and negotiating physical artefacts with all their material specificities and potentialities for failure. The film print brings with it the added responsibility of caring for a unique object, not impossible to replace, but also not without substantial costs and administrative burden. An inexperienced projectionist or an unmaintained projector can easily turn a screening into a logistical and financial nightmare. The relative ease and reproducibility of digital media in this respect has thrown these qualities of film into relief, with many institutions now opting for the path of least resistance.

In order to address this situation, filmmaker and co-founder of the artist-run L'Abominable Nicolas Rey established, in 2016, a Charter of Cinematographic Projection in the twenty-first century. Entitled filmprojection21, the Charter aims to 'bring to light a critical situation'—that is, the dwindling of skills and expertise related to photochemical film projection, but also the disappearance of dedicated screening spaces and a general failure of cultural organisations to defend the presentation of film on film. Signed by over 1000 individuals and organisations involved in the production, distribution and exhibition of film, the Charter functions as a collective gesture to promote and protect the art of photochemical film projection in ways analogous to Tacita Dean's project savefilm.org.[22] The philosophy of the Charter runs counter to the widely-held view that high definition digital projection is able to achieve the same level of image quality as 16mm or 35mm, therefore rendering these formats unnecessary. In fact, it is not image quality that is at stake here, but the recognition that film projection produces a different kind of experience that relates specifically to the materiality of the medium.[23] Therefore, it is not a question of aesthetic choice, but of technical necessity, as the Charter makes clear:

> To continue to be able to project films in their original format is not a luxury, it is a necessary and logical continuity. It is a unique and incomparable experience, which will also allow filmmakers to continue to create in this medium. Who knows? Perhaps, photochemical film, liberated from the burden of its industrial heft, will live to see a new age, a rebirth linked to its proper specificity, an unforeseen and vibrant moment in its long history.[24]

This statement forges an important connection between the cultures of photochemical film production, with their emphasis on the reinvention and reinvigoration of the medium, and the exhibition contexts that enable its circulation and appreciation. Nonetheless, we must not overlook other challenges such as the cost of producing a screening print in the first place.

Whilst the artist-run film labs provide vital access to equipment and technical expertise, it is increasingly common to find works produced on film—often employing artisanal processes such as those discussed in Chapter 3—being transferred to digital for screening purposes.[25] In most cases, this is a financial decision since striking prints is an expensive business and an investment that is beyond the realms of possibility for some filmmakers, especially those at an early stage of their career. Arts funding programmes exist, but in countries like the UK they are increasingly limited and often geared towards projects that can claim some form of 'digital innovation'. So, whilst Rey is correct in stressing the importance of a cultural infrastructure that sees film projection as a necessity not a luxury, the issue extends to a broader artistic landscape that privileges certain kinds of art-making over others. Given that photochemical film production still carries lingering associations with retro, nostalgia and fetishism, it is clear that some very substantial hurdles remain to be negotiated and alleviated beyond the screening room itself. Cinemas, museums, art institutions and archives all have a key role to play in recognising the cultural value of photochemical film and investing in its future. For film archives, this means restoring film prints and ensuring that they are seen by the public, not locked away in a vault while the digital copy circulates in its place.[26] A shift in perspective that sees film not as a precious relic from the past but as a living art form in the present might encourage a corresponding shift in attitude in relation to funding streams, as well as a more open-minded approach in relation to how technological innovation manifests across a range of media—old as well as new. To quote Alexander Howarth, previously the director of the Austrian Film Museum, the continuation of celluloid 'depends on the social awareness that film cannot simply be supplanted by digital technology'. 'That's why', he states, 'it is so important to discuss [the] differences and characteristics, in order to better communicate and understand on a political and public level why it makes sense to "invest" in the preservation of this system or medium'.[27]

Reinventing Exhibition

What is the future of photochemical film projection? Or rather *where* is this future located? In the publication that followed the 2004 gallery installation of his *Invisible Man*, Mike Hoolboom reflects on a post-digital situation that sees film situated, as the subtitle of the publication suggests, between the art gallery and the movie theatre. 'At this moment', observes Hoolboom, 'there remains modest cadres of motion-pictured citizens dedicated to the pure film experience, busy organizing small festivals and large, or hauling projectors into galleries, or reworking the apparatus so they can present film as film in a performance environment'.[28] A decade on, and the situation appears much the same, with 16mm projectors now also hauled into cinemas for those rare moments of mechanical magic. The sight and chattering sound of the portable Eiki is a recognisable part of the contemporary experimental film experience, offering a boisterous counterpoint to the almost inaudible hum of the digital projector. A mainstay of smaller festivals and pop-up events that screen either historical or contemporary experimental films, the transplanted projector, with its own cordoned-off seating and dedicated operator whose actions become a tangible part of the performance, creates an unintentional installation experience and a heightened sense of material awareness. In many cases, then, the tactile engagements that are so much a part of photochemical working practices are further emphasised by the projection event.[29] As Erika Balsom observes, 'to see a film made on film and exhibited on film has taken on the character of a special event, marked out as an encounter with the original'.[30] There are reasons to celebrate this emphasis on uniqueness, but there are also several ways in which the 'special' nature of film projection can be seen as problematic, not least because it is always in danger of slipping into the rarefied (Fig. 5.1).

A number of filmmakers have held a resistant stance against the move towards greater accessibility and reproducibility that characterises the digital era, marking out a unique space for photochemical projection. Despite his embrace of digital technology in later works such as *Corpus Callosum*

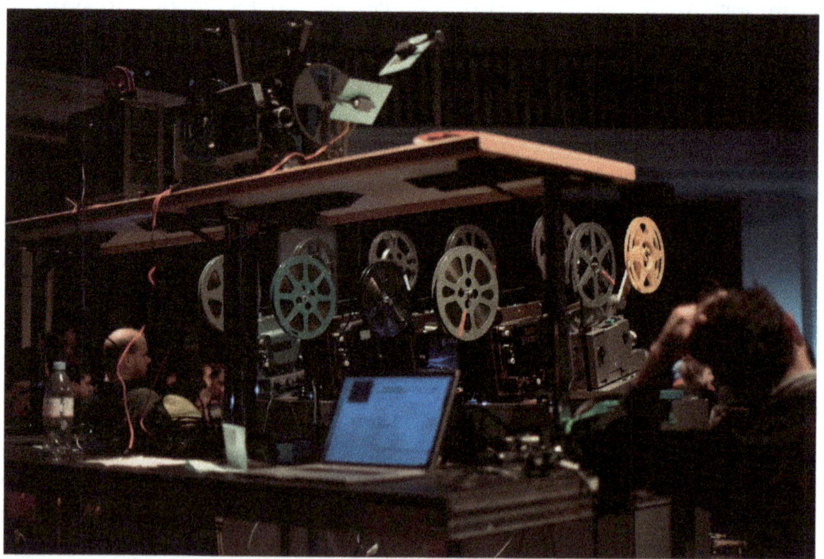

Fig. 5.1 Diffraktion 2017 at LaborBerlin. Expanded film set-up (above: *New Museum of Mankind* by OJOBOCA, and below: *Highview and Cluster Click City Sundays* by Simon Liu) (Photo: Laurence Favre. Image courtesy of LaborBerlin)

(2002), Michael Snow insists on the singular cinematic and photochemical experience of his classic avant-garde film *Wavelength* (1967). Responding to calls to make the film more widely available through home viewing formats such as DVD, Snow released a tongue-in-cheek version entitled *WVLNT (Wavelength for Those Who Don't Have the Time)* (2003). The celebrated 45-minute zoom across a New York loft space is divided into three 15-minute sections, which are superimposed together to create a reinterpreted compact version for a sped-up society. An aesthetic exercise in itself, the new iteration of the film also points to the migration of film to the gallery space, unmooring the spectator from a fixed position whilst also transforming the experience of duration. It is hard to imagine *Wavelength* in the transitory space of the gallery, with all its comings and goings—what Chrissie Illes has referred to as a 'shopping mall mentality'.[31] Even if installed in one of the makeshift black boxes that mimic the cinema experience with its darkened space and set start times, there is something about Snow's film that aligns it with the *dispositif* of cinema.[32] Raymond Bellour has argued that this relates to:

> the lived experience in real time of a cumulative process of remembering and forgetting, each of which nourishes the other, an experience according to which our attentiveness (more or less drifting or concentrated) [...] becomes the testing ground for all the subtle shocks of which any film worthy of the name offers a more or less differentiated variety, according to its own style.[33]

Bellour's fondness for the specificity of the cinema space and Snow's resistance to the circulation of *Wavelength* on any format other than the 16mm print might be perceived as a backward step in the contemporary redefinition of the moving image, which 'reshape[s] cinema's *dispositif* by multiplying screens, exploring other timeframes and intensities, transforming the architecture of the projection room or proposing other relations with spectators'.[34] As I will go on to outline, however, photochemical film projection contributes significantly to this redefinition, activating critical modes of spatial and material engagement in a diversity of screening contexts.

Many of the films discussed in this book were made with the theatrical single-screen projection context in mind, but what constitutes a 'cinema' spans a multitude of settings, from ephemeral DIY spaces and microplexes to one-off screenings—both indoor and outdoor—at festivals of varying sorts. From bookshops and churches to fire stations and ballrooms, cinemas have been constructed from a range of disused and repurposed buildings, ushering audiences into the most unlikely spaces for the collective experience of film projection.[35] Radical exhibition, as Janine Marchessault describes it in her discussion of CineCycle in Toronto, runs through the history of experimental cinema and has been central to the establishment of alternative networks of production, distribution and exhibition.[36] These resistant spatial practices that mark themselves out as non-commodified and often non-hierarchical contribute to the experiential emphasis of photochemical film practice, which increasingly relies on unconventional screening contexts by default. The 'makeshift ambience of the unsanctioned space' thus becomes an important part of the viewing experience, offering an antidote to the more institutionalised sites such as cinemas and art centres.[37] Additionally, argues Donna de Ville, '[t]he informal environment of the microcinema encourages a more direct connection between audience and artist', where the work is often screened in the presence of the filmmakers and usually involves some kind of post-screening discussion.[38] Filmmakers both within and outside the artist-run film lab community frequently organise screenings of work by other artists to facilitate the exchange of ideas but also to provide an exhibition platform that might not otherwise exist in that particular location. This form of creative collaboration and DIY exhibition is partly what sustains a marginal field tending to exist outside of the art world, as well as the more traditional cinema network. In the UK, DIY spaces such as the Cube Cinema in Bristol and the Star and Shadow Cinema in Newcastle have even succeeded in raising funds to purchase the building that houses the cinema, a form of insurance that protects against eviction in a period of rapid gentrification.

Intricately tied to 16mm projection, these radical exhibition practices outside the mainstream provide a context for contemporary photochemical film in the digital era and create possibilities for the continued circulation of historical work, opening up dialogues between cinema past and present. To echo Scott MacDonald on this point, '[g]iven the fact that so much of alternative cinema history has been produced in 16mm, specifically for 16mm exhibition', the important role that these spaces play in maintaining a culture of photochemical film projection cannot and should not be underestimated. 'Fortunately', says MacDonald, 'the current network of microcinemas, run and attended by true lovers of alternative cinema, is helping to keep the full range of film-historical achievement alive'.[39] It is perhaps within this constantly shifting field of DIY exhibition that photochemical film might stake out a future of sorts, liberating it from the 'special' status bestowed on it by the institution.

Bea Haut's 'living loop' single-screen performance *Pending* (2016), which I briefly touched on in Chapter 3, is a lively example of how the performative presence of the 16mm projector can be folded into the work itself, creating a dynamic relationship between the screen, the projector, the audience and the artist. The piece relies on the collective viewing situation while exploding the traditional constellation of filmmaker, apparatus and audience. At the beginning of each screening, Haut appears and explains to the viewers that they are about to become an active part of the film projection. An entire 100ft roll of film is then spooled into their hands and looped carefully backwards and forwards around the screening space, encouraging physical collaborations and material negotiations between friends and strangers alike who are instructed to hold the film above their heads for almost the entire duration of the performance. The film makes a journey through several fingers before being fed into the projector at the back of the room, which in turn animates the characteristically grainy black and white image of the filmmaker holding a ladder in the air. The gestures carried out by the audience at the level of the projection therefore mirror—and are mirrored by—the content of the film. Haut clearly revels in the sense of community that the cinema space is able to bring about, actively rebelling against its association with a passive audience. That the work also requires her presence—not just as a projectionist but as a comic instructor, drawing the audience out of their habitual anonymity and facilitating physical bonds between them—turns the event into something more than just the visual display of photochemical technologies. Seen within the context of Haut's wider body of work, *Pending* is in many ways a nod to Buster Keaton's *Sherlock Jr.* (1924), where the silent-era comic steps directly from the auditorium into the filmic diegesis, thus separating the boundary between the now of the projection and the imagined reality of the represented image. Like Keaton, Haut traverses the two worlds, her live presence in the performance space suddenly mirrored in her projected image that appears on the screen. This performative doubling extends the spatial transgressions of her single-screen films, implicating the projection event and the viewing context in the meta-cinema reflections that to a large extent define her work.

Having been involved in several collectively organised projection events over the years, such as Loophole Cinema (1989–1998) and Analogue Recurring (2012–2017), Haut is especially attuned to the possibilities of radical DIY exhibition practices and the importance of bringing the materiality of the spectatorial encounter to bear on the works themselves.[40] With its exclusive emphasis on photochemical film projection—single-screen, multiple screen and expanded film performance—Analogue Recurring provided a crucial platform for artists working in a marginal form. Like many pop-up films and music events, Analogue Recurring was never just a presentation of films and performances, but an intimate social gathering where audiences could meet artists and discuss the work in a free, non-hierarchical and convivial space outside the dictates of the more regulated and commodified venues.[41] The social event was as important as the projection event, with one feeding into the other. At each Analogue Recurring evening I attended, a simple spread of food—soup, bread, cheese—would be provided for the audience, who gathered around as though at a dinner party, largely unconcerned about when the 'main event' would start. The intimacy of the setting and the emphasis on social interaction both between and during the projections are a defining feature of DIY cinema spaces, bestowing on them a valuable material dimension.[42]

Projection as Installation

The traditional cinema environment—where, as Brakhage ironically observed, '[t]he devout [...] break pop-corn together'—is indeed now one of the least likely places to experience the mechanical film projector.[43] Culturally marginal and relegated to the scrapheap of historical technologies, it finds itself at home amongst the bric-a-brac of radical and resistant DIY communities of recycling, recuperation and reinvention. Trash to one but treasure to another, the portable 16mm projector in particular is a coveted eBay item with a unique cultural status. Its historically symbolic physicality and sculptural presence have drawn it into a wide variety of artistic contexts where it performs its material specificity. Here, installation art—'the art form that cannot quite articulate its name'[44]—meets live film performance or expanded cinema, a field that is similarly 'notoriously difficult to pin down or define'.[45] It is, in fact, the installation-performance axis that increasingly comes to define photochemical film in the digital era.

Whilst there are clearly points of overlap—the American duo Sandra Gibson and Luis Recoder, for instance, engage in both—the most effective way of understanding these two practices is to distinguish between the live and ephemeral *event*, where the artist is physically present with the audience in a one-off situation, and the durational *exhibit*, where a work is installed on a loop or displayed as an object within a gallery space, often without the presence of the artist(s). In the former, the key feature of the artwork is the temporal unfolding of the audio-visual experience over a period of time determined by the performer (generally between 15 and 60 minutes), whereas the latter allows the spectator to control the length and intensity of the interaction. A further distinction can be found in the forms of spatial engagement that activate the formal and conceptual features of the work. Whilst both installation art and expanded cinema work with the architectural specificities of the venues that stage them, one of the defining characteristics of expanded cinema is its chameleon-like ability to adapt to a wide variety of spaces and contexts, from the neutral white cube of the gallery to the grungy basement or club environment. Unlike installation art, which is defined at least in part by its gallery positioning, expanded cinema lacks a proper home, its itinerant nature having more in common with the notion of the radicant that, as I discussed in the previous chapter, characterises photochemical film culture more generally.

Mathilde Nardelli has drawn attention to the 'emergence of what is now an inescapably increasing trend in contemporary art: the pursuit of outmoded technologies'.[46] What she describes as the '"cinematization" of the gallery'[47] is characterised by a material fascination that, in her view, reframes the political gestures of earlier attempts to relocate film apparatus outside the cinema space:

> if artists in the 1960s and 1970s intended to alert the public to the ideological workings of cinematic spectacle via a show of its material objects and dynamics, contemporary artists, it seems, want to lure us with – and are possibly equally lured by – the very spectacle of cinematic materiality, its machines and mechanics.[48]

Nardelli is referring to the development of expanded cinema during a period when 'apparatus theory' began to shape film critical discourse by directing attention towards the ideological foundations of technology and its spatial organisation in a cinema setting.[49] In the UK, this practice emerged primarily through the performances of a group of filmmakers working at the London Film-makers Co-op who called themselves Filmaktion: William Raban, Gill Eatherley, Malcolm Le Grice, Annabel Nicolson and Mike Dunford. Here, the live event of the film projection became a focus in itself and was key to the formulation of an interactive encounter between the filmmaker/artist, the film materials and the audience. Malcolm Le Grice referred to this 'projection situation as material event', stressing that it is 'the only point of actual/material access to the filmic process for the film's viewer'.[50] Rather than being hidden behind the viewer in the soundproofed confines of the projection booth, the material/technological conditions of the cinema experience were made visible, tangible and audible. Addressing the ideological ramifications of the apparatus head-on, these performances broke down the traditional constellation of the viewing situation and foregrounded the illusionist nature of film. In this sense, they extended the structural-materialist agenda from the self-reflexive staging of process within the film frame itself to an experiential awareness of the constituent components—film strip, projector, and the body of the artist.

The gallery space arguably involves a similar form of self-reflexive staging, but Nardelli is right to point out the shift in political emphasis and ideological concerns, which relate directly to the context of technological transition and obsolescence. Here, the focus on materials bestows on outdated technology a special material status—a form of objectification that emphasises film's own 'to-be-looked-at-ness' in the digital era.[51] So long the bearer of fetishised representations, the medium succumbs to an ironic reversal as its mechanical operations, celluloid gleam and intermittent glow indicate an exotic otherness that frames its pastness as a form of beauty.[52] Standing on pristine plinths or polished floors, the film projectors of the gallery installation often seem awkwardly out of place, whilst the looping mechanism that removes the need for a human operator bestows on them a ghostly quality. Yet these dislocations can have a powerful critical function, asking us to question our relationship to outmoded objects and technologies and to see their mechanical specificities in a new light.

In the work of British artist Louisa Fairclough, 16mm projectors are used to describe emotional intensity through layers of bodily symbolism and corporeal communication. *Absolute Pitch* (2014), a collaboration with the composer Richard Glover, takes a linocut print by the artist's deceased sister Hetta Fairclough as source material, interpreting the original as both a sonic and a spatial score. Five projectors with out of focus lenses throw diffuse spots of colour onto the walls of the gallery accompanied by the sound of five different choristers who sing five notes on a pentatonic scale. The film loops criss-cross through the space, visualising the sonic harmony and dissonance and creating a material dialogue between the projectors, which appear to be singing to each other in a game of call and response. In the semi-darkness of the space, one has the feeling of witnessing a private conversation full of internal drama, the projectors taking on psychological depth in the spectatorial encounter. As Fairclough describes:

> The projected colour is that which the chorister visualised as he sung with eyes closed. He sustains the single pitch until his voice falters. There is a corporeality and vulnerability as you hear the boys' breath and the grain of each voice. This is reinforced by the varying heights of plinths with each projector's lens as the height of the chorister's mouth, the plinths and projectors thereby enabling an anthropomorphic reading.[53]

Although it has the quality of a live performance, Fairclough's installation is a perfect example of how the physical absence of the artist enhances the expressive power of the work. Released from human interference, these machines can be read as activating each other through an unseen interconnected energy or agency that imbues their material presence with an affective resonance. The sounds spill into the space, bounce off the walls and inhabit the body of the spectator in a powerful exploration of shared physicality (Fig. 5.2).

In the second iteration of the work—*Absolute Pitch II*—the five filmstrips contain the same note as sung by a different chorister, inviting the viewer to tune into the subtleties of difference in pitch and texture. The lenses are this time completely removed from the projectors' bodies, causing the colours to bleed into one another and flood the gallery space. Whilst the presence of the projectors as outdated objects from a mechanical era is clearly a contributing factor in the material fabric of the installation, the sculptural details and tightly choreographed articulations of the piece go beyond the fetishistic gaze. Emphasis rests, here, on how technologies can be repurposed and reimagined to create a multi-layered and tactile rendering of interior space that responds to the installation context.[54]

Can People See Me Swallowing (2014) demonstrates how film projection can imagine space in complex ways. The site-specific piece was

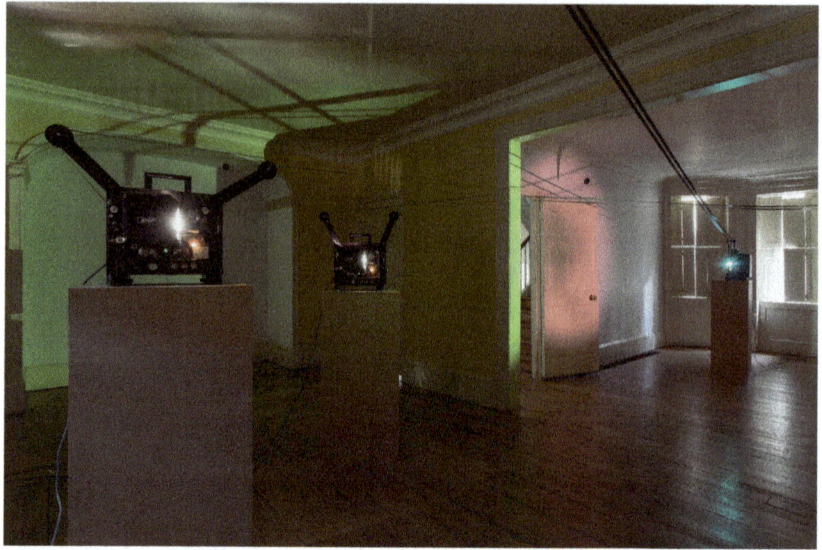

Fig. 5.2 Installation view of *Absolute Pitch II*, Louisa Fairclough, 2014 (Photo: Oskar Proctor. Image courtesy of the artist and Danielle Arnaud)

conceived and designed especially for the stairwell at Spike Island in Bristol, where it was installed for one weekend during the Open Studios public event. Fairclough again uses one of her sister's artworks, this time a pencil word-drawing that delicately articulates the physical experience of anxiety and the highs and lows of living with mania and depression. Central to the drawing is a cotton thread that winds around the page, culminating in four points that each state 'Oh God', while at the centre sit the words 'can people see me swallowing?' Pressed under a laminate covering, where small bubbles of air sit trapped between two surfaces, the drawing seems itself to be suffocating. In order to interpret the work as a projector installation, Fairclough worked again with Glover to design a vocal score that transformed the textual articulations in the drawings into different sounds, sung by Karen Middleton. Four projectors emit a high-pitched incantation of 'Oh God', the voices microtonally apart so that they 'aurally scrape against each other'. One projector emits a deep drone and from another 'can people see me swallowing' is sung at the end of a breath. Approximating the sense of pressure and constraint in the original piece, the voice takes on a vulnerability as the breath struggles to contain the phrase in its entirety.[55] The different sounds are represented through alternating black and transparent film. 'What happens', observes Fairclough, 'is that the projector becomes the body and the lens the mouth'. When the projector sings, a beam of light pours through the space, and just as the loops of film are spun up, down and across the stairwell, so too do the voices 'fall together chorally'.[56]

The key difference between this work and *Absolute Pitch* is the harnessing of a particular space—the stairwell—as an expressive sonic element that is woven into the embodied design of the projector performance. Fairclough refers to the stairwell as a throat, both in its architectural layout and its sonic resonance. 'A voice box in its own right', it becomes an instrument, whilst also functioning as the key conceptual focal point of the work—the anxious swallowing that features in the original drawing.[57] Materiality operates, then, on several interrelated levels—the stairwell itself, the sonic materiality of the voice as it spreads throughout the space, the physical presence of the film loops and the corresponding shadow play on the surrounding walls, the luminous texture of the projector beam, the 'bodies' of the projectors, and, of course, the bodies of the exhibition visitors.[58] Fairclough describes her aesthetic attachment to 16mm film technology through reference to what are otherwise perceived as restraints or weaknesses. 'When I started to use 16mm projectors as core elements in sound, I remember being asked why I would do that because the sound is so bad on 16mm! It's precisely the rawness of the sound quality that interests me'.[59] That the words emitted from these projector mouths are almost intelligible expresses precisely the ambiguity and vulnerability that is at the heart of Fairclough's material explorations.

Sandra Gibson and Luis Recoder demonstrate a similar investment in the reinvention of projection, and their diverse body of installation and performance work draws attention to the creative potential of photochemical film technology as an artistic subject in its own right. Working together since 2000, the duo systematically deconstructs the projector's functionality and its intended use as an intermittent mechanical device that reanimates a sequence of still photograms as moving images. Their attempts to reframe and reimagine the art of projection give rise to radically new perspectives, where the 'idea' of cinema is juxtaposed with a sculptural analysis of its constituent components. *Threadbare* (2013), for example, features a 16mm projector, with film reels attached, entirely wrapped in the celluloid that would normally be flowing through its mechanisms. The element of non-functionality is in some ways a playful nod to the early object-assemblages of the Dada movement, such as Man Ray's *Cadeau* (1921) and *Indestructible Object* (1923), which demonstrate a process of defamiliarisation and a desire to disrupt and reconfigure our relationship with material things. Resonances can be found particularly with *The Enigma of Isidore Ducasse* (1920), where Man Ray wraps a sewing machine in a blanket and ties it with string. The association of the film projectors with sewing machines—both intermittent mechanical devices—has been staged in a number of projection performances, from Annabel Nicolson's *Reel Time* (1973) to Mary Stark's more recent *Film as Fabric* (2015).[60] What distinguishes Gibson and Recoder's work is the arresting of movement, the absence of light and the uncharacteristic silence, the film material stifling the mechanical sounds by rendering the mechanisms inoperable. *Threadbare* is at once visually striking and conceptually elaborate, asking the viewer to consider film materials and mechanics from a radically altered perspective. Employing the technique of juxtaposition, it reclaims the physical properties of the projector through a different kind of sensuous experience (Fig. 5.3).

In *Light Spill* of 2005, a work that has become emblematic of photochemical projection as gallery installation, a single 16mm projector without a take-up reel spits film onto the gallery floor, which builds up into a growing mound of waste. Jonathan Walley has described the work as subjecting film to 'death by projection', a concept explored in Chapter 2 of this book and demonstrated particularly in D. N. Rodowick's view that cinema is inherently 'an autodestructive medium [...] Each passage of frames through a projector – the very machine that gives filmophanic/projected life to the moving image – advances a process of erosion that will eventually reduce the image to nothing'.[61] In Gibson and Recoder's installation, however, the image is already rendered nothing due to the removal of the shutter mechanism. Deprived of one of its most basic technical functions, the projector fails to present a legible image, instead of throwing onto the wall or screen opposite a luminous abstract blur. For John Hanhardt, the piece 'negates the power of the cinematic through its codified languages and returns us to the elemental experience of light and celluloid'.[62] But the significance of the installation arguably extends beyond a contemplation of the essential components of cinematic technology and the negation of an identifiable image; it cleverly references the contemporary association of photochemical film with waste, the accumulation of celluloid on the gallery floor acting as

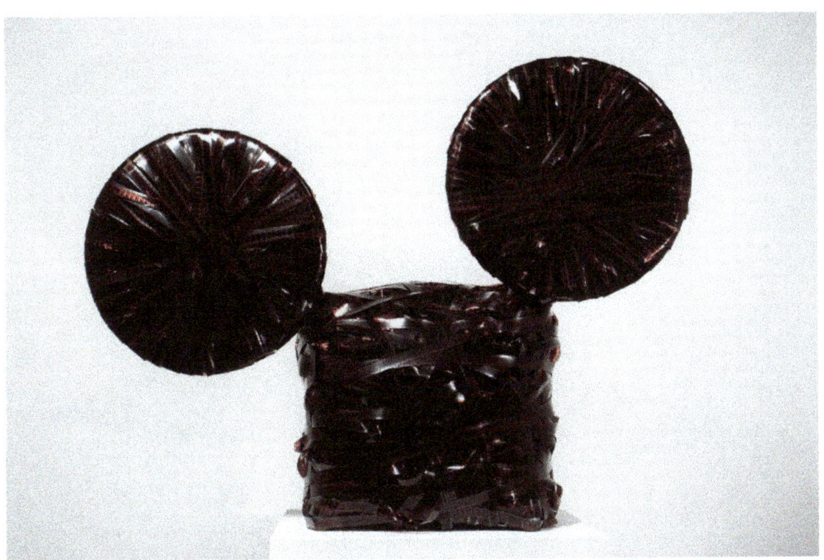

Fig. 5.3 *Threadbare*, Sandra Gibson and Luis Recoder, 2013. Installation view, Gibson + Recoder Studio, Brooklyn, New York (Photo: Rachel Hamburger. Image courtesy of the artists)

a metaphor for its cultural status in the digital era. Surplus footage from a variety of sources depending on the location of the installation is recycled in a way that stages its own material excess. Like *Threadbare*, *Light Spill* revels in the visual spectacle of the celluloid rubbish heap but it also negates the idea of film as something 'precious'. The piece is interesting precisely because it celebrates the reinvention of projection whilst using the very discourse that surrounds it as a springboard for new artistic directions[63] (Fig. 5.4).

Contemporary Expanded Cinema and the Cinema of Attractions

If the gallery has developed as the site of reconceptualisation of the filmic apparatus, throwing into question the traditional notion of cinema through a deconstruction of its materials and meanings, then the

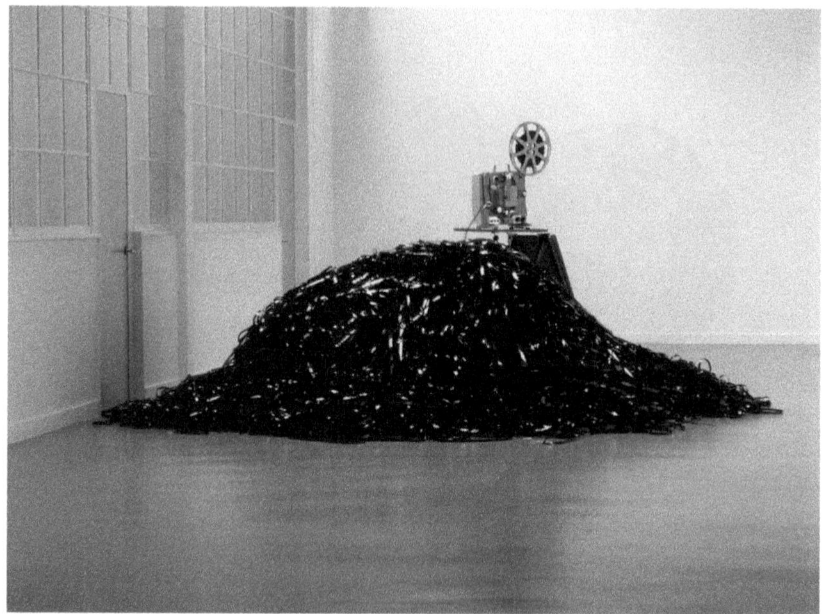

Fig. 5.4 *Light Spill*, Sandra Gibson and Luis Recoder, 2005. Installation view, 'Borderline Behaviour: Drawn Towards Animation', 25 January–18 March 2007, TENT, Rotterdam (Photo: Roel Meelkop. Image courtesy of the artists and TENT)

field of expanded cinema has activated this in a live and increasingly visceral register. The past few years have seen the reassessment and restaging of a number of historical expanded cinema performances. In 2012, to mark the opening of The Tanks—a new space for installation and performance—the Tate Modern gallery in London hosted a fifteen-week programme of performances and events entitled 'Art in Action', including several expanded cinema pieces from the 1970s. 'Interrupting Light' featured works by Guy Sherwin, Tony Hill and Gill Eatherley, amongst others. The gallery is, however, one of the least likely places to come across the recent wave of expanded film work, much of which emerges from or overlaps with the alternative scene of film labs and microcinemas.[64] Walley speaks of the synergy between recent expanded cinema and the artisanal forms of film production that characterise contemporary engagements with photochemical film, arguing that these performances 'put film's mechanical nature on display, and cast the filmmaker as a kind of artisan/inventor/do-it-yourself-er who has mastered all of film's mechanical, optical and chemical facets'.[65]

Indeed, the emergence of one of the first artist-run film labs—MTK in Grenoble—coincided with the resurgence of multi-projector film performance, with the collective Cellule d'intervention Metamkine (filmmakers Christophe Auger and Xavier Quérel and the sound artist Jérôme Noetinger) folding handmade interventions into live manipulations.[66] The lab functioned initially as a hub for the production of materials that would be used in these performances, which consistently drew attention to the specificities of film, often through its live physical transformation and destruction. As the labs grew in number so too did the exploration of artisanal practice as an immersive and frequently spectacular sensorial event. The alchemical spirit that drives the Double Negative collective in Montreal, for example, is channelled into the multi-projector presentations of Karl Lemieux, whose hand-processed and manually manipulated images accompany the live performances of underground rock band Godspeed You! Black Emperor.[67] Mike Rollo points out that these projections 'enhance the immersive nature of these bands' live musical performances'. They are 'not simply backdrops', he states, but rather offer 'synergistic visual content that responds to the music'.[68] Other key examples of expanded film emerging from the artist-run film labs include the work of Stefano Canapa from L'Abominable in Paris, Aurélie Percevault from MIRE in Nantes, Adriana Vila and Luis Macías from Crater Lab in Spain, Elena Pardo from Laboratorio Experimental de Cine in Mexico City, OJOBOCA (Juan David González Monroy and Anja Dornieden) from Labor Berlin, Britt Al-Busultan from Filmverkstaden in Vaasa and Simon Liu and Josh Lewis from Negativland in New York.

This contemporary phenomenon echoes in many ways the expanded cinema performances of the 1970s, but material self-reflexivity is now framed by discourses of obsolescence and a renewed awareness of film's mechanical possibilities in the digital era. In his analysis of several works by Gibson and Recoder, Bradley Eros, Sally Golding and Bruce McClure, Walley argues that '[w]hile "expanded cinema" originally referred to a practically unlimited field of materials and forms, contemporary work in that mode has narrowed its scope, returning the film medium to a privileged status'.[69] The element of performance is more consciously choreographed to incorporate an awareness of film's 'thingness'—its material presence and potential for reinvention in the moment of projection. Emphasising the bulky analogue equipment and various mechanical paraphernalia, contemporary expanded film performance aims to get under the spectator's skin—it is loud, messy, chaotic, often improvised and susceptible to failure. It is perceptually overwhelming, physically immersive and materially abrasive, overlapping with sound or noise art to create multi-layered audio-visual environments. The employment of intense and immersive sonic compositions to enhance the sensorial impact of the material interventions is an increasingly familiar characteristic in recent expanded cinema, with most filmmakers collaborating closely with a sound artist in the live event.

British-Australian artist Sally Golding is a notable exception, her works already incorporating sonic and visual elements in the artisanal production process. In performances such as *Ghost – Loud + Strong*, *Super Grotesquerie* and *Composted Material*, Golding works with what she calls 'darkroom compositions', where sonic fragments, transferred to 16mm using an Auricon camera for producing optical sound, are recomposed and contact printed in an elaborate and time-consuming process. Golding relies on a combination of 'sonic memory' in compiling these sound collages in the dark, which then (e)merge with the responsive nature of the live performance. Harnessing chance, error and discovery, the work comes into being through the element of performativity. 'I'm always constructing the work on the spot to an improvised composition', she explains, 'but I'm developing and learning the work through the performance itself'.[70] Golding weaves together material from multiple sources, using archival images and found sounds, which she then further manipulates during the live event. Dual projections of differing sizes create layers of flickering images, often alternating between blocks of black and clear frames in a manner similar to Bruce McClure. The quality of intermittence already emphasised through the flicker effect is pushed further by the use of various forms of interruption and manipulation of the projector beam. Physically moulding and obscuring it with her hands, the artist plays with the light, which manifests as organic and unpredictable formal arrangements on the screen. In many of the works, these gestures are accompanied by a repetitive strobe light that is operated at different speeds to choreograph different levels of intensity in relation to the projected images.

Taking the audience to their perceptual limits, a flashlight is employed at various moments in the performance, emitting a blinding light to a corresponding high-pitched noise. In Golding's sensorially challenging environments, one has the feeling of participating in some kind of scientific experiment on bodily endurance. Indeed, as the artist describes, both corporeal and psychological responses play a central role in her explorations of sound and light:

> I'm thinking about film performance in relation to conditions of liveness and participation. My interest in materiality relates to the psychology of sensation and perception and so I use everything on the spectrum from minimal to excessive abstraction of light and sound. This is a way of picking through the way light and sound describe the materiality of perception.[71]

The bric-a-brac of analogue materials that make up Golding's performances is always, therefore, harnessed to the exploration of the materiality of projection and the multiple constellations of light, sound, objects and bodies (Fig. 5.5).

Vicky Smith has argued that '[o]ne aspect of expanded cinema that has persisted across the decades is the presence of the artist visibly orchestrating the film production in ways that are not ordinarily evident in industrial cinema'.[72] Despite the absence of the body from Gidal's theory of structural/materialism, it played a significant role in the way artists interacted with film technology during the 1970s, and it was within the field of expanded cinema that the body fully became part of the materialist encounter, alongside projectors, filmstrips and other technological paraphernalia—all 'primary signifiers in their own right'.[73] Le Grice's account of his *Horror Film 1* (1970) neglects to mention the centrality of his own body in the constellation of 'simple loops of changing colour, directly-cast shadows and moving projectors', but it is the physical performance that activates the technological demystification and directs attention to formal transformations.[74] Naked to the waist and with his back to the audience, the artist places himself at the centre of the work, revealing the ripples of performance art that had emerged a decade earlier. So crucial to the craft-based approach to filmmaking that I have outlined in the previous chapters, but largely invisible in the film itself, bodily intervention is brought directly into the live projection event alongside the physicality of the technology, where the audible chattering of the projector(s) provides a corresponding layer of tangibility that fills the viewing space.

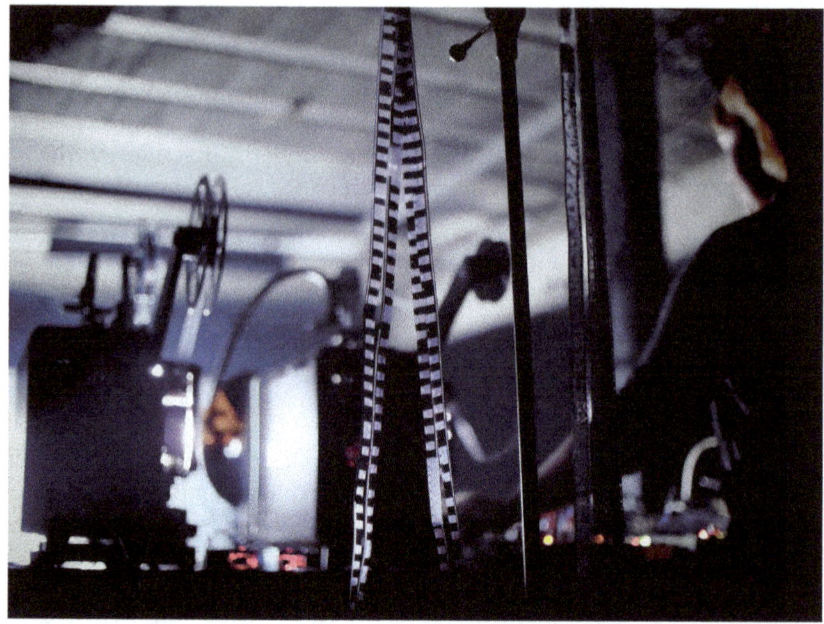

Fig. 5.5 Documentation of *Ghost - Loud + Strong*, performance by Sally Golding at Cable Festival, Nantes, 2016 (Photo: Pierre Acobas. Image courtesy of the artist)

What seems to most distinguish contemporary expanded cinema is the relationship between the presence of the artist as an analogue magician and the visual spectacle being played out in front of the audience. Tom Gunning's concept of the 'cinema of attractions'—an approach to pre-narrative cinema that rescued it from a 'primitive' framing—provides a useful starting point for thinking about this updated form of 'exhibitionist cinema'.[75] The attractions model posited that rather than viewing this period as simply a stepping stone to a more sophisticated form of storytelling, it is possible to see it as establishing a celebration of cinema's visual qualities that 'goes underground' with the arrival and subsequent dominance of narrative codes and conventions after 1906. The exhibitionist tendency of this early cinema is manifested through self-conscious 'acts of showing', which invite the audience to revel in the magical possibilities of the medium. Gunning argues that this cinema was a key source of inspiration for the early avant-garde, also founded on the exploration of film's visual qualities outside the confines of narrative structure.

One of the most appealing features of Gunning's cinema of attractions is its historical portability—its potential to find applicability well beyond the period about which it speaks. But contemporary uses of the attractions model tend to focus on the spectacle of new technology, predictably homing in on digital special effects, interactivity and immersion, and drawing parallels with the idea of novelty so present at the beginning of cinema.[76] The digital era certainly lends itself to comparisons with the early cinematic period, when the filmic apparatus and the simplest of cinematic trickery was a source of amazement amongst both makers and spectators. But equally interesting and far less frequently discussed is the spectacle of the outmoded or the novelty of the old reframed as new and staged through performances that, as Walley has argued, 'partake of a kind of illusionism and an indulgence in visual pleasure that distinguishes them from many earlier works of expanded cinema'.[77]

Greg Pope's *Cipher Screen* (2009–2014) demonstrates most effectively the connection between contemporary expanded work and Sergei Eisenstein's principle of visceral shocks that underpins Gunning's cinema of attractions. The work uses two 16mm projectors with black film loops and a live sound feed. As the film moves through the projector and onto a purpose-built operating table, Pope attacks it with a variety of mechanical tools, scratching, cutting, puncturing and drilling. These interventions are experienced moments later as abstract images on the screen. As the successive layers of physical manipulation build towards a vibrating visual field, the amplified brutality creates a corresponding looping and echoing auditory onslaught, transferring to the body of the spectator the violence inflicted on the filmstrip. Unlike the tendency mentioned earlier to pair the visuals with a separate sound composition, *Cipher Screen* uses the physical interventions on the film as a starting point for a steadily intensifying soundscape. Situated towards the back of the auditorium and hovering at the edge of the spectator's visual field, Pope's presence is central to the affective power of the piece. In her account of *Cipher Screen* at Tate Britain in 2014, Catherine Elwes describes the specific constellation of artist-as-performer, material excess and visceral impact:

> The artist looked like a demented goldsmith as he frantically brutalised the filmstrip, the emulsion dust from the grinding action rising eerily through

> the projection beam. The banshee screeching increased, the tension grew as the film rose to a crescendo of crackling sounds and strobing abstractions.[78]

Cipher Screen highlights the fundamental paradox at the heart of the film material: the images produced result from the erasure of the emulsion from the surface of the strip (Fig. 5.6).

As Pope moves from scalpel to power tools, the excessive nature of the intervention shifts into a space of absurdity, gradually drawing the spectator's attention away from the screen and towards the shadowy figure of the drill-yielding Pope. What is this maniac up to? What is going on? What is the relationship between what I'm seeing, hearing and smelling and the baffling acts of mechanical labour at the back of the room? The audience becomes animated by the feeling of an impending catastrophe, as the image on screen starts to fall away and the film eventually snaps. At the heart of the performance is, of course, the wilful destruction of celluloid, 'an act of avant-garde vandalism', to quote Luis Recoder, that

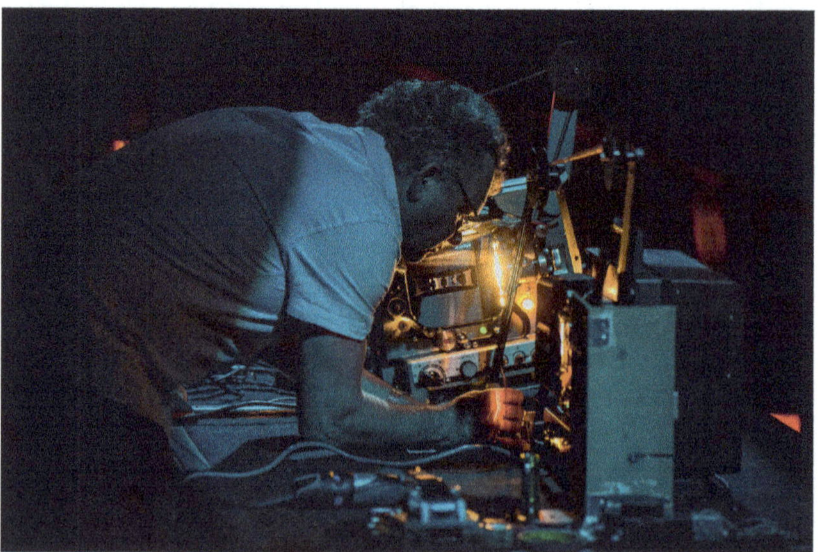

Fig. 5.6 Documentation of *Cipher Screen*, performance by Greg Pope at Inmute Festival, Athens, 2015 (Image courtesy of the artist)

runs through experimental film history, from the Lettrists to Paul Sharits and Jürgen Reble to numerous contemporary examples of expanded cinema (particularly Metamkine in France).[79] There are obvious overtones of Isidore Isou's *Traité de bave et d'éternité* (1951), a film I discussed briefly in Chapter 2, where repetitive forms of surface intervention such as scratching and painting question the authority of the image, 'put[ting] into practice an alternative politics of looking'.[80] Isou's conception of an amplic phase (*phase amplique*) and a chiselled phase (*phase ciselante*) in cinema take on a very literal resonance in relation to Pope's performance. Whilst earlier instances of physical destruction can be linked to the rejection of cinematic illusionism and the problems of representation, recent examples seem more directed towards a heightened awareness of film's physicality and its throwaway status. An abject object, it refuses to disappear, hangs in a state of liminality and disturbs the capitalist drive to upgrade, discard and move on (Fig. 5.7).

Another notable expanded film performance that draws on the avant-garde tradition via the spectacle is *Parallaxe* (2017) by the Paris-based collective Nominoë (Emmanuel Lefrant, Nicolas Berthelot and Stéphane de Courcy). Using four 16mm projectors mounted onto specially built tracks and a combination of three screens, one of them transparent, the trio creates a choreographed moving projection event. *Parallaxe* refers to a visual phenomenon whereby an object appears differently depending on the position from which it is viewed, and the performance explores various optical effects through the specific positioning and overlapping of the four images as they slide across and between surfaces. In its emphasis on geometry and space, the performance feels like a descendent of the 1920s graphic animation films by Hans Richter, Walter Ruttmann and Viking Eggeling. Early examples of intermediality, these paintings in motion, such as Richter's *Rhythmus 21* (1921) and *Rhythmus 23* (1923),

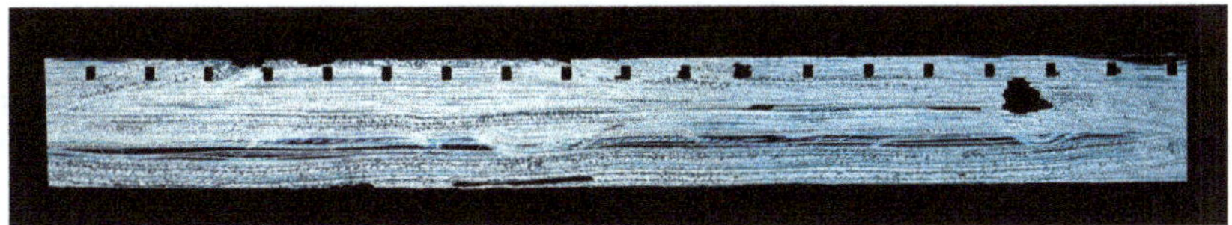

Fig. 5.7 Section of a filmstrip used in the performance of *Cipher Screen* by Greg Pope (Image courtesy of the artist)

drew on the temporal nature of film and the ability to construct an illusion of depth on a flat plane by showing simple shapes getting bigger and smaller and moving in and out of the frame. By removing the emotional drama that dominated narrative cinema, Richter claimed to cultivate a distinctly cinematic form of perception and feeling based on graphic relations.[81] Nominoë's *Parallaxe* revives these ideas in a contemporary context, incorporating an element of theatricality markedly different to the one rejected by Richter. For if Richter's vision of cinematic expression was one of reduction, Nominoë pursues an aesthetic of expansion by incorporating elaborate bodily gestures into a gradually unfolding kinetic spectacle.

Uprooting the projector from its traditionally static position is no easy task, given the weight of the machinery and potential disruption to the projection mechanism. For this reason, very few expanded performances incorporate mobility into the projection event, but the trio gets around this by transposing the technology associated with film production—the tracks on which cameras move—to the performance space. In doing so, this space takes on the co-ordinates of a shooting set, transgressing the boundaries between the normally distinct phases and spaces of cinema production and consumption. Crouched on the ground just below the screen, the three performers sweep backwards and forwards and side-to-side in a majestic mechanical ballet (or '*ballet mécanique*', the title of Fernand Léger's 1924 film, which was surely not far from the artists' minds). The intricate geometric compositions registered on the film—lines, cubes, rectangular forms—take on a three-dimensional quality due to the exact spatial positioning of the screens and projectors, eliciting a sense of awe and amazement that is only enhanced by the physical performance. The eye shifts between stage and screen(s), attention focused not just on the spectacle of the image, but also its coming into being, as Peter Gidal might describe it. Woven together through the electronic soundscapes of Michalis Moschoutis, *Parallaxe* is a powerful example of how contemporary artists are forging new ways of working with analogue film in a live context. The element of spectacle—revealing, showing—draws on its historical roots, but also forces a contemplation of how 'old' materials can perform their very distinct physicality in effective and *affective* ways (Fig. 5.8).

If contemporary expanded cinema is characterised by both material and sensory excess, then a recent performance by four female artists from the Filmwerkplaats lab in Rotterdam is the ultimate embodiment of this.

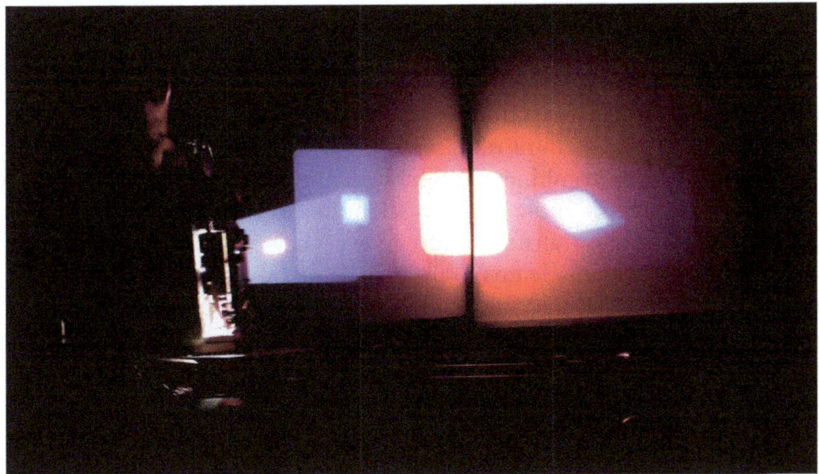

Fig. 5.8 Documentation of *Parallaxe*, performed by Nominoë (Image courtesy of Emmanuel Lefrant)

First performed at the Rotterdam Film Festival in 2016, *Light Leaks* is a highly staged, high-octane piece of photochemical film magic, accompanied another dynamic and immersive electronic soundtrack by Ji Youn Kang that responds to the images in real time. As with much contemporary expanded film performance, the piece follows an arc of gradually building intensity that reaches a point of full-on visual and aural spectacle, an adrenaline rush of excess, and then tails off into an ending suggestive of physical exhaustion or mechanical malfunction. In ways similar to Nominoë's *Parallaxe*, the four performers (Esther Urlus, Lichun Tseng, Nan Wang and Judith van de Made) explore the effects of different spatial positioning, angling the projector beam in such a way that it spreads across the wall. This spatial manipulation of the regular rectangular shape of the projection can be found in a multitude of expanded film works since the 1970s—William Raban's *Wave Formations* (1978), for example, is a five projector piece where adjacent projections of solid red, green and blue are criss-crossed with the beams of two projectors placed next to the wall. In *Light Leaks*, several 16mm projectors are placed throughout the performance space, whilst at the centre of the room a row of three modified slide projectors, developed and operated by Wang, display magnified images of mechanisms spinning and turning in coloured liquid. These handmade constructions relate to an earlier project, in which Wang worked through ways to visualise dust and other minute debris that emerges from the inter-relationship between human and non-human bodies.[82] The motorised 'mini dust sculptures' that are constructed to spin at different speeds combine analogue and digital technology using early technological patents and a modern scientific curiosity.[83] Returning us to Man Ray's inventive transformation of everyday phenomena such as salt and pepper into cinematic rayogrammes, Wang opens up the performativity of matter in a live multimedia context and invites a tactile immersion in the familiar made strange[84] (Fig. 5.9).

This element of the performance has overtones of a mad scientist revelling in some new chemical invention, and the oddly realist quality of the

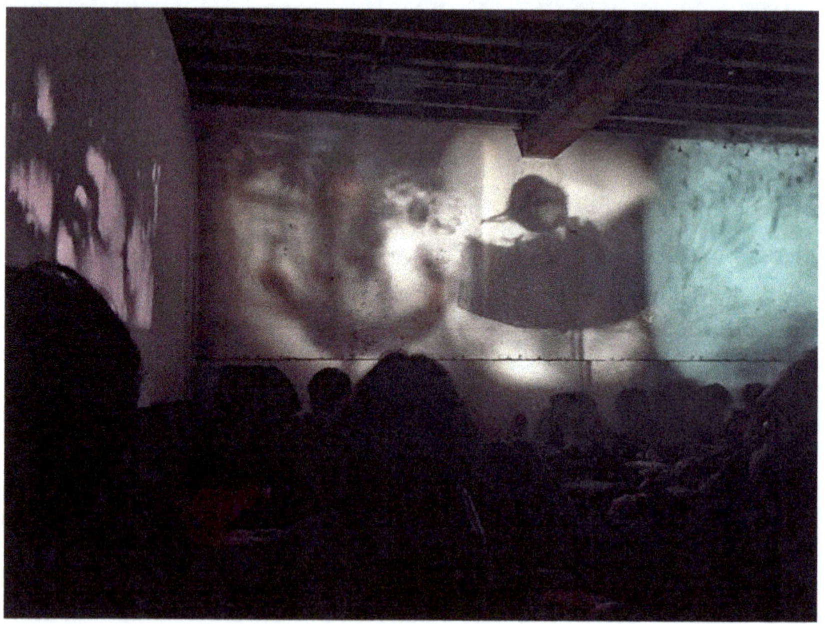

Fig. 5.9 Documentation of *Light Leaks*, performed by Filmwerkplaats at the Rotterdam International Film Festival, January 2016 (Image courtesy of Nan Wang)

magnified details contrasts with the abstract flickering of the 16mm projections. Although the other performers are less 'on stage' than Wang, the sudden appearance of a projector here or a light there makes the spectator aware of their nimble movement around the darkened room, drawing the eye to hidden corners and folding the entire space into the choreography of material details. Like the members of Nominoë, the Filmwerkplaats performers create a dialogue between the static and mobile positions of the cameras, whilst exploring the visceral effects of overlapping projections across three walls. *Light Leaks* had a second outing at the Bains Argentiques film labs meeting in Nantes in July of the same year. Despite the very different spatial co-ordinates of the venue, the work lost none of its ability to plunge the audience into a dazzling play of light and sound. The relationship between visual spectacle, technical invention, sensory immersion and corporeal implication is what makes this expanded piece such a powerful articulation of the multiple potentialities of photochemical film projection.

The death of cinema in its traditional form—the mechanical projection of moving images in a darkened theatre—has led to a reconceptualisation of the screen and the modes of spectatorship associated with it. Mobile bodies and fluid screens increasingly define our contemporary media landscape, opening up new material situations and projection events. Whilst photochemical film projection has disappeared from most commercial screening spaces, it has re-emerged in new contexts and in reinvented configurations, from gallery rooms to radical DIY spaces and from contemplative installation to sensorially immersive performance. It finds its way into environments as diverse as museums and underground clubs, as an 'old' medium carrying the aura of times past or as a lively participant in the material fabric of music concerts. But whilst this plurality offers exciting possibilities, the future of photochemical film as an art form depends largely on the nourishing of infrastructures that value and support its material specificities, both alongside and in dialogue with digital technology. The role of cinemas, galleries, art centres, archives, higher education institutions and funding agencies is crucial in this respect. There is much to be lost in the removal of artistic diversity. It is our cultural responsibility to ensure that future generations have the possibility not only to work with film as artists, but also to experience it as audiences—preserved or reinvented, on film and through film.

Notes

1. MONO NO AWARE in New York will host its 11th festival in 2019, whilst the Baltic Analogue Lab in Riga has run the Process festival since 2016. In 2017, Filmwerkplaats launched a biennial festival of analogue film and sound called Back to the Future Project, whilst MIRE organised the second edition of Prisme in 2019. Diffraktion, LaborBerlin's showcase of work by lab members and friends held its 9th edition in 2019. Other labs organise regular screening programmes and one-off festivals throughout the year, many of which are focused on creating historical parallels with contemporary practice, emerging from and feeding into the work of lab members. A founding member of Bristol Experimental and Expanded Film (BEEF), Vicky Smith curated a three-part series of women in animation, which took a broad historical perspective whilst providing a panorama of technical approaches: 'Go Go Go: Women in Experimental Animation', 8 May, 13 June, 11 July 2019, Cube Cinema, Bristol.
2. Bourikas, a filmmaker and curator, established the artist-run film lab LabA in Athens.
3. Catherine Elwes, *Installation and the Moving Image* (London and New York: Wallflower Press, 2015), pp. 7–8.
4. A more exhaustive survey of expanded cinema can be found in Jonathan Walley's *Cinema Expanded: Avant-Garde Film in the Age of Intermedia* (Oxford: Oxford University Press, 2020).
5. Malcolm Turvey, Ken Jacobs, Annette Michelson, Paul Arthur, Brian Frye and Chrissie Illes, 'Roundtable: Obsolescence and Avant-Garde Film', *October*, Vol. 100, 2002; Malcolm Turvey, Ken Jacobs, Federico Windhausen, Flo Jacobs, Mark Street, Lynne Sachs and Luis Recoder, 'Roundtable on Digital Experimental Filmmaking', *October*, Vol. 137, 2011.
6. In Malcolm Turvey et al., 'Roundtable: Obsolescence and Avant-Garde Film', p. 122.
7. John Belton, 'Digital Cinema: A False Revolution', *October*, Vol. 100, 2002, p. 100.
8. Ibid.
9. Janet Harbord, *The Evolution of Film: Rethinking Film Studies* (Cambridge: Polity Press, 2007), p. 1.
10. Gertrude Koch, Volker Pantenberg and Simon Rothöhler, *Screen Dynamics: Mapping the Borders of Cinema* (Vienna: Austrian Film Museum and SYNEMA, 2012), p. 6.
11. Janine Marchessault and Susan Lord (eds.), *Fluid Screens, Expanded Cinema* (Toronto: University of Toronto Press, 2008), p. 6.
12. Ibid., p. 7.
13. Gene Youngblood, *Expanded Cinema* (London: Studio Vista, 1970).

14. The intermittent nature of mechanical projection has been at the heart of recent discussions about the difference between film and video. In a debate organised by L'Abominable during the 2013 edition of Cinema du Réel, for example, Nicolas Rey stated: 'Souvent, on parle de la résolution, de la finesse de l'image, du grain ou de la dimension organique du photochimique. Personellement, je suis assez sensible à la question du battement. Quand on voit un film, succession d'image de noir due à l'obturateur, l'écran est un noir la moitié du temps, même si ce n'est pas perçu consciemment' [We often talk about resolution, the quality of the image, the grain or the organic nature of the photochemical. Personally, I'm quite sensitive to the question of flicker. When we watch a film, with the intermittent black of the shutter, the screen is black for half of the time, even if this is not consciously perceived]. See also Nicolas Rey and Martine Derain, *Digital(e): L'argentique à l'heure du numérique* (Marseille: Editions Commune, 2015), p. 34.
15. The mechanical similarities between the film camera and the film projector are explored in Peter Miller's *Projector Obscura* (2005), a work that can also be read as a reflection on the specificity of the cinema space. Focusing on seven different cinemas—The Biograph, Gene Siskel Film Center, Anthology Film Archives, Gateway, MFA-Boston, Coolidge Corner and Harvard Film Archive—Miller uses the projector as a camera, running the unexposed film through the mechanism with enough light for the screen opposite to register as an image. If the film is in some way a contemplation on the end of cinema, it also takes us back to its beginnings in a nod to the Lumière brothers' first cine-cameras that were also projectors.
16. This issue is dealt with at length in the series of discussions, exchanges and conversations between curators and archivists, brought together in Paolo Cherchi Usai, David Francis, Alexander Howarth and Micheal Loebenstein, *Film Curatorship: Archives, Museums, and the Digital Marketplace* (Vienna: Austrian Film Museum, 2008).
17. Katia Rossini, 'Who Wanted the Death of Analog Projection? Not Independent Cinemas!', in Luisa Greenfield, Deborah S. Phillips, Kerstin Schroedinger, Björn Speidel and Philip Widmann (eds.), *Film in the Present Tense: Why Can't We Stop Talking About Analogue Film?* (Berlin: Archive Books, 2018), p. 60.
18. Scott MacDonald argues that 'The fundamental issue [...] is not which projection technology is theoretically "better", either in practical or aesthetic terms, but rather, the compelling nature of the films that have been made in 16mm for 16mm exhibition (or in 8mm or Super-8mm for 8mm or Super-8mm exhibition). If we were talking simply about the transfer of information, then medium wouldn't really matter: whichever projection system allowed for the accurate transfer of information to the largest number of people who need the information would be the "best" one.

But the many major contributions to avant-garde film history available only in 16mm are *theatrical film experiences* that are so crucial for a full understanding of film history and so valuable for an understanding of modern cultural history in general that those committed to the full range of cinematic accomplishment have little option but to see that 16mm exhibition continues to be available'. '16mm: Reports of Its Death Are Greatly Exaggerated', *Cinema Journal*, Vol. 45, No. 3, 2006, p. 128.

19. Katia Rossini, p. 61.
20. Sixpack Film was established in 1980 by Peter Tscherkassky and Brigitta Burger-Utzer to provide a distribution platform for Austrian film. See Peter Tscherkassky (ed.), *Film Unframed: A History of Austrian Avant-Garde Cinema* (Vienna: Austrian Film Museum, 2012).
21. Gerald Weber, personal interview carried out at the Rotterdam Film Festival on 29 January 2017. Previously published as part of the Reset the Apparatus! project: http://www.resettheapparatus.net/scrapbook-article/rotterdam-dialogues.html.
22. http://www.savefilm.org/ (accessed 26 October 2019).
23. The differences between film and digital projection are most often articulated in terms of physiological responses to the intermittent flicker on the one hand and the constant electronic signal on the other. Pip Chodorov argues, for example: 'The flickering of the projector with a shutter, a more and more rare experience these days, provokes a psychophysical phenomenon in the retina and visual cortex called the Phi Phenomenon, especially conducive to creating the illusion of motion, like lucid dreaming'. Pip Chodorov, 'The Artist-Run Film Labs', *Millennium Film Journal*, Vol. 60, 2014, p. 36.
24. http://www.filmprojection21.org/charter/ (accessed 26 October 2019).
25. This was one of the discussion points at the recent edition of Process festival in Riga (20–24 March 2019). Whilst the festival focuses exclusively on photochemical formats—Super 8, 16mm, 35mm or a combination of film and digital—many of the works included were screened from digital formats, much to the disappointment of the curators. It turns out that this was due largely to economic constraints. Many of the filmmakers were 'hoping' to get a film print made but were in the process of raising funds to facilitate this. A digital transfer was the easiest and most convenient way to ensure that the film circulated in the meantime.
26. For a recent overview of the issues involved in artists' film restoration see Enrico Camporesi, *Futurs de l'obsolescence: Essai sur la restauration du film d'artiste* (Paris: Éditions Mimésis, 2018).
27. Alexander Howarth in Paolo Cherchi Usai et al., *Film Curatorship: Archives, Museums, and the Digital Marketplace*, p. 116.

28. Mike Hoolboom, 'Showing Pictures: A Conversation Between Yann Beauvais and Mike Hoolboom', in Hoolboom, *Projecting Questions: Mike Hoolboom's Invisible Man Between the Art Gallery and the Movie Theatre* (Toronto: Art Gallery of York University, 2009), p. 119.
29. We might also note, here, that even when the projector is not physically present in the room, projectionists and curators are often keen, in their programme introductions, to remind audiences of the differences between digital and photochemical projection, drawing attention to the possibility of delay, interruption and failure.
30. Erika Balsom, *After Uniqueness: A History of Film and Video Art in Circulation* (New York: Columbia University Press, 2017), p. 174.
31. 'I think the shopping-mall mentality of the museum means that we don't physically absorb anything fully, it just passes through us, through our eyes. And digital and video sort of confirm that – *a different part of our brain reads electronic imagery to celluloid*' (my emphasis). Chrissie Illes in 'Does the Museum Fail? Podium Discussion at the 53rd International Short Film Festival Oberhausen', in Mike Sperlinger and Ian White (eds.), *Kinomuseum: Towards an Artists' Cinema* (Cologne: Walther König, 2008), p. 142.
32. The French term is frequently translated as 'apparatus' but the broader philosophical implications, particularly in the work of Michel Foucault, stretch to discourses, infrastructures and institutions—in short, 'the system of relations'. Foucault, 'The Confession of the Flesh', in Colin Gordon (ed.), *Power/Knowledge: Selected Interviews and Other Writings, 1972–1977* (New York: Pantheon Books, 1980), p. 194. The term has been taken up in Film Studies by Jean-Louis Baudry and Christian Metz, as well as Raymond Bellour.
33. Raymond Bellour, 'The Cinema Spectator: A Special Memory', in Gertrude Koch, Volker Pantenberg and Simon Rothöhler, *Screen Dynamics: Mapping the Borders of Cinema*, p. 16.
34. André Parente and Victa de Carvalho, 'Cinema as dispositif: Between Cinema and Contemporary Art', in *Cinémas: revue d'études cinématographiques/Cinemas: Journal of Film Studies*, Vol. 19, No. 1, 2008, p. 39.
35. In 2016, Bristol Experimental and Expanded Film (BEEF) acquired the lease on an old working men's club, known as the Brunswick Club. The carpeted ground floor ballroom was frequently used as a cinema space, as well as a venue for live film and music performance, whilst the basement bar and skittle alley were transformed into installation and performance spaces. Vicky Smith's insightful essay reflects on the relationship between the material specificities of the building and the events that were staged there during the first year: http://www.beefbristol.org/essay/ (accessed 6 November 2019). Other examples include The Nightingale in Chicago,

The Boathouse Microcinema in Portland, Cinecycle in Toronto, Total Mobile Home in San Franciso.

36. Janine Marchessault, 'On Bicycles and Films: The Case of CineCycle', *Public: Art/Culture/Ideas*, Vol. 40, 2010, pp. 93–104.
37. Donna de Ville, 'The Persistent Transience of Microcinema (in the United States and Canada)', *Film History*, Vol. 27, No. 3, 2015, p. 106.
38. Ibid.
39. Scott MacDonald, 'The American Microcinema Movement in Historical Context', in Andrea Grover and Ed Halter (eds.), *A Mircocinema Primer: A History of Experimental Film Exhibition in the United States* (Houston: Aurora Picture Show, 2010), p. 27.
40. Under-represented in the history of live film performance in the UK, Loophole Cinema was a collective of artists including Haut, Greg Pope, Ben Hayman, Paul Rodgers and Ivan Pope. They hosted large-scale installation and performance work featuring 16mm film and other mechanical ephemera in a variety of spaces across London.
41. It was at one of Haut's Analogue Recurring events that I first encountered the work of Sally Golding, who would come to have a profound influence on my understanding and appreciation of expanded cinema.
42. Another important series based in London is Unconscious Archives, organised by Sally Golding. Emphasis is placed on multi-projector film performance and sound art.
43. Stan Brakhage, 'From *Metaphors on Vision*', in P. Adams Sitney (ed.), *The Avant-Garde Film: A Reader of Theory and Criticism* (New York: Anthology Film Archives, 1978), p. 121.
44. Alison Butler 'Review: Tamara Trodd (ed.) Screen/Space: The Projected Image in Contemporary Art', *Screen*, Vol. 52, No. 4, 2011, pp. 531–535.
45. A. L. Rees, 'Expanded Cinema and Narrative: A Troubled History', in A. L. Rees, Duncan White, Steven Ball and David Curtis (eds.), *Expanded Cinema: Art, Performance, Film* (London: Tate Publishing, 2011), p. 12.
46. Mathilde Nardelli, 'Moving Pictures: Cinema and Its Obsolescence in Contemporary Art', *Journal of Visual Culture*, Vol. 8, No. 3, 2009, p. 244.
47. Ibid., p. 244.
48. Ibid., p. 245.
49. See, for example, Jean-Louis Baudry, 'Ideological Effects of the Basic Cinematographic Apparatus', in Philip Rose (ed.), *Narrative, Apparatus, Ideology: A Film Theory Reader* (New York: Columbia University Press, 1986), pp. 286–298; Christian Metz, *The Imaginary Signifier: Psychoanalysis and the Cinema* (Bloomington: Indiana University Press, 1977).
50. Malcolm Le Grice, 'Material, Materiality, Materialism', in *Experimental Cinema in the Digital Age* (London: BFI Publishing, 2001), p. 165.

51. This term is from Laura Mulvey's essay 'Visual Pleasure and Narrative Cinema'.
52. I have lost count of the amount of times I have heard a Super 8 or 16mm camera being described as both a 'beautiful object' and a 'thing of the past'. Recently, having set up a projector for a demonstration of camera-less animation at a university open day, a visitor looked admiringly at it before asking me if it worked, the assumption being that it had long given up its functionality and was displayed simply for its aesthetic qualities or as an example of old media.
53. Email correspondence from the artist, 12 November 2019.
54. Absolute Pitch was installed at the Whitstable Biennale in 2014. A slightly different iteration of the piece Absolute Pitch II was exhibited at the Danielle Arnauld gallery in London from 19 September to 26 October 2014.
55. Personal interview with the artist, 20 February 2020.
56. Ibid.
57. Ibid.
58. A second iteration of the piece, *Can People See Me Swallowing II*, was presented as a live performance for five singers in a stairwell as Tyntesfield House as part of the In Between Time Festival in February 2015. See http://louisafairclough.co.uk/lines-of-thought/can-people-see-me-swallowing-ii for visual documentation.
59. Ibid.
60. Nicolson's ephemeral performance, of which there remains little documentation, saw the artist punching holes into the filmstrip with a sewing machine and simultaneously projecting the same strip before the audience. After several cycles the film broke down and the performance ended. In *Film as Fabric*, Stark explores her family's connections to the textile industry, bringing together projected images of fabrics, sounds of the sewing machine and performative interactions with the audience whose bodies she measures to determine the lengths of film to be presented.
61. D. N. Rodowick, *The Virtual Life of Film* (Cambridge, MA and London: Harvard University Press, 2007), p. 125.
62. John Hanhardt, 'The End(s) of Film', in Marente Bloemheuvel and Jaap Guldemond (eds.), *Celluloid: Tacita Dean, João Maria Gusmão & Pedro Paiva, Rosa Barba, Sandra Gibson & Luis Recoder* (Amsterdam: EYE Filmmusuem, nai010 publishers, 2016), pp. 101–102.
63. *Threadbare* emerged conceptually out of the earlier installation *Light Spill*—the first work on which Gibson and Recoder collaborated. Having been asked numerous times by gallery visitors about what happens to the mass of film that falls onto the floor, the artists decided to stage its return to the projector in a different form and with a different material

emphasis that still speaks of excess. Personal conversation with the artists, 20 February 2020.

64. Although there are examples of expanded cinema being presented in gallery spaces, the two worlds of DIY photochemical filmmaking and the institutionalised contexts of the gallery often seem counterposed. This is less the case with smaller, independent institutions who may find more value in the counter-cultural spirit of the ad hoc and improvised bric-a-brac of expanded film artists such as Bruce McClure.
65. Walley, '"Not an Image of the Death of Film": Contemporary Expanded Cinema and Experimental Film', in *Expanded Cinema: Art, Performance, Film*, p. 246.
66. See Nicolas Rey, 'Contemporary Issues of Artist-Run Film Lab Practices', in Luisa Greenfield, Deborah S. Phillips, Kerstin Schroedinger, Björn Speidel and Philip Widmann (eds.), *Film in the Present Tense: Why Can't We Stop Talking About Analogue Film?* (Berlin: Archive Books, 2018), pp. 63–71.
67. The band has also toured with former Double Negative member Philippe Léonard.
68. Mike Rollo, 'A Collective Charge: Collectif double négativ/Double Negative Collective', in Scott MacKenzie and Janine Marchessault (eds.), *Process Cinema: Handmade Film in the Digital Age* (Montreal: McGill-Queens University, 2019), p. 222.
69. Walley, '"Not an Image of the Death of Film": Contemporary Expanded Cinema and Experimental Film', p. 243.
70. Personal interview with the artist, 9 November 2019.
71. Ibid.
72. Vicky Smith, 'The Animator's Body in Expanded Cinema', *Animation: An Interdisciplinary Journal*, Vol. 10, No. 3, 2015, p. 224. This is demonstrated in Smith's own film performances *Bicycle Tyre Track* (2012–2014), in which she cycles 'mud' (actually brown paint) across the film strip and then projects the results to the gathered audience; *33 Frames per Foot* (2013), where she covers her feet with ink and imprints her footsteps across the clear celluloid; and *Agitations* (2017–2018), a dynamic and deadpan performance that sees the artist jumping repeatedly up and down on the film strip in order to register marks on the surface. The physicality of the three pieces, with their emphasis on various forms of futile bodily movement that lead nowhere in particular resonates with the 'action films' of Jenny Baines and Bea Haut, which I discussed in Chapter 3.
73. A. L. Rees, 'Expanded Cinema and Narrative: A Troubled History', p. 14.
74. Malcolm Le Grice, 'Material, Materiality, Materialism', p. 167.
75. Tom Gunning, 'The Cinema of Attraction: Early Cinema, Its Spectator and the Avant-Garde', in Thomas Elsaesser (ed.), *Early Cinema: Space, Frame, Narrative* (London: BFI Publishing, 1990), pp. 56–62.

76. See, for example, Wanda Strauven (ed.), *The Cinema of Attractions Reloaded* (Amsterdam: Amsterdam University Press, 2006).
77. Walley, '"Not an Image of the Death of Film": Contemporary Expanded Cinema and Experimental Film', p. 247.
78. Catherine Elwes, *Installation and the Moving Image*, p. 222.
79. Luis Recoder, 'The Death of Structural Film: Notes Toward a Filmless Cinema', *Spectator*, Vol. 27, 2007, p. 26.
80. Kaira M. Cabañas, *Off-Screen Cinema: Isidore Isou and the Lettrist Avant-Garde* (Chicago and London: University of Chicago Press, 2014), p. 41.
81. See Hans Richter, 'The Badly Trained Sensibility', in P. Adams Sitney (ed.), *The Avant-Garde Film: A Reader of Theory and Criticism* (New York: Anthology Film Archives, 1978), pp. 22–23.
82. In Wang's single screen and performance work *Dust Poetry* (2014), 7000 frames of dust are combined with images of plants and insects from the artist's garden.
83. Personal interview with the artist, 16 November 2019.
84. There are also resonances, here, with Man Ray's photograph *Dust Breeding* (1920), a document of Marcel Duchamp's *The Bride Stripped Bare by Her Bachelors, Even (The Large Glass)* (1915–1923), which had accumulated dust over the course of a year. It was not the first time that Man Ray was drawn to the expressive quality of material debris or waste, and much of his work focuses on phenomena that exists on the visual peripheries.

Conclusion: Past Present Future Perfect

In Lindsay McIntyre's documentary *Film's Final Curtain* (2018), several key figures in the film world—both mainstream and alternative—reflect on the medium's commercial demise and the consequences for its continuation as an art form. 'Now, film is out of the box', states Hollywood actress Eva Childs. 'Finally, she has discovered what it was that was inside of her. All she wanted was to be an artist'. Featuring a number of figures discussed in this book—Josh Lewis, Jeanne Liotta, Nicolas Rey, Kevin Rice, Richard Tuohy, Esther Urlus—the film delves into the topic of obsolescence and DIY film culture with a spirit of exuberance and optimism, seeing the 'death' of film as perhaps a necessary step in its creative liberation and rebirth. As archival footage shows factories being demolished and labs being cleared out, the story of film's glorious rise and astonishingly rapid fall is told through a series of heartfelt confessions and upbeat observations about how film re-emerges in new forms and contexts. For Canadian filmmaker Kelly Egan, for example, 'the discourse of the death of film is actually really exciting, because it allows us an opportunity to come together and reimagine what it can be instead of being told what it is. It's a really great revolutionary moment.' For Richard Tuohy, film is 'now a choice. We choose film'. Although they remain bound to the commercial interests of film manufacturing companies—largely Kodak and Orwo—experimental artists are uncovering new possibilities in this old medium and building communities around it. Its

K. Knowles, *Experimental Film and Photochemical Practices*,
Experimental Film and Artists' Moving Image,
https://doi.org/10.1007/978-3-030-44309-2

marginal status, inconvenience, awkwardness and time-consuming working methods are an attractive quality for those who wish to carve out a position of resistance against convention.

Throughout my interviews with photochemical filmmakers, I rarely encountered comparisons with, or criticisms of, digital technology. The artists I spoke to appreciate the creative capacities of this relatively new medium, many of them working across both film and digital to 'get the best of what both mediums have to offer', to quote Emmanuel Lefrant.[1] Let us not forget that the interconnected communities of skills and equipment sharing that sustain photochemical film practice are largely facilitated by digital platforms and globally networked modes of communication and exchange. The purchase of a Bolex camera, a processing tank, film stock and other analogue equipment is usually made online. The most ardent photochemical enthusiast I know—James Holcombe—prefers the light meter app on his smart phone over the trusty Sekonic. The interviews I carried out were mostly via Skype, reaching out across geographical boundaries and time zones and negotiating occasional temporal lags and video fall-out. I made virtual trips to Brazil, Australia, Canada, USA, the Netherlands and France, and had the most inspiring caffeine-fuelled conversations about tactile interventions and chemical processes mediated by a laptop computer. All manner of materialities came to bear on the writing of this book, just as a myriad of real and virtual interactions coalesce in the practice of photochemical filmmaking.

This is not a purist art, photochemical filmmakers do not shun new technologies and the digital is never far away, so integrated is it in our daily lives. Choosing to work with older materials *is* in some sense a form of resistance, 'a *fuck-you* to contemporary fads', in the words of the filmmaker Bradley Eros.[2] But I like to think of the negotiation of alternative positions in more subtle terms and from a less divisive perspective. Working with film allows a particular kind of material engagement and temporal investment that is appealing to some artists but not to others. Being sensitive to the differences between media is not festishistic or nostalgic, but a key part of negotiating and maintaining a diverse technological and artistic landscape. Within the field of experimental film practice, where meaning is often located outside of narrative and even figurative concerns, and where attention is often directed towards the materials of representation, the tools and techniques specific to either film and digital can be compared to the difference between paint and charcoal. As Peter Tscherkassky has stated:

> It may be true that in many fields of audio-visual communication it does not make a big difference whether images stem from a strip of film or are rendered from a digital medium. However, in all cases where it's about film as an art form, the difference between the two media is absolutely crucial.[3]

This is especially the case in the artisanal working methods that have been discussed throughout this book, where the physical manipulation of surfaces and the various interventions in colour and chemistry hinge on material connectedness. Time and again in my discussions with artists, I encountered the sentiment that were film to disappear entirely as an artistic choice, the turn would not be to digital moving images, but to other art forms such as painting. Charlotte Pryce describes her embrace of the pre-cinematic magic lantern in performances such as *W.H. Hudson's Remarkable Argentine Ornithology* (2013) and *Tears of a Mudlark* (2018) as partly an anticipation of the end of film.[4] Returning to even older optical technologies not controlled by large corporations may indeed be the next step in the counter-cultural reinvention of the moving image.

Although this book has focused attention on the reinvention of photochemical processes, artists are increasingly working at the intersection of both film and digital technologies, offering innovative directions for hybrid practice. Experimental filmmakers such as Makino Takashi, Johanna Vaude, Péter Lichter, Thorsten Fleisch, Janis Crystal Lipzin and Nan Wang, to name just a few, have pioneered what Jihoon Kim describes as 'the aesthetics of co-presence', offering a fluid negotiation of medium-specificity.[5] Here, the grain meets the pixel in an overlapping consideration of material characteristics, technological capabilities and unique sensory associations. Mary Ann Doane has argued in this respect that the potential of a medium

> lie[s] in the notion of material resistances or even of matter/materiality itself as, somewhat paradoxically, an *enabling impediment*. The juxtaposition of negativity and productivity is crucial here. A medium is a medium by virtue of both its positive qualities [...] and its limitations, gaps, incompletions.[6]

Doane's account offers a number of useful roads into the subject of hybridity in relation to material engagement and the dialogue between old and new media. It is perhaps, paradoxically, through digital technology that the photochemical medium finds a future, be it through the 3D printing of mechanical parts or the programming of specific tools.[7]

The possibilities for rethinking film in the digital era are multiple, and a landscape of creative diversity offers exciting new pathways for reinvention. Film in its previous incarnation may be obsolete, but the practices and communities I have described in this book make it clear that new directions which reveal the ongoing radical possibilities of material engagement are actively being forged. Reformulating and reimagining Peter Gidal's call for a politics of representation through the staging of process, contemporary artists are finding ways to activate material and mechanical surfaces through gestures of contact, problematising conventional forms of vision and communicating a haptic awareness of the world. For a marginal art form and a form of resistance, the future might be uncertain, but the potential is vast.

Notes

1. Personal correspondence with the artist, 30 January 2018.
2. Bradley Eros, 'More Captivating Than Phosphorous', *Millennium Film Journal*, No. 56, 2012, p. 47.
3. Peter Tscherkassky, 'How and Why: A Few Notes Concerning Production Techniques Employed in the Making of My Darkroom Films', in Scott MacKenzie and Janine Marchessault (eds.), *Process Cinema: Handmade Film in the Digital Age* (Montreal: McGill-Queens University, 2019), p. 93.
4. Personal interview the artist, 29 July 2019.
5. Jihoon Kim, *Between Film, Video, and the Digital: Hybrid Moving Images in the Post-media Age* (New York: Bloomsbury, 2016), p. 2.
6. Mary Ann Doane, 'The Indexical and the Concept of Medium-Specificity', *Differences: A Journal of Feminist Cultural Studies*, Vol. 18, No. 1, 2007, p. 130.
7. Tacita Dean's *FILM* is a good example of this, since although the installation focuses on photochemical processes, the mattes that were used to create the work were produced digitally.

Bibliography

Acland, Charles R. (ed.), *Residual Media* (London and Minneapolis: University of Minnesota Press, 2007).

Anders, Günter, 'Commandments in the Atomic Age', in Claude Eatherly and Günter Anders (eds.), *Burning Conscience: The Case of the Hiroshima Pilot, Claude Eatherly* (New York: Monthly Review Press, 1957), pp. 11–20.

———, *L'Obsolesence de l'homme: Sur l'âme à l'époque de la deuxième révolution industrielle* (Paris: NUISANCES, 2002).

Balázs, Béla, *Theory of the Film: Character and Growth of a New Art* (New York: Arno Press, 1972).

Balsom, Erika, *After Uniqueness: A History of Film and Video Art in Circulation* (New York: Columbia University Press, 2017).

———, *Exhibiting Cinema in Contemporary Art* (Amsterdam: Amsterdam University Press, 2013).

Balsom, Erika, Lucy Reynolds, and Sarah Perks, *Artists' Moving Image in Britain Since 1989* (New Haven: Yale University Press).

Barad, Karen, 'Posthumanist Perfomativity: Toward an Understanding of How Matter Comes to Matter', *Signs: Journal of Women in Culture and Society*, Vol. 28, No. 3, 2003, pp. 801–831.

Barker, Jennifer, *The Tactile Eye: Touch and the Cinematic Experience* (Berkeley: University of California Press, 2009).

Baron, Jaimie, *The Archive Effect: Found Footage and the Audiovisual Experience of History* (New York: Routledge, 2014).

Baudry, Jean-Louis, 'Ideological Effects of the Basic Cinematographic Apparatus', in Philip Rose (ed.), *Narrative, Apparatus, Ideology: A Film Theory Reader* (New York: Columbia University Press, 1986), pp. 286–298.

K. Knowles, *Experimental Film and Photochemical Practices*,
Experimental Film and Artists' Moving Image,
https://doi.org/10.1007/978-3-030-44309-2

Bauer, Petra and Dan Kidner (eds.), *Working Together: Notes on British Film Collectives in the 1970s* (Southend-on-Sea: Focal Point Gallery, 2012).

Belina, Mirna (ed.), *Vertical Cinema* (Amsterdam: Sonic Acts Press, 2013).

Bellour, Raymond, *L'entre-images: photo, cinéma, vidéo* (Paris: La Différence, 1990).

———, 'The Cinema Spectator: A Special Memory', in Gertrude Koch, Volker Pantenberg, and Simon Rothöhler (eds.), *Screen Dynamics: Mapping the Borders of Cinema* (Vienna: Austrian Film Museum and SYNEMA, 2012), pp. 9–21.

Belton, John, 'Digital Cinema: A False Revolution', *October*, Vol. 100, 2002, pp. 98–114.

Benjamin, Walter, *Illuminations*, edited by Hannah Arendt and translated by Harry Zohn (New York: Fontana/Collins, 1973).

———, *Selected Writings, Volume 2, 1927–1934*, edited by Michael W. Jennings, Howard Eiland, and Gary Smith (Cambridge, MA and London: Belknap Press, 1999).

———, *The Arcades Project*, translated by Howard Eiland and Kevin McLaughlin (Cambridge, MA and London: Harvard University Press, 1999).

Bennett, Jane, *Vibrant Matter: A Political Ecology of Things* (Durham: Duke University Press, 2010).

Beugnet, Martine, *L'Attrait du flou* (Liège: *Yellow Now*, 2017).

Beugnet, Martine, Allan Cameron, and Arild Fetveit (eds.), *Indefinite Visions: Cinema and the Attractions of Uncertainty* (Edinburgh: Edinburgh University Press, 2017).

Beugnet, Martine and Kim Knowles, 'The Aesthetics and Politics of Obsolescence: Handmade Film in the Digital Era', *Moving Image Review and Art Journal*, Vol. 2, No. 1, 2013, pp. 55–65.

Bliss, Lauren, 'Second Nature: On the Experimental Work of Richard Tuohy', *Senses of Cinema*, Issue 78, 2016: http://sensesofcinema.com/2016/feature-articles/richard-tuohy/.

Blümlinger, Christa, *Cinéma de seconde main – Esthétique du remploi dans l'art du film et des nouveaux médias* (Paris: Klincksieck, 2013).

———, 'The Filmic Convulsions of Mara Mattuschka', in Peter Tscherkassky (ed.), *Film Unframed: The Austrian Avant-Garde Film* (Vienna: Austrian Film Museum, 2012), pp. 222–231.

Boscagli, Maurizia, *Stuff Theory: Everyday Objects and Radical Materialism* (New York and London: Bloomsbury, 2014).

Bourriaud, Nicholas, *The Radicant* (New York: Lucas & Sternberg, 2009).

Bousé, Derek, 'False Intimacy: Close-Ups and Viewer Involvement in Wildlife Films', *Visual Studies*, Vol. 18, No, 2, 2003, pp. 123–132.

Boym, Svetlana, *The Future of Nostalgia* (New York: Basic, 2001).

Bozak, Nadia, *The Cinematic Footprint: Lights, Camera, Natural Resources* (New Brunswick: Rutgers University Press, 2012).

Braidotti, Rosi, *The Posthuman* (Cambridge: Polity Press, 2013).

Brainin-Donnenberg, Wilbrig and Michael Loebenstein (eds.), *Gustav Deutsch* (Vienna: Austrian Film Museum, 2009).

Brakhage, Stan, 'From *Metaphors on Vision*', in P. Adams Sitney (ed.), *The Avant-Garde Film: A Reader of Theory and Criticism* (New York: Anthology Film Archives, 1978), pp. 120–128.

Brannigan, Erin, *Dancefilm: Choreography and the Moving Image* (New York: Oxford University Press, 2011).

———, 'Micro-Choreographies: The Close-Up in Dancefilm', *International Journal of Performance Arts and Digital Media*, Vol. 5, Nos. 2–3, 2009, pp. 121–139.

Brereton, Pat, *Environmental Ethics and Film* (London and New York: Routledge, 2016).

Broomer, Stephen, *Codes for North: Foundations of the Canadian Avant-Garde Film* (Toronto: Canadian Filmmakers Distribution Centre, 2017).

Brown, Dan, 'Projection as Performance: Recent Directions in Canadian Expanded Cinema', in Scott MacKenzie and Janine Marchessault (eds.), *Process Cinema: Handmade Film in the Digital Age* (Montreal: McGill-Queens University, 2019), pp. 407–425.

Brown, Simon, Sarah Street, and Liz Watkins (eds.), *Colour and the Moving Image: History, Theory, Aesthetics, Archive* (New York and London: Routledge, 2013).

Bruno, Giuliana, *Surface: Matters of Aesthetics, Materiality and Media* (Chicago and London: University of Chicago Press, 2014).

Buell, Lawrence, 'The Ecocritical Insurgency', *New Literary History*, Vol. 30, No. 3, Summer 1999, pp. 699–712.

Butler, Alison (ed.), 'Review: Tamara Trodd Screen/Space: The Projected Image in Contemporary Art', *Screen*, Vol. 52, No. 4, 2011, pp. 531–535.

Cabañas, Kaira M., *Off-Screen Cinema: Isidore Isou and the Lettrist Avant-Garde* (Chicago and London: University of Chicago Press, 2014).

Camporesi, Enrico, *Futurs de l'obsolescence: Essai sur la restauration du film d'artiste* (Paris: Éditions Mimésis, 2018).

Chare, Nicholas and Liz Watkins, 'The Matter of Film: *Decasia* and *Lyrical Nitrate*', in Estelle Barrett and Barbara Bolt (eds.), *Carnal Knowledge: Towards a 'New Materialism' Through the Arts* (London and New York: I.B. Tauris, 2013), pp. 75–87.

Cherchi Usai, Paolo, *The Death of the Cinema: History, Cultural Memory and the Digital Dark Age* (London: Reaktion Books, 2001).

Cherchi Usai, Paolo, David Francis, Alexander Howarth, and Michael Loebenstein, *Film Curatorship: Archives, Museums, and the Digital Marketplace* (Vienna: Austrian Film Museum, 2008).

Chodorkoff, Dan, 'Everything Depends on What People Are Capable of Wanting', in Eirik Eiglad (ed.), *Social Ecology and Social Change* (Porsgrunn: New Compass Press, 2015), pp. 35–41.

Chodorov, Pip, 'The Artist-Run Film Labs', *Millennium Film Journal*, Vol. 60, Fall 2014, pp. 28–36.

Chun, Wendy Hui Kyong, and Anna Watkins Fisher (eds.), *New Media, Old Media: A History and Theory Reader*, 2nd Edition (New York: Routledge, 2016).

Clayton, Sue and Laura Mulvey (eds.), *Other Cinemas: Politics, Culture and Experimental Film in the 1970s* (London and New York: I.B. Tauris, 2017).

Cole, Janis, 'The Harvest of Philip Hoffman', *POV Magazine*, Issue 58, Summer 2005, pp. 4–8.

Colebrook, Claire, 'What Is the Anthro-Political?', in Tom Cohen, Claire Colebrook, and J. Hillis Miller (eds.), *Twilight of the Anthropocene Idols* (London: Open Humanities Press, 2016), pp. 81–125.

Coleman, Rebecca and Liz Oakley-Brown, 'Visualizing Surfaces, Surfacing Vision: Introduction', *Theory, Culture & Society*, Special Section: Visualizing Surfaces, Surfacing Vision, Vol. 34, Nos. 7–8, 2017, pp. 5–27.

Connolly, Maeve, *The Place of Artists' Cinema: Space, Site and Screen* (Bristol: Intellect, 2009).

Cooper, Davina, *Everyday Utopias: The Conceptual Life of Promising Spaces* (Durham and London: Duke University Press).

Cramer, Florian, 'What Is Post-digital?', in David M. Berry and Michael Dieter (eds.), *Postdigital Aesthetics: Art, Computation and Design* (Basingstoke: Palgrave Macmillan, 2015), pp. 12–26.

Crew, Louise and Nicky Gregson, *Second-Hand* Cultures (Oxford: Berg, 2003).

Crutzen, Paul and Eugene F. Stoermer, 'The "Anthropocene"', *Global Change Newsletter*, Vol. 41, No. 1, 2000, pp. 17–18.

Cubitt, Sean, 'Ecocritique and the Materialities of Animation', in Suzanne Buchan (ed.), *Pervasive Animation* (New York: Routledge, 2013), pp. 94–114.

———, *Finite Media: Environmental Implications of Digital Technologies* (Durham: Duke University Press, 2016).

Curtis, David, 'A tale of Two Co-ops', in David E. James (ed.), *To Free the Cinema: Jonas Mekas and the American Underground* (Princeton, NJ: Princeton University Press, 1992), pp. 255–265.

Curtis, David and Deke Dusinberre (eds.), *A Perspective on English Avant-Garde Film Catalogue* (London: The Arts Council, 1978).

Danino, Nina, Jean Matthee, Ruth Novaczek, Sarah Pucill, and Alia Syed, 'Roundtable Discussion: The Women of the London Filmmaker's Co-op', *Moving Image Review and Art Journal,* Vol. 4, Nos. 1–2, 2015, pp. 165–179.

Danks, Adrian, 'The Global Art of Found Footage Cinema', in Linda Badley, R. Barton Palmer, and Steven Jay Schneider (eds.), *Traditions in World Cinema* (Edinburgh: Edinburgh University Press, 2006), pp. 241–253.

Daumal, René, *Mount Analogue: A Novel of Symbolically Authentic Non-Euclidean Adventures in Mountain Climbing* (London: Vincent Stuart, 1959).

Davis, Fred, *Yearning for Yesterday: A Sociology of Nostalgia* (New York and London: The Free Press, 1979).

Davis, Heather and Etienne Turpin, *Art in the Anthropocene: Encounters Among Aesthetics, Politics, Environments and Epistemologies* (London: Open Humanities Press, 2015).

Dean, Tacita, 'Artist Questionnaire: 21 Responses', *October*, Vol. 100, Obsolescence Special Issue, Spring 2002, pp. 26–27.

———, 'FILM', in *Catalogue for the Exhibition* FILM, *11 October 2011–11 March 2012* (London: Tate Publishing, 2011), pp. 15–48.

———, 'Save Celluloid, for Art's Sake', *The Guardian*, February 22, 2011: https://www.theguardian.com/artanddesign/2011/feb/22/tacita-dean-16mm-film.

De Bruyn, Dirk, 'Recovering the Hidden Through Found-Footage Films', in Estelle Barrett and Barbara Bolt (eds.), *Carnal Knowledge: Towards a 'New Materialism' Through the Arts* (London and New York: I.B. Tauris, 2013), pp. 89–104.

———, *The Performance of Trauma in Moving Image Art* (Cambridge: Cambridge Scholars Publishing, 2014).

Deleuze, Gilles, *Cinema 1: The Movement Image* (Minneapolis: University of Minnesota Press, 1986).

DeLoughrey, Elizabeth M., *Allegories of the Anthropocene* (Durham: Duke University Press, 2019).

Demos, T. J., *Against the Anthropocene: Visual Culture and Environment Today* (Berlin: Sternberg Press, 2017).

Deren, Maya, 'Cinematography: The Creative Use of Reality', in P. Adams Sitney (ed.), *The Avant-Garde Film: A Reader of Theory and Criticism* (New York: Anthology Film Archives, 1978), pp. 60–73.

De Ville, Donna, 'The Persistent Transience of Microcinema (in the United States and Canada)', *Film History*, Vol. 27, No. 3, 2015, pp. 104–136.

Doane, Mary Ann, *The Emergence of Cinematic Time: Modernity, Contingency, the Archive* (Cambridge, MA and London: Harvard University Press, 2002).

———, 'The Indexical and the Concept of Medium-Specificity', *differences: A Journal of Feminist Cultural Studies*, Vol. 18, No. 1, 2007, pp. 129–152.

Dunford, Mike, 'Experimental/Avant-garde/Revolutionary/Film Practice', *Afterimage*, Vol. 6, 1976, pp. 96–112.

Duque, Elena, 'Celluloid and Self-Sufficiency: Artist-Run Labs', *CCCB Lab Research and Innovation in the Cultural Sphere*, 23 February 2016: http://lab.cccb.org/en/celluloid-and-self-sufficiency-artist-run-labs/.

Dusinberre, Deke, '*Le Retour à la raison*: Hidden Meanings', in Bruce Posner (ed.), *Unseen Cinema: Early American Avant-Garde Film 1893–1941* (New York: Anthology Film Archives, 2001), pp. 64–69.

———, 'On British Avant-Garde Landscape Films', *Undercut*, Vol. 7/8, 1983, pp. 48–49.

Elsaesser, Thomas, 'The New Film History as Media Archaeology', *CINéMAS*, Vol. 14, Nos. 2–3, 2004, pp. 71–114.

Elwes, Catherine, *Installation and the Moving Image* (New York: Wallflower Press, 2015).

Epstein, Jean, 'Magnification and Other Writings', translated by Stuart Liebman, *October*, Vol. 3, 1977, pp. 9–25.

Eros, Bradley, 'More Captivating Than Phosphorous', *Millennium Film Journal*, Vol. 56, 2012, pp. 42–49.

Euler, Johannes and Leslie Gauditz, *Degrowth in Bewegung(En)* (blog), 13 December 2016: http://www.degrowth.de/en/dim.

Ford, Martin, *The Rise of Robots: Technology and the Threat of a Jobless Future* (New York: Basic Books, 2015).

Foucault, Michel, *Power/Knowledge: Selected Interviews and Other Writings, 1972–1977*, edited by Colin Gordon (New York: Pantheon Books, 1980).

———, *The Order of Things: An Archaeology of the Human Sciences* (London and New York: Routledge, 1989).

Frase, Peter, *Four Futures: Life After Capitalism* (London and New York: Verso, 2016).

Gaal Holmes, Patti, *A History of 1970s Experimental Film: Britain's Decade of Diversity* (Basingstoke: Palgrave Macmillan, 2015).

Gabrys, Jennifer, *Digital Rubbish: A Natural History of Electronics* (Ann Arbor: The University of Michigan Press, 2013).

Gaudreault, André and Philippe Marion, *The End of Cinema? A Medium in Crisis in the Digital Age* (New York: Columbia University Press, 2015).

Gehman, Chris, 'Toward Artisanal Cinema: A Filmmaker's Movement', in Scott MacKenzie and Janine Marchessault (eds.), *Process Cinema: Handmade Film in the Digital Age* (Montreal: McGill-Queens University, 2019), pp. 172–193.

Gidal, Peter, *Materialist Film* (London: BFI, 1989).

———, 'Technology and Ideology in/Through/and Avant-Garde Film: an Instance', in Mark Webber and Peter Gidal (eds.), *Flare Out: Aesthetics 1966–2016* (London: The Visible Press, 2016), pp. 116–134.

———, 'Theory and Definition of Structural/Materialist Film', in Mark Webber and Peter Gidal (eds.), *Flare Out: Aesthetics 1966–2016* (London: The Visible Press, 2016), pp. 37–68.

Graça, Marina Estela, 'Handmade Films: Questioning and Integrating Cinematic Technology', *International Journal of the Humanities*, Vol. 3, No. 3, 2005/2006, pp. 101–105.

Gray, Jonathan M., 'Heteronormativity Without Nature: Toward a Queer Ecology', *QED: A Journal of GLBTQ Worldmaking*, Vol. 4, No. 2, 2017, pp. 137–142.

Gruen, Lori, *Entangled Empathy, An Alternative Ethic for Our Relationships with Animals* (New York: Lantern Books, 2015).

Guattari, Félix, *The Three Ecologies* (London: Bloomsbury, 2014).

Guffey, Elizabeth, *Retro: The Culture of Revival* (London: Foci, 2006).

Gunning, Tom, 'The Cinema of Attraction: Early Cinema, Its Spectator and the Avant-Garde', in Thomas Elsaesser (ed.), *Early Cinema: Space, Frame, Narrative* (London: BFI Publishing, 1990), pp. 56–62.

Hanhardt, John, 'The End(s) of Film', in Marente Bloemheuvel and Jaap Guldemond (eds.), *Celluloid: Tacita Dean, João Maria Gusmão & Pedro Paiva, Rosa Barba, Sandra Gibson & Luis Recoder* (Amsterdam: EYE Filmmusuem, nai010 Publishers, 2016), pp. 101–102.

Hansen, Mark, *New Philosophy for New Media* (Cambridge, MA: MIT Press, 2006).

Haraway, Donna J., *Staying with the Trouble: Making Kin in the Chthulucene* (Durham and London: Duke University Press, 2016).

Harbord, Janet, *The Evolution of Film: Rethinking Film Studies* (Cambridge: Polity Press, 2007).

Harman, Graham, *Object-Oriented Ontology: A New Theory of Everything* (London: Pelican, 2017).

Haug, Kate, 'Interview with Kate Haug', in Carolee Schneemann (ed.), *Imaging Her Erotics: Essays, Interviews, Projects* (Cambridge, MA: MIT Press, 2002), pp. 20–45.

Hawkins, Gay, *The Ethics of Waste: How We Relate to Rubbish* (Lanham: Rowman and Littlefield Publishers, 2006).

Heath, Stephen, 'Repetition Time: Notes Around "Structural/Materialist Film"', in *Questions of Cinema* (London: Palgrave Macmillan, 1981), pp. 165–175.

Henderson, Neil, 'Emptying Frames', *Animation Practice, Process & Production*, Vol. 1. No. 1, 2011, pp. 77–82.

Henke, Suzette A., 'Virginia Woolf's *The Waves*: A Phenomenological Reading', *Neophilologus*, Vol. 73, No. 3, 1989, pp. 461–472.

Henning, Michelle, 'New Lamps for Old: Photography, Obsolescence, and Social Change', in Charles R. Acland (ed.), *Residual Media* (London and Minneapolis: University of Minnesota Press, 2007), pp. 48–65.

Hertz, Garnet and Jussi Parikka, 'Zombie Media: Circuit Bending Media Archaeology into an Art Method', *Leonardo*, Vol. 45, No. 5, 2012, pp. 424–430.

Hill, Helen, Recipes for Disaster: A Handcrafted Film Cookbooklet, 2005: http://www.filmlabs.org/docs/recipes_for_disaster_hill.pdf.

Hoffman, Philip, 'Vulture Aesthetics: Process Cinema at the Film Farm', in Luisa Greenfield et al. (eds.), *Film in the Present Tense: Why Can't We Stop Talking About Analogue Film?* (Berlin: Archive Books, 2018).

Holdsworth, Amy, *Television, Memory and Nostalgia* (Basingstoke: Palgrave Macmillan, 2011).

Hoolboom, Mike, *Projecting Questions: Mike Hoolboom's Invisible Man Between the Art Gallery and the Movie Theatre* (Toronto: Art Gallery of York University, 2009).

Horrocks, Roger, *Len Lye: A Biography* (Aukland: Aukland University Press, 2001).

Howarth, Alexander and Michael Loebenstein, *Peter Tscherkassky* (Vienna: Austrian Film Museum, 2007).

Hüppauf, Bernd and Christoph Wulf (eds.), *Dynamics and Performativity of Imagination: The Image Between the Visible and the Invisible* (London: Routledge, 2009).

Huhtamo, Erkki and Jussi Parikka (eds.), *Media Archaeology: Approaches, Applications, Implications* (Berkeley: University of California Press, 2011).

Jacquin, Maud, 'From Reel to Real—An Epilogue: Feminist Politics and Materiality at the London Filmmakers' Co-operative', *Moving Image Review and Art Journal*, Vol. 6, Nos. 1–2, 2017, pp. 80–89.

Jenkins, Henry, *Convergence Culture: Where Old and New Media Collide* (New York and London: New York University Press, 2006).

Jutz, Gabriele, *Cinéma Brut: Eine alternative Genealogie der Filmavantgarde* (Vienna and New York: Springer, 2010).

Kim, Jihoon, *Between Film, Video, and the Digital: Hybrid Moving Images in the Post-media Age* (New York: Bloomsbury, 2016).

Kinzey, Jake, *The Sacred and the Profane: An Investigation of Hipsters* (Winchester: Zero, 2010).

Kittler, Friedrich, *Gramophone, Film, Typewriter* (Stanford: Stanford University Press, 1999).

Knowles, Kim, 'Blood, Sweat and Tears: Bodily Inscriptions in Contemporary Experimental Film', *NECSUS: European Journal of Media Studies*, Vol. 2, No. 2, Autumn 2013, pp. 447–463.

———, 'Fragments of Memory: Personal Dialogue with the Films of David Gatten', in Edgar Lissel, Gabriele Jutz, and Nina Jučik (eds.), *Reset the Apparatus!*

A Survey of the Photographic and the Filmic in Contemporary Art (Vienna: De Gruyter, 2019), pp. 134–137.

———, 'Locating Vintage', *NECSUS: European Journal of Media Studies*, Vol. 4, No. 2, Autumn 2015, pp. 73–84.

———, '(Re)visioning Celluloid: Aesthetics of Contact in Materialist Film', in Martine Beugnet, Allan Cameron, and Arild Fetveit (eds.), *Indefinite Visions: Cinema and the Attractions of Uncertainty* (Edinburgh: Edinburgh University Press, 2017), pp. 257–272.

———, Self-Skilling and Home Brewing: Some Reflections on Photochemical Film Culture', *Millennium Film Journal*, Vol. 60, Autumn 2014, pp. 20–27.

———, 'Slow, Methodical, and Mulled Over: Analog Practice in the Age of the Digital', *Cinema Journal*, Vol. 55, No. 2, Winter 2016, pp. 146–151.

Koch, Gertrude, Volker Pantenberg, and Simon Rothöhler, *Screen Dynamics: Mapping the Borders of Cinema* (Vienna: Austrian Film Museum and SYNEMA, 2012).

Krause, Adam, 'Toward an Economy of Repair', in Eirik Eiglad (ed.), *Social Ecology and Social Change* (Porsgrunn: New Compass Press, 2015), pp. 83–92.

Krauss, Rosalind, 'Reinventing the Medium', *Critical Inquiry*, Vol. 25, No. 2, 1999, pp. 289–305.

———, 'Video: The Aesthetics of Narcissism', *October*, Vol. 1, 1976, pp. 50–64.

Kubelka, Peter, 'The Theory of Metrical Film', in P. Adams Sitney (ed.), *The Avant-Garde Film: A Reader of Theory and Criticism* (New York: Anthology Film Archives, 1978), pp. 139–159.

Kuenzli, Rudolf E., *Dada and Surrealist Film* (Cambridge, MA: MIT Press, 1996).

Lamoureux, Johanne, Christine Ross, and Olivier Asselin (eds.), *Precarious Visualities: New Perspectives on Identification in Contemporary Art and Visual Culture* (Montreal: McGill-Queen's University Press, 2008).

Latour, Bruno, *Down to Earth: Politics in the New Climactic Regime* (Cambridge: Polity Press, 2018).

Leadbeater, Charles, *The Frugal Innovator: Creating Change on a Shoestring Budget* (Basingstoke: Palgrave Macmillan, 2014).

Le Grice, Malcolm, *Experimental Cinema in the Digital Age* (London: BFI, 2001).

Lipzin, Janis Crystal, 'A Materialist Film Practice in the Digital Age', *Millennium Film Journal*, Vol. 56, Fall 2012, pp. 50–54.

Lynch, David, *Catching the Big Fish: Meditation, Consciousness, and Creativity* (London: Penguin Books, 2006).

MacDonald, Scott, '16mm: Reports of Its Death Are Greatly Exaggerated', *Cinema Journal*, Vol. 45, No. 3, 2006, pp. 124–130.

———, 'An Interview with Carolee Schneemann', in *A Critical Cinema: Interviews with Independent Filmmakers*, Vol. 1 (Berkeley: University of California Press, 1988), pp. 134–151.

———, 'The American Mircocinema Movement in Historical Context', in Andrea Grover and Ed Halter (eds.), *A Mircocinema Primer: A History of Experimental Film Exhibition in the United States* (Houston: Aurora Picture Show, 2010), pp. 21–27.

———, 'The Ecocinema Experience', in Stephen Rust, Salma Monani and Sean Cubitt (eds.), *Ecocinema Theory and Practice* (New York and London: Routledge, 2013), pp. 17–42.

———, *The Garden in the Machine: A Field Guide to Independent Films about Place* (Berkeley: University of California Press, 2001).

———, 'Toward an Eco-Cinema', *Interdisciplinary Studies in Literature and Environment*, Vol. 15, No. 2, Summer 2004, pp. 107–132.

MacKenzie, Scott, '"An Arrow, Not a Target": Film Process and Processing at the Independent Imaging Retreat', in Mette Hjort (ed.), *The Education of the Filmmaker in Africa, The Middle East, and the Americas* (New York: Palgrave Macmillan, 2013), pp. 169–184.

MacKenzie, Scott and Janine Marchessault, *Process Cinema: Handmade Film in the Digital Age* (Montreal: McGill-Queens University, 2019).

Manovich, Lev, *The Language of New Media* (Cambridge, MA: MIT Press, 2001).

Man Ray, *Self-Portrait* (Boston: Bullfinch Press, 1999).

Marchessault, Janine, 'On Bicycles and Films: The Case of CineCycle', *Public: Art/Culture/Ideas*, Vol. 40, 2010, pp. 93–104.

———, 'Women, Nature, and Chemistry: Hand-Processed Films from the Film Farm', in Steve Reinke and Tom Taylor (eds.), *LUX: A Decade of Artists' Film and Video* (Toronto: YYZ Books/Pleasure Dome, 2000), pp. 135–142.

Marchessault, Janine and Susan Lord (eds.), *Fluid Screens, Expanded Cinema* (Toronto: University of Toronto Press, 2007).

Marcus, Sharon, 'Queer Theory for Everyone: A Review Essay', *Signs*, Vol. 31, No. 1, Autumn 2005, pp. 191–218.

Marks, Laura U., *The Skin of the Film: Intercultural Cinema, Embodiment and the Senses* (Durham, NC: Duke University Press, 1999).

———, *Touch: Sensuous Theory and Multisensory Media* (Minneapolis: University of Minnesota Press, 2002).

Martin, Noélie, 'Pratique des émulsions artisanales', *La Furia Umana*, Vol. 33, 2018: http://www.lafuriaumana.it/index.php/66-archive/lfu-33/767-noelie-martin-pratique-des-emulsions-artisanales.

Martineau, Jonathan, *Time, Capitalism and Alienation: A Socio-Historical Inquiry into the Making of Modern Time* (Boston: Brill, 2015).

Merleau-Ponty, Maurice, *Phenomenology of Perception*, translated by Colin Smith (London: Routledge & Kegan Paul, 1962).
———, *The Visible and the Invisible* (Evanston: Northwest University Press, 1968).
Metz, Christian, *The Imaginary Signifier: Psychoanalysis and the Cinema* (Bloomington: Indiana University Press, 1977).
Mildenberg, Ariane, *Modernism and Phenomenology: Literature, Philosophy, Art* (London: Palgrave Macmillan, 2017).
Mirzoeff, Nicholas, 'Visualising the Anthropocene', *Public Culture*, Vol. 26, No. 2, 2014, pp. 213–232.
Morton, Timothy, *Dark Ecology: For a Logic of Future Coexistence* (New York: Columbia University Press, 2016).
———, *Humankind: Solidarity with Nonhuman People* (London and New York: Verso, 2017).
———, *The Ecological Thought* (Cambridge, MA: Harvard University Press, 2010).
———, 'Zero Landscapes in the Time of Hyperobjects', *Graz Architectural Magazine*, Vol. 7, 2011, pp. 78–87.
Mulvey, Laura, 'Visual Pleasure and Narrative Cinema', in Gerald Mast, Marshall Cohen, and Leo Braudy (eds.), *Film Theory and Criticism: Introductory Readings* (Oxford and New York: Oxford University Press, 1992), pp. 746–757.
Nagel, Thomas, 'What Is It Like to Be a Bat', *The Philosophical Review*, Vol. 83, No. 4, 1974, pp. 435–450.
Nardelli, Mathilde, 'Moving Pictures: Cinema and Its Obsolescence in Contemporary Art', *Journal of Visual Culture*, Vol. 8, No. 3, 2009, pp. 243–264.
Narraway, Guinevere, 'Strange Seeing: Re-viewing Nature in the Films of Rose Lowder', in Anat Pick and Guinevere Narraway (eds.), *Screening Nature: Cinema Beyond the Human* (New York: Berghahn Books, 2013), pp. 213–224.
Nichols, Bill, 'Documentary Film and the Modernist Avant-Garde', *Critical Inquiry*, Vol. 27, No. 4, Summer 2001, pp. 580–610.
Niemeyer, Katharina (ed.), *Media and Nostalgia: Yearning for the Past, Present and Future* (Basingstoke: Palgrave Macmillan, 2014).
Noble, Jem, 'As the Mind Tracks Shape … As the Mind Recalls Sound …', *LUMA*, Vol. 2, No. 7, Winter 2017: https://lumaquarterly.com/issues/volume-two/007-winter/as-the-mind-tracks-shape-as-the-mind-recalls-sound/.
Parikka, Jussi, 'New Materialism and Media Theory: Medianatures and Dirty Matter', *Communication and Critical/Cultural Studies*, Vol. 9, No. 1, 2012, pp. 95–100.
———, *The Anthrobscene* (Minneapolis: University of Minnesota Press, 2014).
———, *What Is Media Archaeology?* (Cambridge: Polity Press, 2012).

Parikka, Jussi and Rossella Catanese, 'Handmade Films and Artist-Run Labs: The Chemical Sites of Film's Counterculture', *NECSUS: European Journal of Media Studies*, Vol. 7, No. 2, 2018, pp. 43–63.

Parente, André and Victa de Carvalho, 'Cinema as dispositif: Between Cinema and Contemporary Art', in *Cinémas: revue d'études cinématographiques/Cinemas: Journal of Film Studies*, Vol. 19, No. 1, 2008, pp. 37–55.

Parkins, Wendy and Geoffrey Craig, *Slow Living* (Oxford and New York: Berg, 2006).

Perry, Simon, *Radical Mainstream: Independent Film, Video and Television in Britain 1974–90* (London: Intellect, 2020).

Phelan, Peggy, *Unmarked: The Politics of Performance* (London and New York: Routledge, 1996).

Pick, Anat, 'Three Worlds: Dwelling and Worldhood on Screen', in Anat Pick and Guinevere Narraway (eds.), *Screening Nature: Cinema Beyond the Human* (New York: Berghan Books, 2013), pp. 21–36.

Ramey, Kathryn, *Experimental Filmmaking: Break the Machine* (London and New York: Routledge, 2016).

Rathje, William and Cullen Murphy, *Rubbish!: The Archaeology of Garbage* (New York: HarperCollins Publishers, 1992).

Reble, Jürgen, 'Chemistry and the Alchemy of Colour', *Millennium Film Journal*, Vol. 30/31, Fall 1997: http://mfj-online.org/journalPages/MFJ30%2C31/JRebleChemistry.html.

Recoder, Luis, 'The Death of Structural Film: Notes Toward a Filmless Cinema', *Spectator*, Vol. 27, 2007, pp. 26–30.

Reekie, Duncan, *Subversion: The Definitive History of Underground* Cinema (London: Wallflower Press, 2007).

Rees, A. L., 'Expanded Cinema and Narrative: A Troubled History', in A. L. Rees, Duncan White, Steven Ball, and David Curtis (eds.), *Expanded Cinema: Art, Performance, Film* (London: Tate Publishing, 2011), pp. 12–21.

Reiss, Julie (ed.), *Art, Theory and Practice in the Anthropocene* (Wilmington: Vernon Press, 2019).

Rey, Nicolas, 'Contemporary Issues of Artist-Run Film Lab Practices,' in Luisa Greenfield, Deborah S. Phillips, Kerstin Schroedinger, Björn Speidel, and Philip Widmann (eds.), *Film in the Present Tense: Why Can't We Stop Talking About Analogue Film?* (Berlin: Archive Books, 2018), pp. 63–71.

Rey, Nicolas and Martine Derain, *Digital(e): L'argentique à l'heure du numérique* (Marseille: Editions Commune, 2015).

Reynolds, Simon, *Retromania: Pop Culture's Addition to Its Own Past* (London: Faber and Faber, 2011).

Rhodes, Lis, *Telling Invents Told* (London: Visible Press, 2019).

Richter, Hans, 'The Badly Trained Sensibility', in P. Adams Sitney (ed.), *The Avant-Garde Film: A Reader of Theory and Criticism* (New York: Anthology Film Archives, 1978), pp. 22–23.

Rodowick, D. N., *The Virtual Life of Film* (Cambridge, MA and London: Harvard University Press, 2007).

Rollo, Mike, 'A Collective Charge: Collectif double négativ/Double Negative Collective', in Scott MacKenzie and Janine Marchessault (eds.), *Process Cinema: Handmade Film in the Digital Age* (Montreal: McGill-Queens University, 2019), pp. 214–230.

Rollot, Mathias, *L'obsolescence: Ouvrir l'impossible* (Geneva: Metis Presses, 2016).

Rosenbaum, Jonathan, 'Regrouping: Reflections on the Edinburgh Festival 1976': https://www.jonathanrosenbaum.net/2018/10/regrouping-reflections-on-the-edinburgh-festival-1976/.

Rossini, Katia, 'Who Wanted the Death of Analog Projection? Not Independent Cinemas!', in Luisa Greenfield, Deborah S. Phillips, Kerstin Schroedinger, Björn Speidel, and Philip Widmann (eds.), *Film in the Present Tense: Why Can't We Stop Talking About Analogue Film?* (Berlin: Archive Books, 2018), pp. 59–62.

Russell, Catherine, *Experimental Ethnography: The Work of Film in the Age of Video* (Durham: Duke University Press, 1999).

———, *Walter Benjamin and Archival Film Practices* (Durham, NC: Duke University Press, 2018).

Sadoul, Georges, *Georges Méliès* (Paris: Seghers, 1970).

Saïto, Daïchi, *Moving the Sleeping Images of Things Towards the Light* (Montréal: Les éditions Le Laps, 2013).

Sax, David, *The Revenge of Analog: Real Things and Why They Matter* (New York: PublicAffairs, 2016).

Schlemowitz, Joel, *Experimental Filmmaking and the Motion Picture Camera: An Introductory Guide for Artists and Filmmakers* (New York: Routledge, 2019).

Serra, M. M. and Kathryn Ramey, 'Eye/Body: The Cinematic Paintings of Carolee Schneemann', in Robin Blaetz (ed.), *Women's Experimental Cinema* (Durham and London: Duke University Press, 2007), pp. 103–126.

Shaviro, Steven, *The Cinematic Body* (Minneapolis; London: University of Minnesota Press, 2000).

Sitney, P. Adams, *Visionary Film: The American Avant-garde, 1943–2000* (Oxford: Oxford University Press, 2002).

Slade, Giles, *Made to Break: Technology and Obsolescence in America* (Cambridge, MA and London: Harvard University Press, 2006).

Smith, Vicky, 'Not (a) Part: Handmade Animation, Materialism and the Photogram Film', *The International Journal of Creative Media Research*,

Issue 2, September 2019: https://www.creativemediaresearch.org/post/not-a-part-handmade-animation-materialism-and-the-photogram-film.

———, 'The Animator's Body in Expanded Cinema', *Animation: An Interdisciplinary Journal*, Vol. 10, No. 3, 2015, pp. 222–237.

Sobchack, Vivian, *Carnal Thoughts: Embodiment and Moving Image Culture* (Berkeley: University of California Press, 2004).

Sperlinger, Mike and Ian White (eds.), *Kinomuseum: Towards an Artists' Cinema* (Cologne: Walther König, 2008).

Sterne, Jonathan, 'Out with the Trash: On the Future of New Media', in Charles R. Acland (ed.), *Residual Media* (London and Minneapolis: University of Minnesota Press, 2007), pp. 16–31.

Steyerl, Hito, 'In Defense of the Poor Image', *e-flux journal*, 10 November 2009: https://www.e-flux.com/journal/10/61362/in-defense-of-the-poor-image/.

Strauven, Wanda (ed.), *The Cinema of Attractions Reloaded* (Amsterdam: Amsterdam University Press, 2006).

Sultzbach, Kelly Elizabeth, *Ecocriticism in the Modernist Imagination* (Cambridge: Cambridge University Press, 2016).

Takahashi, Tess, 'After the Death of Film: Writing the Natural World in the Digital Age', *Visible Language*, Vol. 42, No. 1, 2008, pp. 44–69.

———, 'Meticulously, Recklessly Worked Up: Direct Animation, the Auratic and the Index', in Chris Gehman and Steve Reinke (eds.), *The Sharpest Point; Animation at End of Cinema* (Toronto: YYZ Books, 2005), pp. 166–178.

Tscherkassky, Peter (ed.), *Film Unframed: A History of Austrian Avant-Garde Cinema* (Vienna: Austrian Film Museum, 2012).

———, 'How and Why: A Few Notes Concerning Production Techniques Employed in the Making of My Darkroom Films', in Scott MacKenzie and Janine Marchessault (eds.), *Process Cinema: Handmade Film in the Digital Age* (Montreal: McGill-Queens University, 2019), pp. 90–95.

Trodd, Tamara (ed.), *Screen/Space: The Projected Image in Contemporary Art* (Manchester: Manchester University Press, 2012).

Turvey, Malcolm, Ken Jacobs, Annette Michelson, Paul Arthur, Brian Frye, and Chrissie Illes, 'Roundtable: Obsolescence and Avant-Garde Film', *October*, Vol. 100, 2002, pp. 115–132.

Turvey, Malcolm, Ken Jacobs, Federico Windhausen, Flo Jacobs, Mark Street, Lynne Sachs, and Luis Recoder, 'Roundtable on Digital Experimental Filmmaking', *October*, Vol. 137, 2011, pp. 53–68.

Urlus, Esther, *Re:inventing the Pioneers: Film Experiments on Handmade Silver Gelatin Emulsion and Color Methods* (Rotterdam: Self-Published, 2013).

Van Ingen, Sami, *Moving Shadows: Experimental Film Practice in a Landscape of Change* (Helsinki: Finnish Academy of Fine Arts, 2012).

Virilio, Paul, *Speed and Politics* (Cambridge, MA and London: MIT Press, 2006).

———, *The Vision Machine* (London: BFI, 1994).

Walley, Jonathan, *Cinema Expanded: Avant-Garde Film in the Age of Intermedia* (Oxford: Oxford University Press, 2020).

———, '"Not an Image of the Death of Film": Contemporary Expanded Cinema and Experimental Film', in A.L. Rees, Duncan White, Steven Ball and David Curtis (eds.), *Expanded Cinema: Art, Performance, Film* (London: Tate Publishing, 2011), pp. 241–251.

Watkins, Evan, *Throwaways: Work Culture and Consumer Education* (Stanford: Stanford University Press, 1993).

Whiteley, Opal, *The Singing Creek Where the Willows Grow: The Mystical Nature Diary of Opal Whiteley* (New York: Penguin Books, 1994).

Willoquet-Maricondi, Paula (ed.), *Framing the World: Explorations in Ecocriticism and Film* (Charlottesville and London: University of Virginia Press, 2010).

Wollen, Peter, 'Chris Welsby', in David Curtis (ed.), *A Directory of British Film and Video Artists* (Luton: The Arts Council of Wales, 1996), pp. 198–199.

Woloshen, Steven, *Recipes for Reconstruction: The Cookbook for the Frugal Filmmaker* (Montreal: Scratchatopia Books, 2010).

———, *Scratch, Crackle & Pop: A Whole Grains Approach to Making Films Without a Camera* (Montreal: Scratchatopia Books, 2015).

Woolf, Virginia, *The Death of the Moth, and Other Essays* (London: Harcourt Publishers, 1974).

Youngblood, Gene, *Expanded Cinema* (London: Studio Vista, 1970).

Yue, Genevieve, 'Kitchen Sink Cinema: Artist-Run Film Laboratories', *Film Comment*, Vol. 30, March 2015: https://www.filmcomment.com/blog/artist-run-film-laboratories/.

Zielinski, Siegfried, *Deep Time of the Media: Toward an Archaeology of Hearing and Seeing by Technical Means* (Cambridge, MA: MIT Press, 2006).

Zinman, Gregory, 'Echoes of the Earth: Handmade Film Ecologies', in Scott MacKenzie and Janine Marchessault (eds.), *Process Cinema: Handmade Film in the Digital Age* (Montreal: McGill-Queens University, 2019), pp. 108–124.

———, *Making Images Move: Handmade Cinema and the Other Arts* (Oakland: University of California Press, 2020).

Žižek, Slavoj, *The Art of the Ridiculous Sublime: On David Lynch's Lost Highway* (Seattle, Washington: University of Washington, Walter Chapin Simpson Center for the Humanities, 2000).

Zylinska, Joanna, *Minimal Ethics for the Anthropocene* (Ann Arbor: Open Humanities Press, 2014).

———, *The End of Man: A Feminist Counterapocalypse* (Minneapolis: University of Minnesota Press, 2018).

Index

K. Knowles, *Experimental Film and Photochemical Practices*, Experimental Film and Artists' Moving Image,
https://doi.org/10.1007/978-3-030-44309-2

C

GPSR Compliance
The European Union's (EU) General Product Safety Regulation (GPSR) is a set of rules that requires consumer products to be safe and our obligations to ensure this.

If you have any concerns about our products, you can contact us on

ProductSafety@springernature.com

In case Publisher is established outside the EU, the EU authorized representative is:

Springer Nature Customer Service Center GmbH
Europaplatz 3
69115 Heidelberg, Germany

www.ingramcontent.com/pod-product-compliance
Ingram Content Group UK Ltd.
Pitfield, Milton Keynes, MK11 3LW, UK
UKHW021827270726
14058UKWH00001B/18

* 9 7 8 3 0 3 0 4 4 3 1 1 5 *